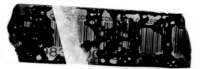

Stepping Up to Power

Stepping Up to Power

The Political Journey
of American Women

Harriett Woods

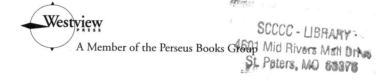

Westview
PRESS

A Member of the Perseus Books Group

＠

To all the brave women who made these events possible.
To the parents whose support gave me courage.
To my own Good Guys, my husband, Jim,
and sons, Chris, Pete, and Andy.

＠

Copyright © 2000 by Westview Press, A Member of the Perseus Books Group

Published in 2000 in the United States of America by Westview Press, 5500 Central Avenue, Boulder, Colorado 80301-2877, and in the United Kingdom by Westview Press, 12 Hid's Copse Road, Cumnor Hill, Oxford OX2 9JJ

Find us on the World Wide Web at www.westviewpress.com

Library of Congress Cataloging-in-Publication Data
Woods, Harriett.
  Stepping up to power : the political journey of American women / Harriett Woods.
    p. cm.
  Includes bibliographical references and index.
  ISBN 0-8133-6815-4 (hc)
  1. Women in politics—United States.   I. Title.
HQ1236.5.U6 W69   1999
320'.082'0973—dc21   99-056832

The paper used in this publication meets the requirements of the American National Standard for Permanence of Paper for Printed Library Materials Z39.48-1984.

10 9 8 7 6 5 4 3 2 1

Contents

Preface

This book anticipates the future by recalling the past. It's a personal story told against the backdrop of tremendous change in women's lives in the second half of the twentieth century, from my mother's lifetime to my granddaughters' future in the new millennium.

There is a lot to learn in the story of women's progress in the last fifty years, a story that coincides with my own reluctant evolution from housewife to national women's political leader. When readers learn about the struggle to get a first newspaper job, who gave money for women to run for office, and how we gambled to create the "Year of the Woman," they may grasp the dimensions of what has occurred and have more confidence to take risks themselves.

In the past few decades, American society literally has been transformed in a revolution that has changed the status of women, with all the accompanying adjustments in personal and public power relationships between men and women. Both men and women have gained the opportunity to discard rigid gender expectations. Within a seeming eyewink of time, we were released from second-class existence to a world of nearly unlimited possibilities. What are we doing with our lives?

It may help to see what other women have done with theirs, particularly those who were faced with unusual challenges. This book begins with a celebration of some important achievers; it closes with a call for new leadership. In between, there is the story of women's political awakening since the 1950s, including the evolution of my own political career, both its successes and its failures. The book examines the strange dance we do around a topic that is key to success in every part of our lives: power. There also are some specific suggestions intended to inspire others to follow in the path of women's political pioneers.

A new millennium is a useful juncture to take a fresh look at how we are doing. It is easy to see that despite much social and economic progress, there is astonishing dissatisfaction with our political system and also with an economic system that seems unresponsive to personal needs. There is an unhealthy spread between the have's and have-not's in our society. Violence escalates, and we are still plagued by the "isms"—racism, sexism, classism. And women still are grossly underrepresented in all positions of power.

What is at stake is the way decisions are made in this country. Power is most often defined as the ability to influence people and events. Some see it as a personal quality; others, as related to positions held or resources controlled. As we shall see, women and men seem to understand and use power differently. What is important for the future is to recognize that no matter how the word is defined, the ability of women to influence events has vastly increased. That carries responsibility.

There will be women presidents in the White House and women CEOs in the executive suites, but it isn't inevitable. Society's leaders say they believe in equal access, but resistance stiffens when we try to take a seat at the table. That is one reason why the number of women in power increases so slowly. The other reason is that too few women are stepping up to power; there are too few risk takers.

The truth about women and power is that people think we have it, but we don't—because we are not using it. Every woman must think this through for herself; everyone must embark on her own voyage of discovery. There are no guarantees that you'll be successful, or that you'll be loved, but if you have a vision, and if you have the courage to pursue it, you can achieve a wonderful and meaningful life.

We are busy today with work, family, education, caretaking, religion, personal enhancement, and recreation. We may not think it matters if we know what happened twenty or thirty years ago. But those events still are part of our lives. They define our choices and shape our collective memory. We are connected by the stories that pass from one generation to the next. They teach and entertain us. We chuckle with surprise, exclaim with astonishment, nod with satisfaction.

When we know where we've been, we're more likely to get where we want to go.

—Harriett Woods

Acknowledgments

Writing is a solitary activity, but publishing a book is a group undertaking, particularly a first book. This one never would have been completed without the encouragement and support of a good many caring people.

Several published writers were generous about sharing their own experiences, women like Kay Mills, Melissa Ludtke, Celia Morris, and Sheila Tobias. Then there were the busy people who took time to read early drafts, like Fran Hoffmann, Pat Reilly, Barbara Freund, my son Andy, and, above all, my long-time political partner, Jody Newman, who always manages to cloak excellent criticism in enthusiasm for the project. It really made a difference.

I was very lucky to find an agent like Audrey Wolf, who believed in the book and never gave up on seeing it published, and an editor at Westview, Leo Wiegman, who thoughtfully read what I wrote and helped to make it better. The review by Professor Wynne Moskop was invaluable, although the final responsibility for the content is mine alone.

There also are those who contributed to this book without really knowing, like my students at the University of Missouri–St. Louis, my political friends, my partners on the tennis courts, and, of course, my family. They're all represented here in some way.

1

The Celebration

If you want to have power over your life, then
you must make sure that more women
have power to make public policy.

—The National Women's Political Caucus

It was an icy night in Washington, D.C., in February 1994, and streets and sidewalks were so slick it was almost impossible to walk. Despite the near-crippling weather conditions, the ballroom of the Mayflower Hotel was full. Looking around, I realized that this probably was the greatest assemblage of female power the country had ever seen. All the years fighting to break through gender barriers had finally produced truly meaningful results.

Strolling through the room, chatting and embracing in high-spirited greetings, were commissioners of major federal agencies, assistants to the president, deputy attorneys general, regional directors of health, judicial nominees, state department officials—and four women of cabinet rank: Attorney General Janet Reno, Secretary of Health and Human Services Donna Shalala, EPA Administrator Carol Browner, and President's Council of Economic Advisers Chairperson Laura D'Andrea Tyson.

Secret service agents had conducted the usual sweep, and a rope barrier had been installed around the speaker's podium in anticipation of the arrival of First Lady Hillary Clinton. The elegant ballroom with its gilded decorations, busy heart of a historic hotel, seemed a fitting site to make modern history. We were celebrating the first year in office for the record number of women who had been named to top-level posts by the Clinton administration. It was a very special night.

The event was being hosted by the bipartisan National Women's Political Caucus (NWPC), and as its president, I exchanged hugs and handshakes with exhilarated officeholders and their friends. I also was chair of the Coalition for Women's Appointments, made up of about sixty women's professional and issue groups, so this event was specially meaningful. I knew about the hard work that had gone into assembling the names, along with the personal contacts, the arm-twisting, the struggles, and the carrot-and-stick maneuvering, so that this number of women could be placed within the new administration.

The effort had demonstrated what was best about the women's movement. In a crisis, or in a great common cause, women do work together. There still were tensions and occasional sharp elbows as individuals jockeyed for position with the new administration, but most women selflessly labored for other women's success. The coalition was able to provide the new administration vital assistance, with seven hundred résumés of highly qualified, individually vetted women, including many who filled breakthrough positions in the military, economic, and scientific areas, such as chief scientist at the National Aeronautics and Space Administration.

That was the carrot. The stick came out in December 1992. The coalition had been working with the Clinton transition team since early fall, even before the election. By late December, we worried that time was running out on key appointments, and women were losing out for consideration in remaining unfilled top posts. Communication with the administration had broken down; it was difficult to get to see anyone. We needed to get their attention. I began sending out to the media a fax news sheet called *The Mirror.* It was headed by a quote of Clinton's statement: "I think I owe the American people a White House staff, a Cabinet and appointments that look like America." Underneath, we simply listed without comment all key appointments to date, by race and sex, and then added them up and noted the percentages. Women were 51 percent of the U.S. population, but they weren't even close to that percentage in the figures on the fax sheet.

The new White House was furious. An annoyed president, determined to show he wouldn't be pushed around by special interests, lashed out at women at a press conference, calling us "bean counters." I was shocked. It wasn't fun being publicly criticized by a president, although *Washington Post* writer E. J. Dionne, Jr., wrote: "What's wrong with bean-counting? . . . Presidential Cabinets always have been the product of a similar kind of bean-counting. What's changed is the nature of the beans we count."

Some women leaders also weren't too happy with me, saying that, by putting out *The Mirror*, the Caucus had just made the president angry. But three decades of making my way within the system had taught me something: Politics is a power game. For women, pressure from an informed public was a big part of our power, and we needed to use it.

In the end, more than 40 percent of the president's appointments were women, including six women at cabinet level, and, most significantly, a record 32 percent of all Senate-confirmed positions.[1] That compared to 22 percent for George Bush. Months later, the president joked about the bean-counting episode as I passed through a White House reception line. I had long since praised him for his appointments, and he had long since sent a very kind note saying that my help with those appointments "was invaluable." We can't really know what made the difference: a sincere Clinton commitment to diversity, key friendships with Hillary, powerful résumés, expert lobbying, political gamesmanship, or public bean counting. What was important was the qualified women who were appointed.

It was obvious many of the president's advisers were unhappy with what had happened, and they blamed his public pledge to diversity for the resulting negative publicity about special-interest pressures. No doubt the pledge did increase expectations among all sorts of groups. That prompted critics to label subsequent appointments of blacks, Hispanics, and women as "quota mongering," but the traditional all-white-male leadership reflected a different kind of quota that had to be challenged. The goal of our women's coalition was the very opposite of quotas; it was to win appointments for women on their merits in the midst of a world that reflected traditional gamesmanship; there always would be a long line of well-connected white men waiting for every opening. Without a specific priority, one of them would get every opening.

We wouldn't have had much to brag about in 1994 if it hadn't been for the president's pledge, and our pressure. That was a lesson women will need to remember in the year 2001.

With this struggle in the background, it is no wonder that I felt so emotional that February night, so moved to see the stunning array of abilities assembled in the ballroom. This indeed would help assure a government that not only looked a lot more like America but acted like it. Women would be in positions of power to influence policy, in which they could address needed changes in the social structures that were barriers to so many people. Their numbers in this room were evidence that the transformation wrought by the women's movement was beginning to pay off in real power.

Spaced around the room, television monitors continuously scrolled a long list of female appointees' names. There were whole areas of government that had female leadership for the first time: the commissioner of Immigration, the commissioner of the Internal Revenue Service, the secretary of the Air Force, the director of the Census Bureau, and the director of the White House Office of Management and Budget.

It would be easy to minimize this celebration, to point out how far we still had to go (even with these recent appointments, still only fourteen women in American history had been appointed heads of executive departments), but this was the time to enjoy our success. Most of these women had taken risks in their lives to reach these positions of power. They had made personal sacrifices. Now they just wanted to celebrate together, to be impressed by their own numbers in a male-dominated political world. The applause and cheers rose as Hillary Clinton and Tipper Gore led the new women cabinet members to a raised platform to be acknowledged. (Only Secretary of Energy Hazel O'Leary had been unable to attend.) They also were cheering themselves for having made it this far, just as they also were applauding all the women who had broken barriers and pushed limits in years past so that women could gain a greater voice.

Who knew better than Donna Shalala, former university president, former assistant secretary of housing in the Carter administration, long-time children's advocate and friend of Hillary Clinton? It was a long climb, but she stayed focused, and she stayed connected with other women. It was Donna Shalala who gave me a place to stay in Manhattan during the tough fund-raising grind in my last race for U.S. Senate in 1986.

Now she was secretary of Health and Human Services, heading one of fourteen executive departments, a member of the president's cabinet—and she still was thinking in terms of women's mutual support. She told the enthusiastic crowd: *"In this administration there are so many women at high levels that you literally can move a major policy issue all the way to the president's desk without it ever touching a man's hands."*[2]

When it came Tipper Gore's turn to speak, she continued the theme, expressing thanks for the people in power who had helped to bring this female progress about, "from the president [pause] on down." *The Washington Post* reported, "The First Lady looked on innocently from the platform and the crowd roared knowingly."[3] Hillary Clinton's influence within the White House on behalf of women was common knowledge.

In response, Hillary Clinton gave credit to another woman, Bill Clinton's late mother, who she said had raised a son with "respect and appreciation for women, women who work, women who raise children, women who are not given the break we think they deserve but keep going every day." She also credited one other person, Jan Piercy, deputy presidential assistant for personnel, who had helped alert women to key positions. Mrs. Clinton joked: "I will admit right now she was one of my room-mates at Wellesley."[4] This verified something we all understood; women needed their own power networks. Without them, we wouldn't be here.

We could sense the spirits of all the preceding risk takers who had made this night possible. Some had famous names, like Secretary of Labor Frances Perkins, first woman named to the Cabinet in 1933 (it would be twenty years before there was another woman named) or Senator Margaret Chase Smith and Congresswoman Shirley Chisholm, one a white Republican, the other an African-American Democrat, who bucked the male system to run for president before polls said it was doable. They had ventured out where none had gone before, with little more than their own determination.

There was Elizabeth Cady Stanton who brought women together for the nation's first women's rights convention in Seneca Falls, New York, on July 17, 1848, but had to ask a man to chair the meeting because it was deemed improper for a woman to play such a public role. A "public woman" was a prostitute. Seventy-two years later, in 1920, women finally gained the vote after incredible struggle, but when they failed to cast their ballots in expected numbers or deferred to their husbands, male politicians began to ignore them. Women advocates continued their activism on issues, like child labor, but it was rare for a woman to try for elective office. As late as 1971, there were just 15 women out of 563 members of Congress and women were only 5 percent of state legislators.

Now, in 1992, after all these years, it seemed that women were fully engaged in the political process. Women were voting, women were running, women were taking power. Not only were there record numbers of senior appointees but there was also a record number of women in Congress: nine women in the U.S. Senate, and forty-seven women in the U.S. House. Women were now more than 20 percent of state legislators. It may have taken the whole twentieth century, but we were seeing results, and that was worth celebrating.

There was another significance to this event. The women surrounding me on the platform, and circulating in the ballroom, were important role models to inspire a new generation of women to believe in themselves and their ability to compete successfully for important positions. There hadn't been many role models for my generation. For me personally, it was my mother and Eleanor Roosevelt. My mother had been a nationally ranked tennis player. Every day I stared at the shining silver trophies that filled our dining room cabinet, and I knew she had achieved something in her own right, and therefore I could too. Roosevelt was a model of compassion, an activist First Lady who reached out to care for all the people in America. She also showed me strength when she ignored criticism to speak out in her own voice.

There also was Amelia Earhart, the pioneering pilot, a slim woman with tousled short hair and warm smile who dressed just like the male flyers but with a bright scarf at her neck. She became a legend when she disappeared on an attempted round-the-world trip in 1937. Asked why she risked her life, she said: "I want to do it because I want to do it. Women must try to do things as men have tried. When they fail, their failure must be but a challenge to others."[5]

Earhart was ahead of her time. Adventurous or powerful women were oddities. I was lucky to have my personal role models. Men held all positions of authority. In public schools, maiden women might be teachers, but men were principals. It took World War II to change women's self-perception of their second-class status. When millions of men were sucked into the military in the early 1940s, the economy needed alternative labor, specifically women and minorities.

There was a wartime poster that became a symbol of the new woman. It showed a muscle-flexing female dressed for factory work—doing a job for which females previously had been judged unqualified. It was powerful visual reinforcement that women could be strong. Women enlisted in every branch of the service to free up men for combat, including the then-new Women's Air Force Service Pilots (WASPs) to fly noncombat assignments. Even young women felt needed. I saved tin foil in huge balls, knitted crooked khaki scarves for the men overseas, and, as soon as I was old enough, took flying lessons. As Earhart had said, women could be risk takers, too.

When the war ended, attitudes changed; women were expected to resume their posture of dependency. There was an underlying understanding that when the boys came marching home, the jobs were to be theirs, and so were the women. Those who continued to work returned to inferior pay and working conditions, in lunch counters and ten-cent stores. Many African-American women went back to domestic service. But the seeds of discontent had been planted among working women, as well as those who had become full-time homemakers.

In many ways, the seemingly placid 1950s set the stage for social revolution, as women realized how little control they had over their own lives. Ruth Bader Ginsburg wrote: "I began law school with a class of over four hundred. It included nine women. Employers were, to put it euphemistically, cool toward the idea of employing women."[6] She also was a young mother, and Jewish. When she began looking for a job in 1959, law firm doors were closed to her.

The doors that closed for me led to newsrooms. I had worked my way up to managing editor of *The Michigan Daily* in college in 1949, and I expected to become a newspaper reporter after graduation with the same prospects as the young men who worked for me. Unfortunately, most editors refused to hire women as general news reporters. The assumption was that we weren't tough enough. During a summer stint at a Chicago newspaper, the city editor tried to scare me off by making my first assignment a twenty-three-story suicide jump into a courtyard. He apparently expected me to weep instead of write. As I looked for a permanent job, the editors all pointed to the society section, where stories focused on weddings, club meetings, and social events. That was not acceptable.

I packed a small bag and, without any appointments or prospects, boarded a train heading east from home-town Chicago to wherever there were good newspapers: Cleveland, Cincinnati, Pittsburgh, Philadelphia, New York. In each town, I'd call the editor from the station, asking for an interview. Amazingly, most of them saw me, but then without fail either said that women didn't belong in the newsroom or that they already had "one."

I finally found a job. So did the young Ginsburg. She turned to teaching and special projects, focusing on laws that treated men and women differently. She went on to win five of six sex discrimination cases before the Supreme Court and in the late 1970s became a federal appellate court judge. We both had learned valuable lessons. If doors are closed to you, find a way around. Don't give in to gender-biased judgments. Be willing to take chances, and try something new because if you maintain your principles, you can earn respect, and that translates into power of accomplishment.

Ruth Bader Ginsburg is a small, reserved woman; it would be hard to guess how much impact she has had within the judicial system. We met for the first time at an inaugural reception that the NWPC held in January 1993 at a Washington, D.C., art gallery. She later recalled that I predicted she would be appointed to the Supreme Court. In truth, I just was reflecting our determination to see a second woman on the court and the knowledge that she was high on everyone's list. It was good luck that we were able to help when the White House did take up her name, by countering false information that was being circulated to damage her chances. It was fascinating to me that our separate struggles for careers had brought us together at this moment, with the power to help one another. It was glorious being in the Rose

Garden the day President Clinton introduced her to be the second woman on the Supreme Court.

Justice Ginsburg deserved appointment to the Supreme Court on the basis of her qualifications, but there's no doubt she won consideration because gender was made an issue. A president no longer could use the excuse that he couldn't find a qualified woman for the job. The 1980s had seen a remarkable increase in the number of women in all kinds of professional positions, from economists and scientists to prosecuting attorneys. Gender was our wedge but good résumés gave us leverage, and aroused public opinion was an effective weapon.

We also had learned that we were no one's priority but our own. There was a lot of lip service about equality, but the statistics demonstrated a lack of follow-up commitment. Our predecessors always seemed to be petitioning for consideration; in 1993, we had to be bolder. All the women advocates agreed that it was time for a gender breakthrough to one of the Big Four cabinet positions: defense, state department, justice, or treasury. These represented the major power bases of government: the military and its contracts; foreign affairs; law and order; and the flow of money. The consensus target was attorney general, head of Justice, because women now were well established in legal fields and there were some excellent candidates.

After the election, while the president-elect remained in Little Rock, Vernon Jordan, one-time civil rights activist, lobbyist, and FOB (friend of Bill), was designated as the Washington contact on appointments. It wasn't easy getting a meeting, so we were pleased finally to arrange what we understood was a private appointment for the coalition with Jordan. When we arrived, the room was full; they clearly had invited every other woman who had contacted them. Probably deliberately, Jordan's office had created an atmosphere that was not conducive to serious negotiation.

Our spokesperson, Judith Lichtman, of the Women's Legal Defense Fund, urged the appointment of a woman attorney general. Others added varied views. Jordan was conciliatory. He is a very handsome black man with the confidence of a power broker and a reputation for charming his way through difficulties, partly relying for credibility on his civil rights credentials. He assured us that women were being actively considered for additional positions, but I left feeling frustrated that we were still lobbing messages over the transom. Fortunately, some members of the team had better results working White House contacts with the new First Lady. A woman was indeed named attorney general: New York attorney Zoe Baird.

Alas for best-laid plans. First, Zoe Baird, and then substitute appointee, Kimba Wood, ran into problems over nonpayment of taxes for domestic workers. By the time Janet Reno was nominated, critics were saying that the president hadn't been looking for the best person, just the best *woman*. True, we answered, but every woman proposed was well qualified. There were plenty of ambitious, well-connected men and without deliberate effort, there never would be a woman selected. Women had to create their connections.

A story about the Reno nomination makes the point. The male political network did not surface her name, even though she had won acclaim in Dade County, Florida, as a prosecutor who created innovative and effective programs to cut crime. Women found her. A prominent political player in Washington who knew her, named Ann Lewis, called me; I checked Reno's credentials with a Caucus leader in Florida and then called the media and the White House. That seemed to set things in motion.

Janet Reno told the rest of the story at the NWPC's annual convention in the summer of 1993. She said: "Harriett Woods was the first person to be quoted in the paper presenting the possibility of Janet Reno. . . . In the Oval Office, the president said: 'So you've got the support of the women's groups!'" Then she looked out at the dedicated volunteers who had labored over the years to put women into power and said: "Thank you."[7]

An article in *Newsweek* right after the Reno appointment noted its impact: "The Old Boys Club that has traditionally ruled Washington is grudgingly making adjustments. With a woman tapped to be the chief law-enforcement officer, a First Lady charged with making policy and four new women senators, there is a new power grid. Rules are being rewritten to take into account the sensibilities of a generation of women coming into power."[8]

In putting later events in perspective, it's important to note that women's political advocacy groups like NOW and the NWPC didn't even exist until the late 1960s; there was little concern in those days about women's views on appointments, or anything else. Women not only couldn't get good jobs or fair wages; we couldn't even get credit cards in our own name. It could be a crime to use contraceptives. Few women were admitted to professional schools like medicine or law. Domestic violence hadn't even been given a name. When I graduated from college, help-wanted ads were divided into male and female; you couldn't apply for a desirable job listed in the male columns, even if you felt you were qualified.

This meant that women who became achievers in the 1970s and 1980s, including many at the ballroom celebration, had triumphed over those situations. They helped to pass laws to end discrimination, win court cases, and get supportive lawmakers elected. There are very thoughtful reflections elsewhere on the women's movement that point out the diverse threads that went into its evolution.[9] For me, as a young mother in the Midwest, the women's movement seemed very distant. What wakened me was injustice at the community level and a passion for reform. Like others of that time, I certainly never intended to become a "woman leader." Now here I was in Washington, leading a woman's group dedicated to getting more women into public office. Life had gradually taught me what many women have had to learn: Women pay a bigger price to get power, and we're more likely to succeed when we support one another.

It had been a long journey, combining individual risk taking and group struggle, a history many younger women do not know or understand. In the months and years after the 1994 reception, there would be more significant appointments of women by the Clinton administration, including Madeleine Albright as the first woman secretary of state, but in many ways, that February night was our zenith for the twentieth century. We thought the future was assured.

Later events would show the struggle was far from over. The 1994 election saw the defeat of many of the women reformers of "The Year of the Woman," as well as a worrisome downturn in the number of women running for state legislative seats. For years we had blamed outside barriers for keeping women from leadership; now we needed to look at the question more carefully, including inside women themselves. Why was it that so many failed to see the connection, that we finally recognized, between the quality of our lives and who makes public policy decisions?

It will take a fresh generation of risk takers to regenerate the momentum, women who have absorbed our history and our commitment to public service but who are clear-eyed in their understanding of the way power is exercised. It would have been good to have them in the ballroom that night. They could have caught the energy that flowed from those who have been part of a great adventure.

My life has been one small part of that adventure, paralleling the evolution of many public women in America. We began at the local level, drawn into the political arena by local problems and a passion for social justice; we took some risks and gradually learned how to create and use power. I did not set out to run for office or devote myself to getting women appointed. One thing just led to another.

That history may be useful to today's young women who are filled with determination for the future without fully understanding that there still are plenty of bumps in the road. They need to hear our stories and learn how we became risk takers and coped with adversity, so they will have more appreciation of the cost of change and more confidence to meet whatever challenges arise in their own lives.

When we know where we've been, we're more likely to get where we want to go. We need a lot more women competing for positions of power. The celebrants in 1994 would agree: a ballroom full of power is wonderful; so is a woman in the Oval Office; but in the next century there must be so many women leaders that no single room can contain our celebration.

We have been trudging uphill far too long.

2

The Awakening

No one should have to dance backwards all their lives.

—**Jill Ruckleshaus**

All during the 1950s, according to a book on that period, the male president of Radcliffe "routinely greeted incoming freshmen by telling them that their education would prepare them to be splendid wives and mothers, and their reward might be to marry Harvard men."[1] The emancipating spirit of the World War II years had disappeared. In her book *It Changed My Life, Writings on the Women's Movement*[2] Betty Friedan has a chapter titled "The Way We Were—1949":

> In 1949, nobody really had to tell a woman that she wanted a man, but the message certainly began bombarding us from all sides: domestic bliss had suddenly become chic . . . . The magazines were full of articles like: "What's Wrong with American Women?" "Let's Stop Blaming Mom"; "Shortage of Men"; "Isn't a Woman's Place in the Home?"; "Women Aren't Men"; "What Women Can Learn from Mother Eve." Suddenly it seemed so attractive to cop out from the competition, the dull, hard work of "man's higher vocations," by simply playing our role as women. No more need to rock the boat, risk failure or resentment from men.

The 1950s have been described as years of normalcy and conventional values. Popular television shows like *Father Knows Best* and *Leave it to Beaver* glorified the traditional family with a father who carried a briefcase and a mother who wore an apron. Republican Dwight Eisenhower was elected president in 1952, supported by a majority of women voters, and reelected in 1956. He was a conciliator. He brought the Korean War to a close and chose the first woman for the cabinet since Roosevelt's days, Oveta Culp Hobby as secretary of Health, Education and Welfare. The appointment of Claire Booth Luce as an ambassador to Italy also was a first. However, these were not signals for women to seek careers. There was a general belief that women's place was in the home, even though a third of women sixteen years and older were in the paid labor force, more than half of all single women, and a fourth of married women.

There were many happy homemakers, of course, women whose husbands earned adequate incomes so that they could stay home, providing housework and child care. But the view of women as free labor carried over to the workplace in terms of lower pay. Working women were treated as domestic servants in a different setting. They still were expected to serve the coffee, no matter what their office titles. Besides, married women should need only "pin money" because their husbands were the primary wage earners. Whatever women did was assumed to be worth less; and to the extent that women accepted that evaluation, they also accepted that women themselves were worth less, forever God's second thought, not quite as good as the original.

Universities wondered why they should waste money on women; 37 percent of college women dropped out before graduation. Barred from most professions and facing the prospect of dead-end jobs, it made sense just to get married. At least a woman would have security. There was no easy, reliable birth control (birth control pills would go on the market in 1961), abortion was illegal, and extramarital pregnancy was a social disaster that could prompt thoughts of suicide. Toughing it out for an executive job wasn't much better. Career women were suspected of being unfeminine. If a woman advanced too far in a profession, "no man will want you."

Five male psychiatrists interviewed in *Life* magazine said female ambition was the root of mental illness in wives, emotional upset in husbands, and homosexuality in boys.[3]

Famed anthropologist Margaret Mead had written in 1949: "It is not new in history that men and women have misunderstood each other's roles or envied each other, but the significant aspect of the American scene is that there is a discrepancy between the way we bring up boys and girls—each to choose both a job and a marriage partner—and then stylize housekeeping as a price the girl pays with stylizing the job as the price the boy pays."[4]

Jim Woods and I were married in 1953. We had met and begun dating as fellow reporters at *The St. Louis Globe–Democrat*, the paper that finally hired me after my long job search. However, we weren't married until after I had run away to Europe for almost a year, unsuccessfully seeking some greater fulfillment than routine reporting, perhaps as a great writer of novels and short stories. Jim offered an alternative future: love, marriage, and family. I was twenty-six and the biological clock was ticking. I had graduated from college determined to establish myself in a journalism career, but it had turned into less-than-satisfying work on a mediocre paper. The European escape also was a failure; there were wonderful days and nights sitting in cafés, but I never did write that novel. Why not marriage and children? They always had been in the future somewhere, and it would feel so good just to stop struggling.

When Friedan was fired from her writing job in the 1950s because she was pregnant again, she says she almost felt relief in seeking security within four walls in suburbia: "I had begun to feel so guilty working, and I really wasn't getting anywhere in that job. I was more than ready to embrace the feminine mystique [centering one's life on husband, children, and home]. . . . There was a comfortable small world you could really do something about, politically: the children's homework, even the new math, compared to the atomic bomb."[5]

If that was truth in New York, it was doctrine in the Midwest. Missouri, like so much of the heartland, was always described as a wonderful place to raise a family, meaning that this is what you were supposed to do. There was solid housing, good schools, lots of places of worship, and just enough entertainment to fill up weekend nights. People identified with their neighborhoods. The first question any new acquaintance asked was not what college you had attended but the name of your high school because it was a clue to everything else: social status, religion, race, kind of home, and much more. This was a well-ordered world where people knew their places. The vast majority had very clear goals: marriage, a good job for the man, and a home of one's own for the woman to care for.

In 1940, 31 percent of women were single; by 1950, the figure had dropped to 23 percent, and by 1960, 21 percent. Women were marrying younger and starting families immediately, having an average of 3.2 children. Three million women had gone to work during World War II. Another 350,000 women served in the armed forces. Wartime jobs paid well, the challenges were exciting, and judging from contemporary comments, women enjoyed the opportunity to stretch their minds and muscles, but when the war ended, so did all the encouragement to women workers. Women were forced out of better-paying jobs, and government-sponsored daycare centers were terminated. The message from society, government, and the popular magazines changed from "go get jobs" to "go get married, stay home, and have babies." An article in *Seventeen* magazine advised: "Being a woman is your career and you can't escape it."[6]

There was something else. The tremendous economic engine that had provisioned the war needed new customers. The GI Bill underwrote startup businesses in shopping strips along the new highways that extended out to the new suburbs where new government-financed homes were filled with new young families who needed new furnishings and new cars. It was an achievement to own your own home but also to escape from a central city whose population had been altered by war. Thousands of blacks from the Deep South migrated north in search of factory jobs and stayed on in overflowing public housing. It was a brewing crisis that no one wanted to face.

Jim and I started out in an apartment in a sprawling development close to a major highway outside St. Louis. It was described as a garden complex, with well-established trees and curving streets to break up the rows of three-story brick buildings. From the air, St. Louis appears filled with trees, and so does much of Missouri, but the parklike atmosphere of our development was a tradeoff for distance. We had one car that Jim usually drove downtown to work. Without it, there was just a shuttle to a bus line. I felt isolated. There was the apartment to decorate; there was learning to be a housewife (a kindly neighbor watching my struggles in the laundry room taught me how to fold sheets); and there was preparing meals every day. I told everyone that I was a happy homemaker, that it didn't bother me at all to have given up a career as a newspaper reporter. I assumed, as did most women at the time, that marriage meant staying home; no one suggested there was a choice.

In truth, all that free time made me feel not only restless and bored but guilty. I should be doing more; if I weren't going to work, and that seemed certain, then I should start a family. People didn't approve of married women who went to work, but they loved women who were pregnant; having a baby would be "doing something." We had three boys within four years. The first one I watched with adoration for hours, even while he slept. I smothered him with attention and compared notes with other mothers as we sat outside on the grassy lawn rocking the carriages. After the third, I determined there would be no more. I loved each one dearly, but my life had disappeared in a pile of diapers. Besides, as Jim noted: "You can have a backyard full of boys trying to have one girl."

I had been determined to make it as a reporter, then equally determined to find fame and fortune in Europe; now I was determined to build a life around my marriage. Jim and I had quite different backgrounds. He was from Missouri's "Little Dixie," a part of central Missouri that was settled by pioneers who had made their way from Virginia to Kentucky into Missouri carrying their southern sentiments with them. His parents were devout Southern Baptists who flouted convention by keeping beer in the refrigerator; mine were Reform Jews who didn't worry too much whether services were held on Saturday or Sunday. Each family had its beliefs, but also a warm flexibility. I figured there would be a good genetic mix for our children.

We shared a great deal: newspaper jobs, commitment to advancing the cause of working people and an enjoyment of all kinds of music. We had courted while listening to Dixieland jazz in cubby-hole bars and riverfront dives. I knew that he was a wonderful man, a person of extraordinary integrity without the intellectual pretensions of too many of my other acquaintances. He knew who he was, and he wasn't threatened by an ambitious, restless wife. Perhaps he assumed that once married, I would fall into a traditional role. There was no way to anticipate then how far off that assumption would be.

With the second pregnancy, we bought a house in an urban suburb, University City, one of the few places in the area where it was possible to get bagels, a guarantee of cultural comfort. University City is a community filled with parks, solid older homes, and a population that thrives on diversity. It is home to symphony players, university professors, professionals, and blue-collar workers, people of all racial and ethnic hues. Years later I discovered that it was the site of the first "Women's Republic" in the United States, convened in 1904 by the city's founder, E. G. Lewis, a risk-taking developer who published a national women's magazine in a unique octagonal building that now serves as city hall.

In the mid-1950s, it didn't take long for the sentimental stage of marriage to pass. The children were wonderful, and Jim's job and union leadership provided stimulating conversation at night, but I wanted to find something for myself again. As Friedan noted about this period, more and more women had attained higher education but found themselves with nothing to do with it. There was so much of me that wasn't being used. A full-time job seemed unfeasible; besides, I really wanted to be home with my children. So I painted and wall-papered the house, baked bread, entertained toddlers, started a discount paperback book store in the grade school cafeteria, wrote book reviews, joined a Great Books group, played tennis in the park and violin in the Philharmonic, took art lessons, and, in desperation, even enrolled in a college correspondence course in education before abandoning it in horror at the required rote learning.

Margaret Mead observed: "The modern wife and mother lives alone, with a husband who comes home in the evening, and children, as little children who are on her hands twenty-four hours out of twenty-four, in a house that she is expected to run with the efficiency of a factory—for hasn't she a washing-machine and a vacuum cleaner?—and from which a great number of the compensations that once went with being a home-maker have been removed."[7]

I was faced with what Friedan called "the problem without a name"—that she then gave a name and the title of her book *The Feminine Mystique.* Should I accept a life that would be defined solely by the success of my husband and children? Then who was *I*? In 1963, when it was published, her book would spark a movement, but it was the experiences of the 1950s that set the stage. So many middle-class women had gone to college or had been gainfully employed during the war or before marriage only to find themselves stuck alone in some subdivision, restless and hungry for change. On the one hand, we seemed to have security, and our lives were supposed to be easier with modern household appliances. On the other hand, there was a feeling of isolation, of being trapped, of having permanent secondary status in a world of male power figures while trying to find a "me" that was separate and distinct.

The turning point was unexpected. Every afternoon, I would look forward to getting all three tots down for their naps at the same time so I could relax and read. Our street was a shortcut for cars trying to avoid a traffic signal. Right outside our house, there was a manhole with a loose manhole cover, and just when everything was quiet, some car speeding through the shortcut would hit that manhole cover with a bang and wake the children. So I went to the local governing body and said, reasonably: "Please either fix the manhole or block off the traffic." Of course, they told me that they'd have to think about it, that they had many other priorities, and so on. Then I did what women were learning to do all over the country when confronted with community problems: I took out a pen and a yellow legal pad and went door to door, collecting signatures of neighbors. It worked. Forty years later, the street is still blocked off.

I learned that if you care about something deeply enough and you're willing to take the initiative, people will join you. I also learned that numbers count. With that wisdom, one can lead nations. Madeleine Kunin, in Vermont, became politically active because her children had to walk across an unguarded railroad crossing on the way to school. Barbara Roberts, in Oregon, began lobbying the legislature because she had a child with special needs whom the public schools refused to educate. Both eventually became governors of their states. I had small children and too much traffic on my street and became a state senator and then lieutenant governor. We dipped our toes into local controversy and gained courage to learn how to be leaders.

Thus are political careers born. As the 1950s progressed into the 1960s, more and more women whose lives had been centered in the home would turn community causes into paths to political careers. Of course, there was much more to my story than success in blocking traffic from our street. There would be larger issues to confront and roles to discover in the community. That path led through the League of Women Voters. Women's organizations played an important role in giving future women leaders skills and confidence. I joined the league, but it could just as easily have been the American Association of University Women, the Business and Professional Women, the National Council of Jewish Women, Zonta, Alpha Kappa Alpha, or any of dozens of others. Middle America was full of women's organizations and clubs. In his nineteenth-century classic, *Democracy in America*, Alexis de Tocqueville described the proliferation of grassroots organizations as a unique characteristic of the New World. Every community had its male clubs and fraternal organizations. Women were excluded, so they created their own.

Women who felt trapped at home were looking for intelligent conversation and a place where a woman who wasn't welcome in the man's world could build a meaningful world of her own. It's true that I had refused to work in the society sections of newspapers where women's activities were recorded, and yet now I eagerly joined a woman's organization. There was no contradiction. In the 1950s, women's organizations were serious business for a homemaker. Joining women's groups affirmed that women had ideas and experiences that shouldn't be overlooked. They provided a link with the male world that had been missing for most of us.

When I was in eighth grade, my life ambition, as revealed in the school newspaper, was to be an "aeronautical engineer." That was a remarkably unrealistic goal. There may have been one or two women engineers in those days, but I never had heard of them. Math wasn't even my best subject. But the boys talked about airplanes and engines, and I figured that whatever the boys wanted to do, I did too. It already was clear that males got bragging rights for doing things that were more adventurous and challenging. Boys took chances in the way they played their games. Fathers went off each day for business that everyone understood was special and important.

Certainly we girls had plenty of confidence in grade school. It seemed perfectly natural for me to be elected student council president while one of my male buddies became vice president. Men might rule the world, but not the eighth grade. On the other hand, there was absolutely no notion that this implied future leadership in the real world. A *New Yorker* profile, in 1998, of Vice President Al Gore noted that both Gore and President Bill Clinton "essentially started running for office when they were in grade school" because they wanted to be like President John F. Kennedy.[8] There was no such female role model for me. Running for public office wouldn't occur to me until I was almost middle-aged.

Women's organizations were a transition. They meant lots of meetings and too much time spent on procedures, but at least the League of Women Voters, with its roots in the battle for suffrage, assumed women were smart enough to have ideas about public policy. Too often women were relegated to auxiliaries of the men's groups as an extension of their housewifely duties. We had entered the second half of the twentieth century. It was time for women to be respected for their own ideas, about taxes and urban renewal, in addition to their assumed expertise about family care. We needn't be confined to neighborhood gabfests gossiping about someone's problem child or errant husband.

Talking in the league meant discussing serious policy issues in formal meetings, often convened at someone's house. We also could share personal experiences without having to disguise our feelings or lower our voices. We didn't have to think about deferring to male authority. There was a comfort level, or in Gloria Steinem's words: "Women understand. We may share experiences, make jokes, paint pictures, and describe humiliations that mean little to men, but *women understand.*"[9]

Our lives gradually expanded. Like many other housewives, I started part-time work as soon as the oldest child hit school. It meant getting dressed up and out of the house once or twice a week to visit stores, marketing products for magazine advertisers. It was not something I really enjoyed, but it was a job with enough earnings to pay the babysitter. Jim earned a respectable income as a newspaper editor, but with three children to raise and educate, we watched our pennies. A bakery delivered a huge sack of powdered milk every few weeks, which was stirred into water for the kids to drink. That worked fine until they were old enough to eat at the neighbor's and discovered that better-tasting milk came ready-made from a container.

When younger women ask now about balancing motherhood and career, I am very cautious about giving advice. The choices in the 1950s were different, just as mine were different from my mother's in the 1930s. My mother didn't have the hands-free modern appliances, but she had household help that doubled as child care. A generation later, we could still manage on one income only because we had lower expectations. We owned just one car; we bought a house near a bus line so Jim could use public transportation to go to work, leaving me the car to chauffeur children. We also didn't have the pressure of paying back tens of thousands in debt from student loans, as do so many of today's young couples. But frankly, there really had been no great ambition among most married women to work. There were very few jobs available to women in the 1950s that were worth foregoing childbearing or worth adding the cost of babysitters.

The phrase "family-friendly workplace" hadn't passed anyone's lips because there wasn't a critical mass of career women in the workplace to make work-home stress an issue. Nor was there a women's movement to articulate the need for support if women were to have real choices. We struggled for answers one at a time. For me, flexibility and freedom meant part-time paid work so that I could have a day out, plus writing magazine articles and book reviews.

There was plenty to write about. *The Kinsey Report* created a furor by stating that 50 percent of women admitted having premarital sex. Rachel Carson awoke environmental conscience with *The Sea Around Us*. Brave black students confronting violence in Little Rock, Arkansas, brought home the issue of school integration. A list-waving senator named Joe McCarthy stampeded a nation with his claims that society was infiltrated by Communists. And the refusal of a tired Rosa Parks to move to the back of the bus in Birmingham, Alabama, started a bus boycott in 1955 that catapulted Martin Luther King, Jr., and the civil rights movement into national consciousness. History may record the Eisenhower years as a period of normalcy, but there was a lot going on.

Despite our knowledge of issues, we tended to be rather naïve about practical politics. Many of us became enthralled with the presidential candidacy of Adlai Stevenson, the intellectual Illinois governor who was deemed a man of the people because a photographer took a picture of him wearing a shoe with a very visible hole in the sole. He became a rallying point for progressives who feared the loss of the old Roosevelt social goals as the country confronted an aggressive Soviet Union. We admired Stevenson's intelligence, courtly manners, and liberal ideas. Determined to get him endorsed in our area, a few of us tried unsuccessfully to pack the local Democratic club. The regulars not only defeated us but chastised us for coming around only at endorsement time.

They had a point, so when my friends all left, I stayed, humbly paying my dues by licking envelopes and handing out flyers. Eventually I was promoted to precinct captain, and I learned the basic skills of turning out a vote, simple things like going door to door to identify the friendly voters in the precinct, and then checking to be sure they went to the polls on election day. Township clubs were required to have both a committeeman and a committeewoman. It was assumed that the committeeman was the real authority, but in our club, the committeewoman carried a great deal of weight because of her ability to get things done and the power of her personality. We all played a game, knowing she was the stronger leader, but the man had to be the figurehead.

Joining organizations meant I was putting down roots, becoming known in the community as other than my children's mother and husband's wife. I also was expanding professionally. One day, I called the manager of the public television station to ask for writing jobs, and he blurted out: "Can you moderate a discussion? I'm having a panel tonight on University City urban renewal—and we've just lost our moderator." Nothing ventured, nothing gained. After all, I had led a Great Books group at the library. That's *sort of* a moderator, and we had studied urban renewal in the League of Women Voters, so I had the facts. Over the next couple of years, as a volunteer moderator at KETC-TV, I learned television by doing. Eventually a commercial station, KPLR-TV, compelled to do public service by new FEC rules, hired me to launch their public affairs department.

Risk taking had paid off again. Whatever gave me the confidence to leap into moderating a television panel with no apparent experience had resulted in a new career that would produce useful skills. The lesson was this: Your best chance to move forward is to seize opportunities as they come along. Success is never guaranteed, but if you do your best, there is no absolute failure.

The television job was a tremendous opportunity, and something of a gender issue, although I didn't think of it that way. Almost all the women on television were weather girls trying to communicate temperatures while appearing attractive. Although Phil Donahue was launching his tremendously popular talk show for women in this time frame, the idea of a woman hosting such a discussion program wasn't even considered, ironic in light of the later extraordinary success of women like Oprah Winfrey and Rosie O'Donnell. I was just delighted to have the job.

In the next ten years, I produced and/or hosted almost every kind of local discussion show, from policy debates to audience participation to phone-ins to a video magazine that anticipated *60 Minutes,* even originating the first prime time local series for a black audience, produced and hosted by a black woman. There were programs on serious social problems, as well as personalities and attractions in the community. It kept me well informed and also taught me to use the more conversational tone demanded by television, imagining that I was speaking through the camera lens to just one person at home in his or her living room. I was able to give a voice to many who previously were unheard in the community, but I never produced a series aimed at concerns of women. The assumption of television executives was that women's programming consisted of soap operas. That made me a pioneer in changing attitudes about women's role in television.

A majority of women were still at home: 44 million homemakers compared to 24 million in the paid workforce. Women could still get excused from jury duty just by saying they were women; they were still denied the most basic property rights and were still paid less than men for doing the same work. The grievances were building up that would push women to become political players. They were beginning to realize that they were, indeed, dancing backwards. It would take only a little more to inspire the awakening.

A handful of political women had begun the process. Before the 1960 election, they gained the promise of presidential candidate John F. Kennedy to create a commission that would look into women's accumulating economic and social grievances. In 1961, President Kennedy kept his word, creating the Commission on the Status of Women and naming Eleanor Roosevelt as the commission's first chair and Esther Peterson, head of the Women's

Bureau in the Department of Labor, as executive director. The action didn't attract big headlines, but it was a breakthrough.

It was the first time women had an official place on the national agenda.

3

Flexing Muscles

If you don't like the way the
world is, you change it. You have an
obligation to change it. You just do it one step at a time.

—**Marian Wright Edelman**

In 1964, the committeewoman of our local Democratic club, Margaree Klein, decided to run for state representative. There were only 3 women out of the 163 members in the Missouri General Assembly at the time. I loyally enlisted in Margee's campaign. It surprised me when many progressive women chose instead to support a young man in the primary. He was a great candidate and became a terrific elected official when he won the race, but their choice of a male candidate over a female made it clear that electing women wasn't a priority.

The 1960s were a strange decade for women, a time of tremendous national change that swept us into involvement in other issues before we could concentrate on our own. It was a decade that began with idealism and hope and ended with assassinations and mayhem in the streets. It was a time when expressing passion about war, racism, and the rights of others gradually freed women to express long-repressed resentment about their own secondary status. It was a decade when America lurched forward through minefields of confrontation to achieve at least some measurable national progress: putting a man on the moon, starting medicare and the Head Start program, and passing the

Civil Rights Act that included women. It also was a decade when women began flexing their political muscles by launching the first national women's political organization.

The decade had a great send-off. John F. Kennedy, the youngest man ever elected president, and the first Catholic, seemed to represent a new spirit. "Ask not what your country can do for you—ask what you can do for your country." Television, which still seemed an innovation in the 1950s, but was a necessity in the 1960s, instantaneously transmitted the president's inaugural challenge, as well as his handsome, youthful image, to households all across the country. His words told Americans they could make a difference, while his image told them America was prosperous, powerful, and free.

The truth was, however, that the prosperous nation had a less attractive underside. There was poverty, ignorance, and hunger in both city and countryside. In a best-selling 1962 book, *The Other America*, Michael Harrington described this poverty as largely invisible because it was off the beaten track for the more prosperous.[1] It was compounded by deep-rooted racism: Blacks were locked into urban ghettos in the North and humiliated daily in the South, and everywhere were denied access to jobs, education, the ballot box, even public facilities. Thousands of young people heard Kennedy's speech as a challenge to tackle these problems.

Thousands of women also were inspired by the issues of the 1960s, and that was important because it moved us to undertake public action for the first time and prepared us for what would follow. That included my own activism around the issue of housing discrimination. Years before, when my mother had taken us on adventurous automobile tours, there was one region we never visited—the Deep South. We wouldn't go there because of the mistreatment of blacks, forced to use separate water fountains and subject to sadistic lynching. As children, we had inhaled social justice with our junket. Now I had children myself, and I felt obligated to move out from a protected, home-centered life to take responsibility for the community's actions, even at the cost of not being liked by everyone.

Being liked was important for women; girls traditionally were taught to be pleasing and never to get involved in controversy. However, the urgencies of the decade made proprieties seem less important to young people in the 1960s, and there were a lot of them. By 1965, 41 percent of all Americans were under twenty, products of the post-World War II baby boom.[2] It was the young who embodied the 1960s spirit. Some would join a new Peace Corps; others became campus activists, holding teach-ins on the Vietnam War; still others risked their lives in the battle for African-American voting rights. A few became black revolutionaries, setting fire to their own neighborhoods; and some just turned on and tuned out, to the beat of new rock music, drugs, and the illusion that it was "love, love, love" that ruled the world.

For young urban blacks, it was hate, not love; they had long-standing grievances over low-paying jobs, poor public services, bad schools, and being hassled by white law enforcement officers who treated their neighborhoods like reservations. In 1965, 200 of the 205 police officers covering a Los Angeles neighborhood called Watts were white, even though the community was 98 percent black.[3] That August, a confrontation between a white officer and a black resident over a traffic incident turned into a six-day riot. A watching crowd began to throw rocks, and rumors escalated the violence. The entire area was devastated, with blocks of burned-out buildings and hundreds of people killed and injured.

St. Louis escaped, but similar riots occurred in other city ghettos as young male blacks released their anger, despite the appalling destruction to their own neighborhoods and the disapproval of older leaders like Martin Luther King, Jr. Wasn't there violence everywhere? The 1960s were the decade of assassinations: President Kennedy in 1963; black nationalist Malcolm X in 1965; and there would be Martin Luther King, Jr., and Robert Kennedy in 1968. Although mainstream black organizations continued to talk about integration to the middle class, black youth wanted separation, black studies and black dormitories at their colleges, black power, and finally, black revolution, with a handful who called themselves "Black Panthers" decking themselves out in military-style uniforms and shooting it out with the police.

The Vietnam War added fuel to every fire, including women's political frustration. During the 1960s, the number of American military personnel in South Vietnam escalated from a few military advisers to hundreds of thousands of troops engaged in frustrating,

bloody battles. There was growing resistance as casualties mounted and the media showed horrifying images of Vietnamese children burned by American napalm. The initial policy of widespread
deferrals for college students meant that it was the working class
and blacks that disproportionately were suffering the casualties. I
remember attending the Women's Hearing on the War in St.
Louis, which drew a variety of women's organizations advocating
an end to the war. There were a lot of speeches, but as one
speaker said, women were just beginning to reach for political
power. We just talked.

Eventually there were hundreds of thousands of antiwar
activists including college students, religious leaders, business-
men, civil rights leader Martin Luther King, Jr., and a Beverly
Hills group called "Another Mother for Peace."[4] The final straw
was the massive Tet offensive launched by the North Vietnamese
in 1968. Even though the drive was stopped, it contradicted the
official propaganda about a weakened enemy, and disapproval of
the war became so strong that President Lyndon Johnson
announced in March that he would not run for reelection.

There was another war being fought in the 1960s, inside
America, that would have a profound influence on the women's
movement. Young African-American college students began sit-
ins at segregated lunch counters in the South in 1960, vowing
they would keep it up until they were served. They responded to
physical attacks with a nonviolence that became the hallmark of
a new civil rights movement. The idea spread. "By the end of
1960, some 70,000 people in over 150 cities and towns had participated in sit-ins. Close to 3,600 of them had been arrested....
Through local actions, the young protesters learned a hard lesson
they would carry with them for years. It was up to them, they
decided, not the federal government or Big Business or even
their elders, to change their country's direction."[5]

Sit-ins were followed by busloads of Freedom Riders testing
segregated bus terminals and then by a massive voter registration
effort. Official white resistance with terrible brutality was por-
trayed on television and created sympathetic support in the
North. In the summer of 1964, 1,000 mostly young white volunteers, both male and female, went to Mississippi to help register
black voters. The project was sponsored by the Student Nonviolent Coordinating Committee (SNCC) and run by a man named

Robert Moses who believed in empowering the poor themselves and in using everyone without regard to race.[6]

Three of the workers were murdered almost immediately, two whites, Andrew Goodman and Michael Schwerner, and one black, James Chaney, who were part of another civil rights group, the Congress for Racial Equality (CORE). Many others were arrested and brutally beaten, but the project succeeded in getting enough poor blacks registered to help build the integrated Mississippi Freedom Democratic Party (MFDP). In 1964, the MFDP sent delegates to the Democratic National Convention to challenge the all-white official delegation and gained national attention for the kind of repression still being practiced by governing officials within the United States.

Women were the heart of the MFDP, and the strongest heart and loudest voice belonged to a young black mother named Fannie Lou Hamer. She was a poor sharecropper from Ruleville, Mississippi, who had been forced to leave the plantation where she worked with nothing but the clothes on her back because she insisted on trying to register to vote. Millions of Americans heard her describe to the Democratic convention credentials committee how she escaped gunshots intended to kill her and how she was falsely arrested and beaten in jail so severely that she suffered permanent injury. "All of this is on account we want to register, to become first class citizens, and if the Freedom Democratic Party is not seated now, I question America, is this America, the land of the free and the home of the brave?"[7]

President Johnson wanted to avoid controversy before the election and deliberately preempted the television time to keep the public from hearing Hamer's testimony. But the networks replayed it in prime time, prompting an outpouring of support from all over the country.

Hamer wouldn't win the delegation battle until the convention of 1968, and she never was able to win public office herself, but she became a familiar figure in feminist circles. She attended the founding meeting of the National Women's Political Caucus in 1971 and was an outspoken advocate for women in the civil rights movement. She complained that when the struggle began making progress, educated males took over as leaders, even though it was women at the local level who still carried the burden of the confrontation.

A fellow grassroots worker, Unita Blackwell, who became the first black woman mayor in Mississippi in 1976, told author Kay Mills that women became civil rights leaders because they were the accustomed providers of services in the community, particularly in the churches. "So in the black community the movement, quite naturally I suppose, emerged out of all the women that carried these roles. We didn't know we was leaders."[8]

Women also were unrecognized leaders in Missouri in the 1960s. Some were African Americans who emerged from the churches and city ward organizations, the black sororities and civil rights organizations, to take leadership in the battle for civil rights, and in the new war against poverty: Marian Oldham, a teacher and civil rights activist who would one day become the first black curator of the University of Missouri; Gwen Giles, a community organizer who would one day become the first black woman state senator; and Pearlie Evans, who would help elect the state's first black congressman, Bill Clay, and as his assistant, wield unprecedented local political power.

There was another thread of feminist political activity. Labor union women had long been vocal in the push for better working conditions in the trades they dominated, acting through unions like the International Ladies Garment Workers Union, and the Communications Workers of America. Men still filled the top union positions, but women provided the energy to achieve better contracts. They gradually realized that they could lose in legislative chambers everything they had gained at the bargaining table. A number of union women became recognized leaders in political action. A few ran for public office. The issues of the sixties helped bring them together with the new feminists.

White women, often the wives and friends of male leaders, had been helping to run political parties for years; in the 1960s, they were joined by white liberals like me who were moved by big issues like civil rights, urban blight, and the Vietnam War to seek a bigger voice in choosing candidates. However, to be very honest, I was helping Margee try for a legislative seat out of friendship, not great issues nor even gender advocacy. Margee was a local committeewoman who had built her own political base of support so that she could run as a conventional politician. We never talked about gender; instead, we used lessons from community organizing and observations of the civil rights and antiwar movements to get attention.

We could see that demonstrations and controversial issues attracted the media. We seized on a hot new environmental problem and organized the Greater St. Louis Clean Air Committee, with Margee as chair. The entire committee was three housewives. To get publicity, we staged a protest in front of St. Louis City Hall wearing gas masks. As others did in the 1960s, we were learning that staged television events were the way to reach the public. The air pollution division in the Department of Health, Education and Welfare (HEW) was so impressed with our publicity that a man was dispatched from Washington to work with us. Our initiative lasted only a little longer than the election campaign, but it had helped arouse interest in air pollution and showed the value of a political woman picking a scientific-sounding subject for a theme.

There still was skepticism about women's competence to hold public office. Women weren't very visible there in the 1960s. There were 234 women state legislators scattered across America in 1963, but many had arrived by appointment or anointment rather than a truly competitive election—early women officeholders in America often were widows of men who had previously held the positions. No one much talked about sex as a political factor. The Civil Rights Act of 1964 as originally proposed did not cover discrimination against women; it was intended to discourage only racial, religious, and ethnic discrimination, not anything related to sex.

The same kind of brush-off occurred after the Civil War when women who struggled for emancipation of slaves saw the U.S. Constitution amended to give African-American men the right to vote, while the same right was not extended to women of any race. Women were considered a form of property in the 1860s, and they still were treated as such one hundred years later. Police didn't interfere when husbands beat their wives because the women belonged to the men for whatever use they chose. Men, not women, had ultimate authority over children as they did over the entire household; women could not complete any kind of financial or credit transaction without their husband's signature. Most women just accepted this as their reality. It was only by accident, by a miscalculation, that women won some coverage in the final version of the 1964 Civil Rights Act.

The legislation was being pushed by new-to-office President Lyndon Johnson in the aftermath of the assassination of President Kennedy in 1963. It would eliminate most discrimination against blacks, and a southern Congressman, Howard Smith, hoped he could kill the bill by amending it to cover sex. At first he seemed successful; members guffawed at the very notion of making discrimination against women a crime. Then Congresswoman Martha Griffiths of Michigan, one of just fourteen women in the U.S. House, rose to her feet.

Congresswoman Griffiths had an interesting history. She and her husband and fellow attorney, Hicks Griffith, had been involved in reform politics in Michigan for years, but when she ran for Congress in 1954 as a former state legislator, the Democrat Party leaders rejected her and endorsed her opponent in the primary. "They nearly died when he turned out to be the head of the White Citizens Council. But . . . I beat him two to one," she said. She was opposed by powerful Michigan labor leaders, even though she had helped labor in the state assembly, because "they didn't want an individual voice speaking up. You were supposed to take orders."[9] Congresswoman Griffiths told an interviewer that her independence from power blocs turned out to be an advantage; it freed her to become a spokesperson for women in Congress.

In 1972, she would lead the successful fight to pass the Equal Rights Amendment (ERA) through the House despite opposition from unions, which at that time thought the ERA would kill protections for women built into labor contracts. That involved an extraordinary achievement of bullying and lobbying enough members to sign a discharge petition to get the ERA proposal out of a hostile committee and onto the floor for debate. Now in 1964, there were similar problems with the unions concerning Congressman Smith's "sex" amendment to the civil rights bill. Liberal Congresswoman Edith Green of Oregon worried that if the amendment were adopted and the civil rights bill passed, it could cost women their job protections.[10] But Griffiths saw an opportunity for women's progress, and she would not be deterred. She rose to her feet and asked fellow congressmen how they could go home having given legal protection to everyone but those nearest and dearest to them—their wives, sisters, and daughters. The men were backed into a corner. "Sex" was added, and to everyone's surprise, the bill still passed.[11]

The previous year, after twenty years' effort, Congress had passed the Equal Pay Act to provide equal pay for equal work without discrimination on the basis of sex. Passing both the Equal Pay Act and the amended Civil Rights Act marked a major shift that was a tribute both to the new women in Congress and to women's increasing economic and political importance. An equal-pay law was long overdue. While working as a reporter, I had been on the bargaining committee of the St. Louis Newspaper Guild. We had tried to increase wages for the classified advertising solicitors, who were paid much less than those who sold the regular display ads throughout the paper. All the classified solicitors were women, and the display salesstaff were all men. It looked like blatant sex discrimination, but there was no law forcing management to provide equal pay. I could imagine what extraordinary courage it took for an individual woman to complain if there were no union to help. Traditional attitudes kept women in second-class status. Would the new laws really help?

I was taking an increasing interest in the operations of government. The League of Women Voters had asked me to monitor the University City Human Relations Commission once a month. Attending was an excuse to get out in the evening while Jim babysat, so I attended religiously. When a vacancy occurred on the commission in 1962, it seemed natural for the council to appoint me to fill it. "She's always there." For the first time in my life, I was part of government, sitting on the decision-making side of the table. Now I had to take responsibility, remember that motions needed seconding, that solutions sometimes required compromise, and that the city council had the real power. It was humbling but also exhilarating. "Your mother, the commissioner," I told our grade-school boys.

The appointment put me in the middle of a major policy battle over housing desegregation. Even though racial discrimination was flagrant in the North, certainly in a border state like Missouri, most Americans wanted to believe that civil rights concerned only the South. University City, a progressive community, was the first St. Louis suburb to ban discrimination in public accommodations. Now the issue was whether to ban discrimination in housing, and that seemed more threatening. Sharing space in a neighborhood was more permanent than sharing space in a restaurant. For most Americans, owning their own home was a long-held dream. It was treasured private turf. It was their equity. Surveys showed that the majority of Americans weren't ready to welcome a black family next door.

Some of us had started an organization called "Freedom of Residence" to help blacks to locate anywhere in the metropolitan area they could afford to buy property. White realtors wouldn't sell property to blacks, no matter their income level, unless it was within a neighborhood that already had been "broken" by a minimum number of blacks as whites fled. There even were separate sales systems with white "realtors" and black "realtists." The battle on the commission was difficult. Opponents of a law barring racial discrimination in the sale of housing argued that they really favored integration but they were afraid University City, as the lone open suburb, would attract so many blacks that whites would flee and integration would fail. For me, on the other hand, it was a simple matter of right and wrong, justice and injustice. We needed to bar discrimination and meet the threat of white flight by countering the myths that encouraged it.

Street wisdom said that black neighbors would create deteriorated property, overcrowded schools, declining public revenues, and neglected public facilities, causing a loss of home values to present residents. But history demonstrated that it was the blacks who were victims of what was happening in the transfer of property and that racial discrimination played a major role.

A federally financed study of urban decay in St. Louis, published in 1972, chronicled a pattern of white flight from older, deteriorating middle-class housing.[12] More than 400,000 whites left the city between 1950 and 1970, using rising postwar incomes and FHA-and VA-subsidized financing to acquire attractive new suburban property.[13] At the same time, massive land clearance in the name of urban renewal was forcing blacks out of existing housing in the city. Discriminatory sales practices bottled them up within a city that had very limited geographic boundaries (because of a shortsighted decision back in 1876 not to extend city lines).

The new absentee owners of housing previously owned by whites were able to extract profit from black renters "through crowding, doubling, conversion to multiple units, merger of small units to accommodate large families."[14] Taxes often remained fixed, so they created a profit by cutting maintenance. This led to devaluation and blanket "red-lining" of vast areas of the city by insurance companies and lenders who refused to do business there. "A normal real estate market then ceases to exist for the affected area. Speculators move in, acquiring houses at greatly distressed value for resale to the poor—usually at a price three to four times what was paid in cash."[15]

This is what white suburbanites saw looking back to the city, and instead of blaming the process, blamed the blacks. They didn't see the many middle-class black neighborhoods where individual homeowners maintained property and values. They didn't know any blacks because of the segregated society. When I first came to St. Louis in 1950, there was only one place a black could eat in the downtown area, the basement cafeteria of Scruggs Vandevoort Barney department store. So I made a point of eating there. A dozen years later, the black I knew best in St. Louis was our cleaning woman.

There were few opportunities to meet across racial lines. An exception was Ruth Porter, the dynamic black woman who provided leadership for Freedom of Residence at a time when there were few examples of women heading such an inter-racial organization. However, the more I came to know and respect African Americans in the common struggle of the 1960s, the angrier I became at the humiliation they suffered on a daily basis.

University City could play a very key role because it was in the path of the feared black expansion. Could we break the destructive pattern? If you don't like the way the world is, then change it, even if it's one step at a time. We had an opportunity, but we also faced a very tough assignment. If I had built any political muscles, now was the time to flex them.

It didn't catch my attention that far away in New York, representatives of all the state commissions on the status of women were meeting on a totally different agenda, one that really didn't hold my interest at the time: attaining equality for women. The commissions all had been issuing reports documenting discrimination against women, including double wage standards. A number of women complained about government failure to pursue sex discrimination cases under the new laws passed by Congress, and they urged adopting an expression of concern. Those in charge resisted; they said that women were in no position to rock the boat. That really irritated the activists, who sought out Betty Friedan, who was covering the meeting as a journalist, and asked her to help create a new national organization that would be a true voice for women.

While the speeches droned on, Friedan sat at a conference luncheon table and drew up an organizational concept on a paper napkin. It called for women to act *now*. Twenty-eight women contributed $5 each to help fund the organization.[16] The National Organization for Women (NOW) was created. In October 1966, the founding conference met in Washington and elected Friedan president. They then had three hundred members and an annual budget of $1,500. Their goal was to win enforcement of antidiscrimination laws and to end the economic inequities between men and women.

Activist women who were committed to so many other causes finally had realized that they had a cause of their own, their own status as women. They also had found a more effective way to flex their muscles, through organization. The contemporary women's political movement was born.

I hardly noticed. In 1967, I became a member of the University City Council and had some very big challenges of my own.

4

Plunging In

Women "have opened so many doors marked 'Impossible'
that I don't know where we'll stop."

—**Amelia Earhart**[1]

All over the country, women were testing the possibility of
public office, plunging in first at the local level. No travel was
required; therefore, they met less criticism about being absent
from family. It made the transition much easier. Patsy Mink was a
Honolulu City Council member first, and then a state senator
before becoming a Democratic member of Congress in 1965.
Republican Marge Roukema of New Jersey, elected to Congress
in 1980, started out as a member of the Ridgewood Board of
Education. Democrat Juanita Millender-McDonald, elected in
1996, was a Carson City, Nevada, Council member before going
on to the state assembly and then the U.S. House.

A study of women entering Congress in 1998 showed that 70
percent of the fifty-three women lawmakers had previously held
elective office, fifteen of the thirty-seven more than one position.
Six had served on county governing boards; fourteen had been a
mayor or city council member; three, municipal judges; and two,
members of school boards. Twenty-seven had served in the legislature. The 1960s were the years when that trend began. Women
frequently took appointed office on boards and commissions.
They had an impact on local office in this decade, as they would
on state office in the 1970s. Women who had become active in

the community were elected to local school boards and city councils, to which they brought their own energy and style.

However, despite years of public advocacy, running for public office never had occurred to me; the idea of asking a lot of strangers for support and money was embarrassing. I considered myself a rather private person and had no idea how someone got enough votes to win a contested election. A career in public office might never have happened if a departing city council member in University City hadn't nominated me to be appointed by the city council to fill his unexpired term. That meant I wouldn't have to run immediately. I could get into office by appointment, something that was fairly common for women in those days.

Still, there were many reasons to say no. I had a full-time, if flexible job in commercial television, and my children were thirteen, eleven, and nine, with the usual busy schedule of music lessons, sports, and school events. Husband Jim was about to become international president of his union, The Newspaper Guild, requiring more frequent absences from home.

Of course, no one said, well, *men* on the council have full-time jobs and busy children and spouses.

The council appointed me by a split vote over a male nominee, 4 to 2. It was a shock to discover that not everyone thought I was wonderful. Upon the swearing in on May 1, 1967, *The St. Louis Post-Dispatch* ran a full-page feature story headlined "The Four Careers of Harriett Woods. . . . She Keeps Busy As Housewife, Television Personality, Editor and City Council Member."[2] This was my first experience with the extra media attention given to women who enter politics. We were a novelty act. The story revealed that in the period since my restive identification with the feminine mystique, I had become another cliché: "Supermom." Guilt about not using abilities was replaced by guilt *for* using them. Stay-at-home mothers might risk being seen bringing in takeout food, but Supermom provided a home-cooked meal every single night. The price of doing more outside the home was having to do it all inside as well. People remarked how lucky it was to have a supportive husband and family. I had my own somewhat cynical definition of "supportive." It was: Women are still responsible for it all.

Actually, Jim adapted well to having a wife in the public eye. He was good-humored about my comparative notoriety, introducing himself at receptions as "Mr. Harriett." Political friends still cite him as the model political husband, always there when needed but never intrusive, a spouse who never wanted to run the campaign. He's a whiz at polishing shoes and doing his own laundry and has learned to cook three one-pot meals: a stew of sausage, cabbage, and vegetables; a macaroni and ground beef concoction he calls "slumgullion"; and something named "hamburger-gravy," which tastes just like it sounds. Years later, when I was often out of town and our sons were grown but single, they would come to share his table, never complaining about eating the same thing time after time after time. But there was no confusion that I had primary responsibility for keeping house and putting dinner on the table.

Even when I was serving in the Missouri Senate, I cooked all weekend so there would be dinners prepared for the three days I was gone. Finally one evening, arriving home exhausted from a week in the legislature only to find the family waiting for me to prepare the meal, I burst out: "What's wrong with you? You're all old enough. Why don't you fix your own meals?" They replied: "But you never asked."

Despite all the changes in male and female roles today, it remains true that a man will expect support for his career demands while a woman feels she must ask permission. Even those of us who were lucky in our partners anguished constantly, especially about the needs of children. Every politician-mother has her stories about being torn between family and work. There were times when we blew up, wishing we could pitch our unsupportive children out the door. In her memoirs *Living a Political Life*, Madeleine Kunin describes watching her first solo half-hour television interview as a legislator, with her children gathered around her. Children: "Boring, it's so boring." Kunin: "Keep still, please. I mean it, I really, really mean it." Children: "Now can we switch the channel?" Kunin: "I want to listen to myself. I can't hear a thing with all your fighting." She adds: "What if the listening audience could see me now, I thought with amused horror, here in my living room yelling at my kids?"[3]

Then there's the embarrassment felt by adolescent boys when their mother is conspicuous. Madeleine Kunin writes: "A friend asked my son in junior high school, 'Hey, is Madeleine Kunin your mother?' Without hesitation, he replied, 'No, she's my aunt.'[4] During the late 1960s, one of my television talk shows preceded a very popular teen program called *Soul Train*. The morning after each show, my sons were greeted by schoolmates who minced along school corridors, calling out my closing line in falsetto voices: "'Til next time, I'm Harriett Woods." My sons pleaded with me to change the time of the show; they didn't mind what I did as long as none of their friends knew about it.

We know our children love us and ultimately are proud of what we do. The difficulty is that we aren't convinced ourselves of our right to put our needs first; we are prey to every grievance, and worry constantly how good a job we are doing as wife and mother. It's this anxiety that causes many to hesitate, to avoid risk taking and to wait to run for office, or take a major job, until children are older. On average, women have been ten years older than men have been as first-term members in state legislatures. That shortens careers. Young fathers can spend the week at the state capital without criticism; not so mothers.

A study by the Center for the American Woman and Politics in 1991 found only 15 percent of women officeholders were forty or younger, compared to 28 percent of men.[5] It is still rare to find women candidates for major office who have small children. Pat Schroeder was the first young mother to be elected to Congress, in 1972. Her daughter was just two, which gave Schroeder a highly visible argument for daycare legislation. Fortunately, attitudes are changing along with society. Many women now start political careers before marriage. In 1998, Jane Swift delivered a baby girl just before her election as lieutenant governor of Massachusetts, and Blanche Lambert Lincoln was elected U.S. Senator from Arkansas as the mother of two-year-old twins.

Still, women continue to face the issue of balancing work and family in a different way from men. The legal discrimination is gone, but we still see ourselves through the same gender lens. It was worse thirty years ago because there was no general recognition of the value of a woman having a career; we still responded to the postwar priorities: Men come first. It was all right to work if you needed the money, but women ambitious for careers were considered selfish. "Four careers" made a catchy title for that newspaper article, but it simply was nonsense to think one person could handle four careers at once. For example, a television executive said that in order to move up in the business, I'd have to go east. I never entertained it as a real possibility, or discussed it with Jim. His job was in St. Louis, and the children had complicated local lives. I might look the career woman, but there was no way to bring in a substitute mother, or to expect the family to give my goals priority over theirs, particularly when those goals seemed very unrealistic for a woman. Barbara Walters had just managed to get on camera after years behind the scenes of the *Today* show; she didn't rise to be an anchor until 1974. Sitting in mid-America, there was no choice; it was family first.

Despite this, we were determined to make a difference. Observing my frantic attempts to address every issue immediately, City Manager Charles Henry dryly commented: "You know, I really don't think you can solve all the city's problems in the first two weeks." Nearly every night in University City I attended meetings of neighborhood associations to build confidence of homeowners in the face of real estate panic selling. There were special programs to build understanding among black and white neighbors, and diligent patrolling of alleys on the lookout for derelict cars or overflowing garbage cans. It was very hard work; it took time.

Few of the male council members matched the effort. They expressed admiration but shrugged as if to suggest that they would do more if they just had a woman's free time! We were fortunate to have an excellent council, with intelligent, dedicated members. Perhaps the biggest difference was my interest in outreach and personal communication. My hand-typed newsletters, filled with X'd out errors, gave constituents a candid appraisal of city affairs that helped maintain confidence, and the city soon began its own newsletter to all citizens. The morale of city personnel was also important so I attended staff meetings on neighborhood maintenance issues to underscore the importance of their work.

I joined the city council as I was turning forty, and won two elections over the next seven years. It seemed then that the forties were the best years of my life. I felt as if I was coming into my own as a person and a woman. Appearing on television had given me physical self-confidence, a sense of being at home in my body in a way that had been missing as an adolescent and even as a young adult. Serving on the city council through diffi-cult battles provided a different kind of confidence, the ability to hold my own on ideas and to be part of solving problems. Occasionally I was assertive in an insensitive way. For example, I smoked tiny cigars in order to give up cigarettes, out of a mis-taken notion that this was safer. My male seatmate rightfully complained, but I asserted my right to continue to puff in his face.

I joined the council to deal with the burning issues of our times, and I joked that they turned out to be trash, traffic, and dogs that pooped on other people's lawns. But over time, it was the big issues that were the catalyst to move women from the sidelines to center stage. For me, it was housing; for future Senator Barbara Mikulski, it was the underprivileged; for Congresswoman Bella Abzug, peace and women's issues; for Congresswoman Claudine Schneider, the environment. Each of us began with a passionate desire to impact some issue and some-how ended up with political careers.

Our efforts often began as lonely crusades. There weren't any women's political support systems in the 1960s outside of our per-sonal friendships. There were few women in power positions to provide mentoring and fewer men who took women seriously enough to offer guidance. Stokely Carmichael, radical leader of the Student Nonviolent Coordinating Committee (SNCC), said that the best way women could serve the civil rights movement was "in a prone position." The traditional women's groups were rarely help-ful once they became political. They were fearful of taking any stand that could be divisive for their members. Politics was a man's business. So those of us who were taking first steps down new paths had to find our own way, building credibility through com-petence and risk taking. We tried to prove ourselves by working harder than the men and by watching for opportunities.

Of course, one had to do something with those opportunities when they occurred. During door-to-door campaigning for school and city taxes, I met hundreds of older citizens living in aging walk-up apartments and small houses. They had been left behind by the flight of children to the new subdivisions. They were iso-lated, with no place to go and no way to get there and often pinched financially, yet we expected them to support tax in-creases. Listening made me their advocate, pushing the city to establish a meal center for seniors, to start senior transportation services, to put in curb cuts to make it easier to move through the streets, and most crucially, to initiate with the support of seniors themselves, an innovative approach to property tax relief for elderly homeowners and renters that eventually passed statewide.

Looking back, this may have been an example of how a woman's compulsion to work a little harder to prove herself produced a benefit. I stumbled on the "circuitbreaker" idea while looking for ideas in laws from other states at nearby Washington University Law Library. Wisconsin had a unique approach to help seniors called the "circuitbreaker" because it was designed to cut in at the point of property tax overload, like the circuitbreaker in a home electrical system. I drafted a similar proposal for Missouri and took it to the meeting of a social action group at the Jewish Community Center branch in University City. There were only five or six seniors there, but they really liked the idea. It would allow them to continue to pay their taxes as responsible members of the community, but then receive refunds for that portion of the property taxes or rent equivalent judged excessive in relation to their household income.

It took five years to pass it through the legislature, and I learned a lot in the process. The first year, we chose as sponsor the first person to say yes, an elderly, first-term Republican whose desk was practically in the hall. The legislature was run by Democrats. The next session, we made a more expedient political choice for sponsor. There was opposition; it took intensive lobbying, a lot of paperwork and many speeches by an ever-broadening support base; but by the time it passed, the proposal had a thousand proud parents. Missouri Property Tax Relief for the Elderly, upgraded over the years, remains the single largest source of nonretirement revenue for lower-income elderly, who know it isn't a handout, but a recognition of their past contributions to the community.

We also were making progress on University City's other problems. Residents needed reassurance that property values wouldn't drop because of deterioration as predicted with racial integration. We passed a law requiring an occupancy permit at the time property is sold, tied to inspections that enforce existing housing and building codes. This meant residents couldn't discard housing as they did used cars; they had to put it into shape at time of sale, or even better, maintain it in good condition through the years. The system also discouraged overcrowding caused by the doubling up of families because schools wouldn't admit students who weren't listed on the permits. Initially, we were attacked by both the real estate industry and some civil libertarians who claimed we were trying to keep blacks out. In fact, it was our first black residents who had been the biggest boosters for the system, in order to prevent the cycle of deterioration from which they had fled.

Everyone began fixing up their property—repairing windows, installing needed electric outlets, tuckpointing chimneys—knowing they would have to do it eventually if they ever sold their homes. Property values did drop during the initial panic, but the occupancy permit, a crackdown on real estate signs, and multiple efforts to build community spirit turned things around. These were exhausting years on the council, with contentious public hearings and emotional exchanges as we groped toward answers that would preserve an open community in the face of fears and real estate exploitation. Blacks and whites gradually learned to know one another as neighbors, and in the long run, we actually were better off than before integration began.

As University City reached the year 2000, the population was roughly half and half black and white, and although the challenge of achieving truly integrated neighborhoods and schools hadn't been solved, housing values were at an all time high. Best of all, through the courage of University City in going first, the myth that integration brings blighting was destroyed.

It's interesting to conjecture that University City in those days had a lot of the qualities now associated with feminine leadership: an emphasis on candid communication, outreach, collaboration, and honest government but also a readiness to take a stand on principle. It certainly was a good training ground for a woman politician. Good communities require constant effort. During the years sitting around with other mothers discussing children, I came to understand that neighborhoods thrive when people socialize together. One of my early newsletters startled constituents by proposing that "every community needs a good pub," a place for folks to get together and relax.

So it was no surprise that I supported a license for just such a restaurant-pub to locate in our struggling commercial area,

despite the vocal opposition of nearby seniors who were traditionally my biggest supporters. They opposed more liquor licenses.
The authorization squeaked through by one vote, 3 to 2. It was
risk taking of a different sort, taking a chance on people and their
dreams. The pub, called "Blueberry Hill," went on to become
exactly the gathering place we needed, sparking other development around it.

Not all my ideas went so well. For example, there was the
proposal to turn a public school in an endangered neighborhood
into a "community school" that offered public services, daycare,
recreation, and adult classes. It wasn't in my ward, but it seemed
like a wonderful idea so I talked the council into approving it.
Feeling triumphant, I scheduled an announcement meeting at
the school. Residents practically booed me out of the building.
Who asked you for a community school? No one talked to us,
they said. Eventually, with their support, portions of the proposal, like the child care center, became reality. Of course, I
learned a very important lesson. Just because you have power
doesn't mean you should use it. Listen first.

Throughout this time period, more and more women were
engaging in community actions that put them in the public eye.
Women in political leadership had become a hot topic for club
programs. This semicelebrity couldn't hide the fact that elected
women still were isolated within a male power structure. Women
were winning their elections on the same basis as male colleagues, but we weren't acknowledged as equal once we arrived.
This was particularly annoying within municipal organizations
where it was common to have all-male governing boards.
Leaders claimed this occurred because officers had to be mayors,
a position women rarely achieved at that time.[6] The mayor
requirement was elitist as well as sexist because the vast majority
of municipal league members were council members.

Something had to be done. It was my first feminist cause,
although I certainly never would have described it that way at
the time. It just seemed unfair to work long and hard within the
organization and not have the opportunity to move into a position of leadership. I could fret about it, I could walk away, or I
could take action. There was a network to build on in previous
joint efforts on issues such as property tax relief for the elderly
and revenue sharing. This led to the kind of camaraderie that

develops working on a common cause, with staff members as well as fellow local officials.

In 1972 I finally was elected to the board of directors of the National League of Cities (NLC), the second woman ever selected. There were just 100 women at that national convention, among 2,000 total delegates. I promptly convened a women's Caucus, including a press conference, through which several of us jointly demanded greater representation for women. When cameras showed up, the male leadership paid attention. The next edition of the organization's magazine featured four women as "new voices in city hall." We explained to the writer that the purpose of our separate NLC women's Caucus was to focus on inequities; we hoped the separate Caucus would rapidly disappear as no longer needed. A decade later, a woman was elected NLC's national president.

It seemed that part of our responsibility as women leaders was to break barriers. That wasn't as hard as it sounds in the 1960s because there were so many barriers to break. The president of the local bank invited me to join his board of directors and extended an invitation to speak to a statewide bankers' meeting, I discovered there that I was the first woman outside director of any bank in the entire state of Missouri. It was absurd, but it accurately reflected the status of women on corporate boards and in executive suites all over the country.

The speech to the bankers became an opportunity to point out how much money they were losing by ignoring women. After all, women who can't get loans can't open business accounts; and women who are treated as though they are financial idiots won't be able to manage their own affairs after a divorce or as widows. When young women employees are put in teller cages and stay there for the rest of their working lives—in contrast to young men who are rotated up to management—it's a waste of costly training and talent. The bankers came up afterward to praise the speech; but they didn't seem in any hurry to make changes.

Suddenly everything seemed to have a gender angle. As we moved into the 1970s, each breakthrough taught us more about the system from which we had been excluded. It was a revelation when the governor nominated me to serve on the state highway commission (the first woman, naturally). A member of the highway patrol picked me up at my house to drive me to a private airfield where the chief highway engineer waited to provide personal escort service in a department plane to the meeting, just 125 miles away. An ashtray embossed with my name was at my place in the meeting room. So this was how the boys did business! The message was clear: Feeling important is important. There are big bucks involved in road contracts; there are summer jobs to be handed out to the sons of campaign donors; there is incredible power in the wheeling and dealing that go into deciding where highways will be built.

It had been assumed that a woman couldn't play these games. We just play them differently, I said to myself. A few years later, an investigative reporter would write: "In many ways, the Missouri Highway Department is like a secret organization—a kind of club that operates oblivious to the outside world."[7] The department kept all its long-term plans secret. That wasn't in the public interest and was a handicap to urban planners. These plans were public documents, so I promptly handed a copy to representatives of the St. Louis regional planning agency. The state highway engineers ground their teeth, even more so when I insisted on reading the next five-year plan before we adopted it. Alas, after about six months, a constitutional wrangle wiped out the highway appointment. I joked that the engineers turned my official picture to the wall and breathed a sigh of relief.

An emphasis on open government was almost a characteristic of elected and appointed women, as we plunged into service in local, state, and national legislatures. One of the main reasons that Congressman F. Edward Hebert of Louisiana, chairman of the House Armed Forces Committee, didn't want Pat Schroeder on his committee was that she asked too many questions. He made her literally share a single chair at committee meetings with another congressman, Ron Dellums. (Hebert didn't like blacks either.) She reports in one of her books that she was undeterred by sitting on half a chair and said of her battle to expose inefficiency and waste: "I had always believed government was not a fungus: It could survive in sunshine."[8]

Schroeder represented a new breed of women entering Congress, women with professional skills and an independent spirit. In 1960, just 230 women in the nation received law degrees, 5 percent of all those awarded; by 1976, there were

6,208 women, receiving 19 percent of all degrees awarded, and by the end of the 1970s, women were receiving almost a third of all law degrees.[9] Some became associates in large law firms, but many set up on their own, to develop advocacy in cases involving domestic violence and sexual discrimination, and in a few cases, they used their degrees as a credential for election to public office, just as men had been doing for years.

The newly emancipated women of the 1960s, still treated as outsiders by the power brokers, were building their own paths to power. Women like Margaret Heckler, Ella Grasso, Shirley Chisholm, and Bella Abzug would be followed in the 1970s by a parade of stars: Pat Schroeder, Barbara Mikulski, Yvonne Braithwaite Burke, Millicent Fenwick, Geraldine Ferraro, Elizabeth Holtzman, Barbara Jordan, Martha Keyes, Lynne Martin, Mary Rose Oakar, Claudine Schneider, and Olympia Snowe. Inspired by their 1960s role models and with new confidence in their ability to address the great issues of their day, women were plunging into politics.

The question for those of us further down the pipeline was this: Were we ready to risk moving on up?

5

Opening Doors

A Woman's Place Is in the House . . . and in the Senate.

—Slogan of the 1970s

Women do the lickin' and the
stickin' while men plan the strategy.

**—Former Mayor Moon Landrieu of New Orleans, quoted in 1973.
Mary Landrieu, his daughter, was elected to the U.S. Senate in 1996.**

In 1976, I ran for election to the Missouri Senate. It was a major leap for someone whose primary political experience was in nonpartisan local office. It simply wouldn't have been possible without the savvy and muscle of the new women's political movement. The general assembly controlled millions of dollars and critical policy decisions affecting all of our lives, and there was serious resistance to women moving inside where those decisions were made. The men who guarded its gates were not interested in giving place and power to any female. We would have to push that door open.

The 1950s had been the years of women's discontent. The 1960s were their years of social commitment. Now the 1970s were the years when we politically came of age. In 1970, women's wages had fallen to 59 cents for every dollar earned by men. The 59 cents figure became a symbol connecting suburban homemakers with working women. We all felt the indignity of being paid less just because of gender, and we wore "59¢" buttons to meetings as a reminder of every other injustice we faced. We joined new organizations dedicated to correcting these injustices by putting women into public office.

The decade saw an explosion of women's political activity, involving new legislation, major conferences, party reform and electoral politics. On August 26, 1970, an estimated 50,000 turned out to march in New York City on the first Women's Equality Day, marking the fiftieth anniversary of ratification of the amendment that gained women the vote. Six years later, the United Nations "Decade for Women" began, to include a number of international conferences to discuss women's economic and social status around the world. And in 1977, American women won government funding to hold their own official conference in Houston, which produced an aggressive twenty-five-point plan of action to bring women into full participation in society.

Within just a very few years, women had forced politics to expand to take up their concerns. Topics that once could not be mentioned in polite society, like rape, domestic violence, and sexual harassment, now were part of public policy and political action. Women's evolving economic participation also forced Congress to pay attention. In 1972 it passed an extension of the 1964 Equal Pay Act to include professional women and domestics, and it also passed Title IX of the Education Act mandating an end to sex discrimination in federally assisted educational programs, a change that would make so much difference in sports. There also was the Equal Credit Opportunities Act in 1974 to eliminate flagrant discrimination in all consumer credit practices. In 1973, the Supreme Court finally affirmed an order forbidding sex-segregated help-wanted ads. And the Equal Rights Amendment whipped through both the House and Senate and was sent out for ratification to the states in 1973.

These victories were not won easily. Most progress was being achieved through women's own efforts, stimulated by an awakening to "sisterhood," and a new responsibility women felt for one another. They had applied the lessons of the 1960s, and like the black students who sat down at lunch counters in the South a decade before, decided they wouldn't depend on government or business—or men. They would do it themselves. The first emergency rape crisis hotline opened in Washington, D.C., in 1972. By 1976, there were four hundred independent rape crisis centers across the country offering counseling and support.[1] The first battered women's shelters in the United States opened in 1973 in Tucson, Arizona, and St. Paul, Minnesota. By 1979, there were more than 250.[2]

The new issues in women's lives were reflected in new organizations with names like 9 to 5, the National Association of Working Women; the Alliance of Displaced Homemakers; the North American Indian Women's Association; the Coalition for Labor Union Women; the Older Women's League; and the National Black Feminist Organization.

Popular culture began to reflect women's changing status and attitudes. Amid *Gunsmoke, Little House on the Prairie,* and *The Waltons* on television, there was the *The Mary Tyler Moore Show* about a single working woman and *Charlie's Angels,* about glamorous female adventurers. Those women still deferred to their bosses, but *Maude,* an outspoken homemaker, did not. She even discussed having an abortion on national TV. There were also strong women in motion pictures: Jane Fonda as a prostitute in *Klute;* Ellen Burstyn, as an escaping housewife in *Alice Doesn't Live Here Anymore;* and Sally Field, as a feisty factory worker in *Norma Rae.* Each won an Academy Award for female characters who refused to be victims, who took risks, made their own decisions, and opened their own doors.

At the local level, it still was a big step from cloistered homemaker to political officeholder, even for women like me who already were balancing private and public roles. We felt empowered by all the changes in society but still accepted that some positions might be beyond our reach. We were deterred by a society that judged women differently and didn't encourage them to fill nontraditional positions. There were a lot of jokes about macho, "bossy" women, and none of them were kind. To change this environment would take some risk taking and new organizations. We needed some strong personalities with greater political experience to lead the way.

It was women located at the centers of media and political action, principally in New York and Washington, who became our political mentors. They had the national spotlight to vocalize women's grievances, to get everyone's attention, and to pull us

together. The three most prominent were Betty Friedan, Gloria Steinem, and Bella Abzug. Betty Friedan was the author of a best-seller, the intellectual who had roused suburban women to rebellion and led NOW in its early days. Gloria Steinem, a writer and editor with striking good looks, blue aviator glasses, miniskirt, and waist-long blond hair, was the media darling and movement communicator who disarmed male skeptics even as she skewered them.

But it was Congresswoman Bella Abzug who played the pivotal role in the 1970s for me and for other women who had chosen the route of candidacy and campaigns. She was the role model of practical political risk taking, someone who took the chance of running for office and therefore the one who had a political platform with visibility and leverage. She used it aggressively. She was elected to Congress in 1970 from a base of peace activism, party reform, and advocacy for women. She was not a quiet freshman. She immediately proposed a resolution requiring U.S. withdrawal from Vietnam within six months, and she took the floor constantly in debate.

A contemporary book notes: "Ms. Abzug was not merely a woman; she was a difficult woman. . . . Unpopular with the party leadership, she also was one of the least popular freshmen in Congress, a 'loudmouth' continually in the vanguard of unpopular causes as far as the leadership was concerned."[3]

But there also was this, from a newspaper columnist: "The things she is against, most decent people are against: killing, war, waste, the mutilation of our national priorities. . . . Bella can infuriate you, cause you to despair, and drive you to make novenas, but it would be a terribly lonely town without her."[4]

Bella Abzug herself said: "I'm a target because I'm a woman. I've been a leader of the peace movements, a leader of the movements of the underrepresented, a leader in the woman's movement, yes, and in the demand of women for more representation, politically as well as economically, for equal pay for equal work, a leader in the fight for child care. . . . I think that there is resistance to accepting women yet in politics, . . . and I think that as we seek more political power and more economic equality there will be more resistance to us."[5]

She wrote in her book *Gender Gap* that she had been an "instinctive feminist" all her life. She told the story of her father's death when against all traditions of Orthodox Judaism, she recited kaddish for him along with the male relatives. When no one tried to stop her, she said she "came to understand that one way to change outmoded traditions was to challenge them."[6]

Harvard Law School refused to admit her in 1942 because it did not admit women. She graduated from Columbia University's law school instead and went to work full-time as a civil rights, labor, and general-practice lawyer while marrying and having two children. She said she began wearing her trademark big-brimmed hats to court to make sure the judges understood she wasn't a secretary, and she ended up wearing them everywhere, including the floor of the U.S. House. There were just 13 women in the House out of 435 members when she was sworn into office. Bella said she was convinced that the numbers wouldn't grow unless women got organized. If the door wouldn't open when one person pushed, bring a brigade.

Betty Friedan also had been talking up the need to focus on electing women; after some jousting about who thought up the idea first, they joined forces. Bella Abzug convened a strategy group of key activist women in a House hearing room that led to a much larger meeting of some three hundred women from around the country, in the Statler-Hilton Hotel in Washington. The National Women's Political Caucus was born on July 10, 1971. Liz Carpenter, who had worked in the White House for Lyndon and Lady Bird Johnson, handled the press. She later wrote: "Everyone had a different issue—peace, wages, civil rights (but) . . . top priority was to run for office and win voices in Congress and in the state legislatures, to create a Caucus in each state, to find women who would fight for women."[7]

Bella Abzug had very definite ideas about how women should construct a political movement and woe to those who disagreed with her. Betty Friedan favored supporting women for office "within fairly minimal guidelines," according to Abzug. Abzug adamantly rejected this and carried the day. The founding statement said that the NWPC would support only those women candidates "who declare themselves ready to fight for the rights and needs of women, and of all under represented groups." "I was not prepared to spend time getting just any woman elected," Bella Abzug said.[8] She wanted a movement for social change. Friedan also cared deeply about the issues, but she was concerned that mainstream women would be driven away by the use of very liberal language and tight endorsement requirements. She was overruled. The issue would be argued again and again over the years as the NWPC and other progressive groups sought to attract a broader range of women as members while retaining their founding principles.

In the fall of 1971, Bella Abzug came to St. Louis for a previously scheduled speech at the Jewish Community Centers Association just a few weeks after the National Women's Political Caucus was organized in Washington. She had been energized by recent events and energized the local women in turn, telling them that the only way to change society was to get women organized politically. A number of the women who heard her went out and did just that. They founded a St. Louis Women's Political Caucus and began to look for a likely race and a woman candidate to elect.

The timing was good. District lines for elected representatives at all levels had just been redrawn in Missouri, as they were everywhere in the country, to reflect shifts of population recorded in the 1970 census count. Members of the new St. Louis Caucus looked for a district that would be friendly for a woman candidate, an open seat without an incumbent who would be tough to oust, a district where voters had shown the kind of liberal attitudes that signaled they might welcome someone who shared the NWPC agenda. Too often women had simply taken their chances wherever they were. Taking this much care in picking a target showed a new political maturity.

We found what we wanted in a central suburban district in St. Louis County, but a politically well connected young man with perfectly acceptable stands on the issues had already staked it out. In times past, women would have politely stepped aside, but the new Caucus had a new motto: "We don't defer." We were ready to give fate a push; all we needed was a candidate. Few women had public records; there weren't any women mayors in the area and very few women city council or school board members. The "back-to-school" movement was just beginning among restless homemakers, so there were few with professional credentials.

The Caucus members gave up on finding someone with conventional qualifications and instead found someone who reflected the alternative political paths women had been traveling. Her name was Sue Shear. She was a petite, middle-aged homemaker with a deep commitment to social justice and women's rights and a reputation for stubborn persistence combined with a warm femininity. The ideal political woman of the 1970s had to be strong and soft at the same time. Society expected her to be womanly enough to reassure them about her sexual identity but tough enough to justify electing to an office traditionally occupied by a man.

She also was expected to have experience at a time when men held all the power positions so it was unlikely a woman would get any. Shear had devoted her political energy to helping others get elected. In those days that meant helping men like U.S. Senator Stuart Symington, whose campaign office she had managed. It never had occurred to her that she could run for office herself. There were issues of age and family, too. Surely, she said, she was too old at fifty-five to be starting out in the legislature. Besides, her businessman husband, Harry, could never manage in her absence. Men didn't worry about those issues, her friends said, and pleaded the importance of the race to other women. Then Harry surprised everyone by urging her on, and one of her three children, a son in his early twenties, volunteered to manage the campaign.

Sue Shear proved to be an extraordinary campaigner who outworked her opponent with an energetic door-to-door campaign that became a model for the rest of us to follow. Women might not have business buddies to raise money, but we could persuade the voters with personal contact. The new Caucus members flooded the neighborhoods, and Shear won a tough primary and the general election that followed, the first woman elected in Missouri with a specific mandate for gender reform. The election had shown us how to open those closed doors that seemed so intimidating; we just needed women with the courage to turn the doorknob.

The Missouri legislature that Sue Shear joined in 1973 was not an easy place for women, resembling many others across the country. There were just 12 women out of 199 members in the whole general assembly, 11 of them in the house. It was an extremely conservative body, particularly when dealing with issues like the Equal Rights Amendment and abortion. There were strong, hostile pressures from religious bodies like the Roman Catholic Church and the Assemblies of God, which is headquartered in Missouri. Representative Shear was ridiculed on the floor for proposing antidiscrimination statutes and hooted down for efforts to impose state standards on daycare centers.

The fact that they attacked her actually was a sign of their weakness, revealing fears that her thoughtful proposals might pass unless they isolated her, but that wasn't much consolation. Sometimes she was near tears, and after I entered the legislature and was staying in the same motel, there were mornings when it took pep talks to help her prepare as we walked up the hill to the capitol. She battled on with incredible tenacity over the next twenty-five years, and when she retired from the legislature at age eighty, she had won the respect and affection of fellow legislators, as well as their votes on many key issues, such as early childhood education and the needs of women in prison.

Representative Shear had the company of other progressive women who were winning seats in the house during the 1970s, several from the other major urban area including Kansas City. She also had the mentoring of Representative DeVerne Calloway, the first black woman elected to the legislature, who brought the tough love of a survivor of civil rights and poverty struggles. There was no such support in the senate, where there was just one woman, a former state representative from Kansas City named Mary Gant, who opposed the Equal Rights Amendment. When rumors circulated that the state senator from my district planned to retire in 1976, women urged me to run.

I was interested, but not if it meant being identified solely as an advocate for women's issues. I had seen what happened to Sue Shear. Political women in the 1970s faced a dilemma. A major reason for getting elected was to add a different voice to decisions, but anyone labeled "an advocate for women's rights" was given second-class status by male leadership. The disinterest and contempt for matters that weren't on the male priority list translated into contempt for those who espoused them. That gender bias extended to judgments on women's style. Women who didn't have a commanding manner in debate were downgraded, even though they might be very effective in committee work and negotiation. The last thing I wanted was to wear a gender badge.

What was the point in opening the door if you were isolated once you got inside?

The issue of "running as a woman" bothered me deeply. It's instinctive to insist on equality. That's a matter of justice; but my public commitment had preceded the contemporary women's movement, flowing from other causes like civil rights and at-risk neighborhoods. I had worked with men most of my adult life. My interest in running for the senate stemmed from work on urban and elderly issues, not feminism. There was power in the senate to control money, jobs, and policies on matters important to me. That's why I wanted to go there.

In an oral history for the Archives of the University of Missouri–St. Louis in 1977, I said: "I am really not a woman's candidate . . . a woman's politician" and then rationalized: "I am really the stronger spokesman for women . . . by not being the woman's issue legislator."[9]

Of course, I was kidding myself. There were so few women in public roles that the pressure to be a gender spokesperson was overwhelming. I often was the token female in male groups and would find myself responding when someone made a joke about women's libbers or some other sexist remark. It was aggravating to rise to the bait, but even worse to keep silent and let them think I agreed. Besides, I knew that it was impossible to control the labels others stick on you.

Whatever I might prefer, the decision to run had to include the gender concerns. Women still attracted more attention, and they were given a different kind of scrutiny. Even though our three sons were now teenagers, there were questions about the propriety of a woman abandoning her family to be gone to the state capital three and a half days a week. I was the one who cooked every meal to prove I was a good wife and mother. Could I let go without guilt? Would I be able to accomplish enough if elected to make the family sacrifice worthwhile? It was at this point that I really began to pay attention to the new women in Congress.

These were women who had paid their own political dues, moving up from state legislatures or local offices, often without regular party support, so that they felt independent and ready to advocate reform. Some were unattached; others had busy husbands and long commutes. Personal arrangements didn't affect the quality of their performance. It was no accident that Barbara Jordan and Elizabeth Holtzman seemed to make such an impression on the television public watching the Watergate hearings. Women leaders seemed freer to be candid, to speak up for principle. If they could do it at the national level, surely I could take up the challenge in the Missouri Senate.

There was psychological support from another source. *Ms. Magazine* was founded in 1972 by Steinem, with Pat Carbine. It nationalized the women's movement by offering an attractive publication that anyone, anywhere could buy and read, spreading women's news and ideas quickly across the country. The magazine's name came from the term of address many women were using in the 1970s to assert their own identity. They refused to be named by others as "Mrs." or "Miss," with the automatic assumptions that went with being single or married. For many, the act of putting Ms. before a name was a statement about our separate, equal value. It also solved the practical problem of addressing a woman whose marital status was unknown.

Women all over the nation were struggling with the idea of opening doors—to jobs, to education, to political office. I didn't attend the first convention of the National Women's Political Caucus, which attracted 1,200 to Houston in 1973, but those who did came away with fresh energy to put more women inside the chambers where decisions were being made. The feeling was not unanimous, however. Even as they tried to open doors, others were trying to close them. There was a growing backlash against the women's movement. Commentators derided women's aspirations as exceeding their abilities; traditionalists deplored the impact on families if women pursued careers. Feminists were described as man-hating extremists, and at the same time, as wanting to be men. They were defying nature, critics said; they should accept their biological difference and the secondary status that went with it.

The conservative right wing in the 1960s and 1970s had at its core a fervent antiCommunism and America-first nationalism that was represented by the John Birch Society, Alabama Governor George Wallace, and among women, Phyllis Schlafly, a Republican attorney from Alton, Illinois, who ran the *Eagle Forum*, and *Stop ERA*. Her book *A Choice, Not an Echo*, provided philosophical support for the presidential candidacy in 1964 of conservative Barry Goldwater. All these extreme conservative voices claimed to be defending the nation against threats to its founding principles, and to family and traditional religious values. They saw the contemporary women's movement as undermining all three but also as an easy target for attack.

So did a tennis hustler named Bobby Riggs who taunted women players as second-class athletes and said he could beat the best of them with little effort. He intimidated a few women players before top-ranked Billie Jean King took him on. It was a measure of the growing interest in the issue of women's rights that the resulting tennis match, advertised as a "Battle of the Sexes," drew 40 million viewers to their television sets in 1973. For many, it was entertainment, but it was an emotional encounter with serious symbolism for all of us. When Billie Jean won, we sighed with relief. We knew that the tennis match itself was a ridiculous test of women's equality, but winning respect in one arena helped to win it in all.

The percentage of women legislators was inching up far too slowly. It was only 4 percent for the country in 1971 and would still be only 6 percent in Missouri ten years later when the figure had jumped to 12 percent nationwide. Women were the majority, we kept saying. The slow progress in Missouri was an embarrassment. Some of us had to take advantage of opportunities to run for office; my opportunity had come, and all I had to risk was losing.

I went to see the incumbent senator in my district, Maurice Schechter, to learn his plans. He was evasive. He said there was a male local official filing for the office who promised to withdraw if he decided not to retire. He advised me to wait. That made me uneasy. Could the senator's fierce opposition to the ERA influence him against a woman candidate? Waiting too long wasn't wise. I needed to start early because I was relatively unknown in many parts of the senatorial district.

A few years before I had approached the mayor of my city who was rumored to be retiring after many years in office and expressed interest in running for his job, but said I would defer if he wanted to continue. Of course the mayor immediately filed for reelection. I wasn't about to make that mistake again. This time, I told the incumbent senator that I definitely was running, but out of respect would wait to give him plenty of time to announce his retirement as he wished. However, unlike his male friend, once filed, I wouldn't withdraw.

Brave words. In fact, without the help of the senator and the party machinery, I didn't have a clue how to run for the senate. All my experience was in nonpartisan city races that could be won with a few neighborhood coffees and some printed fliers. The senate district was ten times the size of my council ward, and much more diverse. Although active in my own political township organization, I didn't know the key party committeemen in other, more working-class areas, where endorsement was supposed to deliver the vote in primaries.

As we had suspected all along, the incumbent senator used his retirement announcement in early 1976 to endorse his male buddy. By that time, we were launched. The Caucus women had offered their support; they made it sound simple: "We'll lend you a campaign manager to get started. We'll identify primary voters so you'll know whom to target going door to door. Just get a card file to sort your contacts by precinct and you're in business." No one mentioned money, although, of course, there was no way to do without it, even in a low-budget, door-to-door campaign.

Raising money quickly became the principal challenge. I hated asking for it. Women who were so enthusiastic about my candidacy didn't write checks. Women were just beginning to establish professional credentials; they wouldn't be moving in large numbers into better-paid careers until the 1980s. Most of them still viewed money as an allowance they received from someone else and didn't control. Women were homemakers and didn't contribute to charity, let alone a political campaign, without a husband's approval. They didn't even have their own checkbooks. Men did, but they didn't contribute to a woman candidate.

Six months after starting the campaign, my all-volunteer staff was sitting around the dining room, which served as campaign headquarters, bemoaning how tough it was to get contributions. The campaign treasurer (the family lawyer) read off the amounts received so far: $25, $10, an occasional $50. Then he said: "Here's a check for $100!" Everyone exclaimed: "Who gave Harriett $100?" He answered: "Harriett's mother!" (She also donated the first $1,000 in my U.S. Senate race.)

The state senate campaign was the classic women's effort of the 1970s: lots of volunteers, little money, even less party support, and exhausting door-to-door walks evenings and weekends for months, good weather and bad. The campaign issues reflected my public record: opposition to "the throwaway society," a discarding of neighborhoods, the environment, and older people. My opponent, Frank Munsch, promptly announced that the issues were the Equal Rights Amendment and abortion, and he was opposed to both. The press presumed that as a woman candidate, those had to be *my* issues; they knew they would arouse more reader interest than the environment, so the newspaper headline read:"ERA and Abortion Top Issues in 13th District."

Fortunately, the homemakers of St. Louis included the best administrator I've ever met. Jody Newman volunteered to manage the campaign and eventually ran my two U.S. Senate races. She fit Friedan's pattern, a young mother at home with children, with great education and a previous career, who restlessly sought stimulation. She was typical of the women risk takers who were behind the scenes in the 1970s, taking their own first steps toward power. We became equal partners in politics.

My base of support was in University City, and in neighboring upper-middle-class areas. That kind of background was typical for many early women candidates. To win, many had to get a sizeable vote from working-class neighborhoods where we were not as well known and where the active politicians didn't think any woman was electable. In one key area, the political club offered a rather cool reception, despite our dropping word to their members, who belonged to labor unions, that I had been a union shop steward years earlier while working as a newspaper reporter.

Fortunately for me, the club leadership split in an internal power struggle, and a few men agreed to help our campaign not because they liked me particularly but just to beat the other guys. They had never supported a woman before. As we knocked on doors, they were surprised at the friendly reception. Ordinary folks answered our knocks saying: "It's about time for a woman in office!" "Woman" seemed interchangeable with "outsider" and "change." It was a response that women candidates would hear for years to come.

Going door to door, my stomach did clutch nearing houses with religious statues in the yard. The *Roe v. Wade* court decision had legalized abortion just three years earlier, and the antiabortion movement was making this election a test of its strength. "God is Pro-Life" signs were going up on every parish lawn; priests denounced me from the pulpit; church bulletins identified me as a baby killer; leaflets with gruesome pictures blanketed cars in church parking lots. In one case, I was "disinvited" to a political meeting that happened to be scheduled in a church-owned building. In reality, the person answering the knock at a door guarded by a religious symbol was just as likely to offer support. It was a question of not being intimidated, of reminding voters that the abortion issue didn't belong in politics, and of winning respect for the principle that families should make their own private decisions on this matter, even if we differed on the answer.

Ultimately abortion did not decide the election. What did was our intense canvassing of Democratic-leaning precincts, concentrating on doors of frequent voters in areas with favorable voting patterns. This was old-fashioned politics, mastered by new-fashioned women. It helped that I had previous experience organizing neighborhoods, working with fellow municipal officials, communicating for years on television, supporting social justice causes, and advocating for the elderly. It helped that I had a husband and three teenage sons whose picture on brochures was evidence that the candidate couldn't be a dangerous feminist! But as much as anything else, it was the personal energy; people pledged their votes after watching me run up and down front steps for a whole block in 90 degree St. Louis heat.

Judging from this experience, women still needed to be overqualified to compete; it had taken everything I had done in the past dozen years to beat an opponent with virtually no record. I was elated by victory but saddened by the realization that much of the campaign had been fought over my opponent's definition of "women's issues." Could I use the victory to address issues of taxation, the environment, housing, and the elderly and go beyond gender stereotyping?

My middle son Peter was quarterback of the University of Missouri football team. There is nothing more important in the Midwest than the state university football team. When the out-state press discovered the connection, my stature increased; reporters immediately labeled me "Pete's mom" and asked what it was like being a mother and a state senator. I was happy to be identified with my son, I said, but "I want to be known as the senator from the 13th District who just happens to be a woman." Never mind all that, the reporters said, "What will your election do for the ERA?" The ERA's not my main priority, I insisted.

Little did I know.

6

The Men's Club

Dear Senator-Elect Vuich:
Congratulations on your election.
You have successfully crashed the last
publicly funded gentlemen's club in California.

**—Open letter from David Roberti, Majority Leader, California Senate, to
Senator-Elect Rose-Ann Vuich, *Los Angeles Times*, December 5, 1976**

Missouri has a beautiful capitol; its dome rises dramatically
above the banks of the powerful Missouri River in the center
of the state, in Jefferson City, named for the president who
added this territory to the Union. The building is filled with historical
artwork, stone-carved mottoes, tapestries, Thomas Hart
Benton murals, walnut woodwork, lavish murals, and massive
mahogany doors with engraved brass doorknobs. Footsteps echo
in the marble corridors. The building is a monument to state government
that is meant to provide an impressive setting for the
men who run it. There are state capitols like this all across the
country.

It is a very male world; it certainly was when I arrived in 1977.
Men were the legislators, the lobbyists, the bosses. Women
served as support forces: secretaries, phone operators, waitresses.
A standard quip at the time was that women around the capitol
belonged behind the typewriter or in bed. Entering this world felt
like Alice going through the looking glass. The worst part was
that, as an outsider, it was hard to learn the rules of the game.

When I was sworn in, the only other woman senator, an avowed antifeminist, didn't offer any welcoming counsel. There were a handful of friendly women in the House but they weren't familiar enough with senate protocol to give much guidance. My male predecessor, who should have mentored me, was downright hostile.

This was a particularly tricky time to be ignorant. A new president pro tem was elected to lead the Senate, and I had voted for the loser, instinctively picking the more urban candidate. That wasn't good; the pro tem controlled everything, like committee assignments and the priority for considering bills. But there was one comfort: The man I supported, Jack Gant, promised to watch out for me no matter what happened. He even had me sign behind him on the bills he introduced: "You don't want to handle any bills of your own the first term."

Four weeks into the session, he was appointed a judge and left the legislature. I not only lost my mentor, I inherited sponsorship of the resolution he had introduced to ratify the Equal Rights Amendment. So much for avoiding identification with women's issues. News that I was sponsoring the ERA resolution fulfilled the senators' worst expectations. My hostile predecessor had warned them to be on guard against the arrival of a woman "libber." It wasn't helpful when a newspaper story about the two women senators contrasted us by labeling me a career woman, a term of opprobrium to senators uneasy about women's increasing independence. Women were supposed to be at home, or in traditional women's jobs, not wearing business suits or going to graduate school, which described many of my friends.

To make matters worse, just weeks into my first term I publicly criticized the Senate leadership for buying film equipment to publicize senators on home television stations, a waste of tax dollars. The Senate is a club; such criticism might be good citizenship, but members interpreted it as a slap at the institution. Still, high turnover in the preceding election meant that even freshmen like me were given titles; I became vice chair of the education committee. The chair of the committee couldn't figure what to do with a female. The first time he was to present one of his own bills, he tried to turn the gavel over to every man on the committee, but they all just pointed at me. Eventually I helped him on some matter and received a companionable punch on the shoulder, apparently a safe-sex version of the ball player's congratulatory pat on the fanny.

The ERA sponsorship was much more difficult. The story of the ERA in the Missouri legislature is a lesson about women and power. The legislative bodies that were deciding whether women would have equal treatment under the law were filled with men. There certainly were male legislators who championed equal justice, and our cause, but they couldn't fully share our experiences, and besides, they were in a decided minority. Fourteen years into the future, women would explode in protest when an all-male judiciary committee sat in judgment on sexual harassment charges in the Anita Hill–Clarence Thomas hearings. There were no such protests about the handling of the ERA in 1977.

After it was all over, in the final count, three-fourths of women legislators across the country supported ratification compared to only 59 percent of men. In the fifteen states that never ratified, 79 percent of women legislators supported the amendment, compared to 39 percent of men.[1] The numbers just reinforced the difficulties women faced without equitable representation.

The ERA actually had been around for a long time. It was first introduced in Congress back in 1923, not long after women won the vote. The amendment was reintroduced in modified form over the years, but it was not passed by Congress until 1972. The proposed constitutional amendment was straightforward: "Equality of rights under the law shall not be denied or abridged by the United States or by any State on account of sex." Women viewed it as correcting an unfair omission; we had been left out of the Constitution from the beginning. Although Congress recently had begun to pass laws to end sex discrimination, there was great uncertainty achieving reform one statute at a time; a constitutional amendment would be a mandate to wipe out sex-based legal barriers, and it would be enforceable by the courts, preventing future backsliding.

The ERA was popular; most women had experienced the frustrations of second-class treatment as workers or wives. The call for equal rights also fit into the civil rights advocacy of the 1960s, and it became the emotional centerpiece for the flourishing new women's movement of the 1970s. The ratification effort politicized the traditional women's organizations that had been so fearful of taking up political issues, and it attracted thousands of recruits to the new political organization, the National Organization for Women. ERA NOW was a wonderful sign for rallies and public actions.

Amending the U.S. Constitution is a two-step process. An amendment originating in Congress must be passed by both House and Senate and must then be ratified by three-fourths of the fifty state legislatures. In 1972, the amendment had whipped through both houses of Congress by overwhelming votes. It was ratified by twenty-two states within a year without any major opposition. Soon the total was thirty-five states, representing the overwhelming majority of the nation's population. Just three more states were needed for the required three-fourths when organized opposition began to have an impact.

Conservative religions and right-wing political groups saw the constitutional change as threatening social controls built on traditional male authority. Women were warned that enforced equality would cost them the support of their husbands, that it would mean serving in combat, that they would lose privacy and be forced to use unisex toilets. Men were told that women would take their jobs.

Such views had particular appeal in states like Missouri where rural-dominated legislatures thrived on the status quo. I can remember being pleased upon first arriving at the capitol to see a female figure high atop the dome. Then someone explained that it was Ceres, goddess of agriculture. In the late twentieth century, the majority of Missouri's population lived in metropolitan areas (which did not include Jefferson City), but political seniority and adroit redistricting kept power effectively in the hands of rural legislators who controlled state funds and favors. Women's equality was viewed as a liberal, urban idea that threatened their control.

By the time I took up the resolution for ratification in 1977, a number of states had rejected the ERA. Missouri was one of the few remaining possibilities to obtain the final three votes, along with Florida, Illinois, and North Carolina. It was a rather intimidating responsibility. The prospects were depressing. Although the more liberal Missouri house, with an urban leader, had given approval to the ERA in an earlier legislative session, the Senate previously had defeated it by a vote of 20 to 14. The prediction was worse for 1977.

Senate leadership impatiently told me to get rid of the issue; either bring it to a quick vote (and inevitable defeat) or withdraw it. They were tired of being badgered by lobbyists for both sides. National ERA leaders implored me not to give up and to put off any vote as long as possible because a bad defeat would endanger votes in other states that had better chances. I hated my situation. The effort was doomed; fellow senators were antagonized; why should I endanger my new senate career in the name of women's rights? But women assumed that my presence would make a difference and continued to dream that we would somehow find the votes. I was committed to equal rights; the dilemma was how to do the least damage to the national chances of the ERA while facing reality in Missouri.

Advocates on both sides filled the hallways, supporters wearing historic suffragette costumes, opponents passing out cookies. Proponents included frustrated women from the 1950s who saw the ERA as critical to assure equal treatment for women; opponents included women who viewed the ERA as the final blow to traditional family values. This was war, and the legislature was the battleground. They all saw me as holding decisive power, but in electing me, voters had provided women with a voice, not the muscle to control the ERA's future. The real power remained with the men in leadership, and they had made it clear to all within the club that the ERA should be defeated.

The Senate committee hearing was an object lesson. Fifteen busloads of teenage Bible students from Christian schools in southwest Missouri (home of the Assemblies of God) were brought in to oppose the bill, along with the head of an organization called "Women Who Want to Be Women." Another of the opposition witnesses was Janet Ashcroft, wife of newly elected Missouri Attorney General (later U.S. Senator) John Ashcroft, who said there were only "rather minor" problems of sex discrimination.[2] The Ashcrofts were part of a religious right that argued that God didn't intend women to be equal.

As chief sponsor, I told the committee that the amendment would neither perform miracles nor perpetrate the horrors predicted by some, but it "would give a clear signal to all employers as well as courts, official boards and government groups that the people of the country believe in equal treatment and that the burden of proof should be on those who deny it rather than those who seek fair play." Without a clear statement in the Constitution, legislative reforms and even favorable court rulings could be reversed at any time. Women were more than half the population, nearly half the nation's workforce, and half the voters, but except for the suffrage amendment, women simply weren't in the Constitution.

My son Pete appeared before the committee, loyally testifying that he and other members of the Missouri Tigers football team also favored passage.

The committee hearing was a show trial; it had been agreed in advance that the resolution would be reported to the floor for debate on a certain day without recommendation. Basically, I would present it alone. No one else would speak on either side; there would be a quick vote, and it would be over. As the day of debate approached, I racked my brain for some way to avoid the inevitable humiliating defeat. A few close advisers joined in late-night strategy sessions as assistant Sue Luebbering juggled the frantic phone calls from national ERA leadership. We finally came up with a plan.

The galleries were packed on the appointed day. The Missouri Senate is a good setting for high drama; the public looks down from a semicircle of galleries into a marble arena where actors pose at dark wood desks on a red plush carpet. Great emphasis is placed on decorum. It was silent as I rose to speak, nervously referring to my text. An ERA legal team, including law professor Joan Krauskopf from the University of Missouri, had prepared a carefully organized notebook, tabbed by topic, but I knew that what the crowd sought was drama and emotion. Most of the senators had left their seats and drifted to the back of the chamber to show their indifference. Everyone but the members of the public knew that the vote would mean the ERA's defeat.

Then came the unexpected. Senator John Scott of St. Louis, an ERA opponent, suddenly rose to his feet to make a substitute motion to send the ERA to a statewide vote of the people. The leadership was stunned. This might win approval because passing the decision on to the people would let senators off the hook. Such a vote couldn't be used to ratify the amendment, but it would give women voters a chance to overwhelm the ballot boxes. One of the senior members rushed to his seat, waving his arms for attention. Somehow they had lost control. In haste, he moved to table Scott's substitute motion. No debate was permitted, and in the confusion, his motion to table passed 17 to 16. Under parliamentary procedure, tabling of the substitute also tabled my original motion to ratify the ERA because by rule it was attached. Therefore, it no longer could be considered.

The ERA ratification was defeated—but only by one vote. We had lost, but a single-vote defeat might not be too discouraging to other states where ratification still was possible.

I left the chamber to face the television cameras, sighing loudly about losing the ERA by so narrow a margin, trying not to reveal in any way that the incident had been planned. My demeanor was a study in soulful regret. Then I felt a tap on the shoulder. Opponents had caught on. "Oh Harriett," a senator said solicitously, " we're not going to let you leave without a *real* vote on ERA!" It was too late to run for an exit and the highway. Violating every parliamentary procedure, the Senate suspended the rules, reversed the tabling and closing motions, took up the original resolution on the ERA and clobbered it, 22 to 12.

The majority of the members actually didn't care one way or another about the size of the margin of defeat, but the conservative ideologues did. They truly wanted to teach uppity women a lesson. They wanted to kill the movement for equal rights so badly that it would never come back. For them, this was a moral crusade. Men were meant to be in charge, to head families, churches, institutions, and legislative bodies. A constitutional guarantee of equal rights for women was a threat to that power, and they were determined to stop it.

A few years later a change was proposed in the Missouri criminal code to make wives and husbands equally liable for providing support in an ongoing marriage. The same senators took the floor to block the change, threatening a filibuster rather than ever granting that men and women could have equal status as head of household. Natural law ordained otherwise.

The ERA defeat didn't destroy my effectiveness on other issues—senators rather admired the way we planted the substitute motion to almost avoid a big defeat—but socially the senate was a lonely place. With just thirty-four members, it was a small club that seemed even smaller because of party and interest groupings. It was awkward contacting male senators to go to dinner; on one occasion a senator obviously was uncomfortable being seen alone with me in a restaurant. The other possibilities for socializing were late-night drinking sessions, which grew wearisome in a hurry, and pick-up basketball games to which I wasn't invited. The alternative was to spend time with women representatives in the House, who were glad to laugh with me over the latest male gaff.

They also knew what it was like to be singled out: "We're noticed, we're watched, and we're focused in on by the men," a House member said in a newspaper feature story on women in the legislature. "There's a reluctance, particularly among rural legislators, to look upon women as anything other than mothers and party friends," said Karen McCarthy, a Kansas City legislator, and future congresswoman. However, another woman insisted that "men take you seriously if you believe in your legislation and are willing to work for it." The reporter quoted a male leader saying that women show too much emotion, aren't skillful enough in debate, and "need to assert themselves on the floor or in Caucus or they'll never get a bill through." Harriett Woods was cited as an exception: "She's put her experience as council member, public speaker and TV reporter to good use."[3]

Very flattering, but that previous experience didn't prevent mistakes that were prompted by a gender self-consciousness. At least once I insisted on being the Senate sponsor for a house bill even though a more senior senator probably deserved the opportunity. It was a needless struggle for credit that reflected a fear of allowing myself to be pushed around, of appearing weak as a woman among men. On another occasion, a senator decided to present toy guns to the women senators as a joke during a debate on crime. Why just women? That struck me as humiliating, so I dashed for my office and locked the door. They finally sent the sergeant of arms to get me. As silly as the gun joke had been, my fury had just made it worse. I knew I simply should have laughed it off.

The problem is that when there are only a few women, every woman is expected to be both women's advocate and women's role model—a heavy burden. It is much easier when there are more women to share the responsibilities, as became clear with the arrival of a third woman senator in 1978. Gwen Giles came from St. Louis, an African American who had risen through community work and the network of Congressman William L. Clay.

We shared agendas. At last there was someone with whom to put up my feet late at night and let it all hang out. At last there was someone else to carry women's issues. It was astonishing how much better I felt.

I really enjoyed legislating. It was a fascinating process. In order to be effective, it was important to learn what to expect from all the players, whether paid lobbyists, citizen advocates, or fellow legislators. It was important to work hard and always be prepared for hearings and debate. It also was important to develop a broader base of support in order to respond to advocates and citizens who asked for help. Inside the senate, I was hemmed in by the traditional hierarchy; outside, I could generate interest from the public through publicity and coalition building.

In 1978, a national nursing home scandal erupted. The elderly and the mentally ill were being warehoused for profit by operators who went into business to milk the medicare and medicaid programs created in the mid-1960s. States licensed nursing homes. Earlier, I had requested and won chairmanship of a committee on senior issues because nobody else wanted it. That now was a power position that gave me jurisdiction over a very hot item. Everyone said that powerful financial interests in the nursing home industry would resist reform; they had the political muscle to sway the legislature. A counterforce had to be created; I invited everyone with an involvement in nursing homes—from senior advocates and social workers to doctors and the operators of the biggest chains—to gather at a local university with a faculty member, skilled in conflict resolution, serving as a facilitator.

"I am going to write a new nursing home law for the state of Missouri," I said. "Do you want to help write it?" They were afraid to leave the room. The notion that a bill would be written without their input was enough to engage even the most hidebound of industry representatives. We began a process of brainstorming ideas, listing the problems and then possible solutions, breaking into topic groups, negotiating, and drafting. Then we repeated the process elsewhere in the state. Six months later we had a bill in which a great many people had a stake.

There still was a bitter struggle; there were twenty-eight amendments proposed in the senate alone. But at critical moments, I could suspend debate and send out a call for help to the thousands of people who by now had become involved. With crucial leadership from the more liberal house, which supported even stronger enforcement provisions, we passed the Nursing Home Reform Bill in a single session, to everyone's astonishment. It became a national model for nursing home legislation, creating a patient bill of rights, mandatory staff training, and tough penalties for fraud that corrected some of the worst problems.

In a study of women state legislators, the Center for the American Woman and Politics (CAWP) of the Eagleton Institute at Rutgers found that women officeholders are much more likely than male legislators to bring citizens into the legislative process and by doing so, to change the way government works.[4] Perhaps if the male club had made room for me, I would have adopted their style; instead, like other women at that time, I created my own path, building on past community efforts and media experience. That would turn out to be a very important benefit for my political future.

Public outreach certainly made a difference. The plight of the elderly was a cause that mattered to a great many people in the state. Creating a partnership with state employees, social service workers, and citizen advocates, we were able to pass a whole body of laws in the next few years that literally transformed the treatment of seniors in the state, creating not only nursing home reform but the Division of Aging and provisions for protective services for the elderly living at risk in the community. This was a different kind of power, and it drove the guys crazy. They couldn't believe all the attention I received for these initiatives despite their efforts to keep me out of the capitol inner circles.

All across the country, women legislators were adopting new styles and constructing new agendas. In Congress, a handful of the new breed created the Congressional Caucus for Women's Issues in 1977 to build support for previously neglected issues of special concern to women and families. We tried to do the same in Missouri, but for many years differences on the abortion issue kept women from working together, to be followed by more intense and divisive partisanship.

There was a great deal that needed to be improved in the way the legislature operated; many of the rules and committee structures kept the body from being responsive to the citizens. In 1980, a group of state senators in Missouri staged a palace revolution to try to broaden leadership and reform the way we were doing business. One goal was to give the urban areas more of a voice. I was the only woman among about ten men involved, but when we lost, I immediately was falsely fingered as the ring-leader. The old guard preferred to excuse their male buddies and *cherchez la femme*. As punishment, those of us involved were stripped of our committee chairmanships, and my favorite legislation was targeted for the big round file.

Still, they couldn't keep me from floor debate. The senior Republican was a viper-tongued debater named Richard Webster who ran the senate behind the scenes like a Mafia boss, distributing favors and imposing punishment. He was rarely challenged on the floor because of his quick tongue. In my current outcast state, I was sorely tempted. One day when he proposed one of his anticonsumer bills, I rose for recognition and badgered him with questions until he lost his temper and called me a "broad." That was considered a personal attack and a violation of all senate rules of decorum. In the bizarre power struggles within this all-male body, making him lose control in that way was a point for me. A newspaper commentator observed how difficult it was to serve in a chamber "where women who don't know their place have no place."[5]

Despite such exchanges, there really were more good moments than bad. There continued to be opportunities to shape important public policies—in mental health, education, and occupational licensing—and to help a great many people who needed a friend in government. It also was apparent, as we moved into the 1980s, that women in office were winning increasing respect. By persisting in our jobs, we had become part of the political landscape, and we were being joined by others. The number of women in state legislatures throughout the country tripled, from 344 in 1971 to 908 in 1981. These were women who were applying what they had learned at the community level to state policy-making.

A few broke through to leadership posts, as committee chairs or floor leaders, but the CAWP study indicated that regardless of party, women had different priorities and a different style from men. In general, women were more liberal in their attitudes on major public policy issues. Although women legislators differed widely in their individual priorities, the study found they all tended to be more active than male legislators on women's rights legislation and more likely to give priority to policies related to women's traditional roles as caregivers in the family and society. Clearly women felt that if they didn't push these issues, the issues wouldn't get attention.

In 1980, Ronald Reagan was elected with a conservative agenda premised on a less activist government. Although he received a majority of votes from both women and men, women gave him notably smaller margins. There were many reasons, economic and social, for these differing votes, but the bottom line was that more women had voted for Democrats than had men, in contrast to the 1950s when more women had voted for Republicans. National women leaders who spotted the differential coined the term "gender gap" to describe the variance in voting by sex.

Ratification of the ERA was hanging by a thread; time for legislative action would run out in 1982, and if the effort failed, women would lose political momentum. The idea of a gender gap in voting could be a powerful weapon with which to intimidate legislators in last-ditch ratification efforts. "Despite the fact that there was no evidence that the gender gap was related to views about the ERA, [they] promoted the gender gap in their efforts to pressure state legislators to vote for it," one study noted.[6] Women's votes, feminists said, could decide elections. We were delighted to hear it. Even though women have as many different reasons for deciding how to vote as do men, the fact that for the first time women had voted in greater numbers than men made male politicians take notice.

In 1980, I was reelected to the state senate by an overwhelming margin and was figuring that two four-year terms in the Missouri Senate would be enough. That didn't mean I wanted to quit public service and lose the ability to use government to help people. It just seemed wise to move on. Around that time, I attended a conference on "Women and Power" at a local women's college, the first time a conference that combined those words was held in Missouri. Afterward, acquaintances who were fired up by the idea of breaking political glass ceilings urged me to run for federal office. They were astonished when I answered that I was "too old." (I was fifty-three). I really believed it. Like most women who had taken time out for marriage and children, I was playing a catch-up game, getting everywhere just a little later than my male peers. In a society obsessed with youth, "older" carries negative connotations, so being an older woman became part of our powerlessness.

A small group of women who had taken an interest in my future sat down to consider all the options. We were looking mainly at the possibility of running for the position of county executive, the top elected official in our region. They put me through one of those exercises that are supposed to reveal unconscious preferences. To our surprise, it turned out that my dream was not to be an executive but to be a legislator and to serve in the highest assembly in the land. I wanted to be a United States Senator. How unrealistic! No Democratic woman ever had been elected to the U.S. Senate in her own right.

Coincidentally, a magazine article appeared suggesting that my political star would rise higher but specifically dismissing the thought of my running for U.S. Senate in 1982 against Republican incumbent John C. Danforth. He was much too formidable. "Even though she doesn't quail at a challenge and has become an advocate of not staying in office too long, . . . she knows how to count the odds. Washington would seem to be an improbable dream in an unfamiliar land."[7]

Women didn't have that kind of power—or did we?

7

The Great Adventure

I would rather lose standing on
principle than win standing for nothing.

—Harriett Woods, U.S. Senate Concession Speech, November 2, 1982

By the early 1980s, very few women ever had served in the U.S. Senate, no more than two at any one time, and most who did serve succeeded deceased husbands. Even recently elected Nancy Landon Kassebaum, a Republican from Kansas, had used the leverage of her father Alf Landon's fame as a former governor and presidential candidate. A Democratic woman had never been elected to the U.S. Senate in her own right.

In 1982, Republican Senator John Danforth of Missouri was running for reelection after six years in office. He was viewed as invulnerable. He had been a popular Missouri attorney general, was an ordained Episcopal priest, and also an heir to the Ralston Purina fortune and family name. None of the obvious Democratic possibilities, such as congressmen, major city mayors, or state-wide officials, wanted to take him on. By 1982, I had been in the Missouri Senate for six years and was being urged to try for higher office. In exploring all the possibilities, I blurted out that I had always hoped one day to be a United States Senator. The Democratic Party needed a candidate now. Why not go for it?

The campaign against incumbent Senator Danforth would be a long shot. However, there were some attractions to trying. The economy was in a downspin. Missouri was experiencing double-digit unemployment. Significant issues in the Reagan presidency needed to be debated, such as budget cuts that squeezed the elderly and middle class, issues that fit my areas of concern. Second, I was ready to move on politically to a statewide race. Although the chances of winning seemed slim, I would be building statewide name recognition for a future attempt if that should be necessary. And finally, I genuinely believed if elected that I could do a better job for Missouri than the incumbent. And if it seemed like jumping off a cliff, at least there was a safety net: I was in midterm and would still be in the state senate if I lost. So I began to make noises about the senate race, checking in with party and elected officials around the state. It seemed the Democratic field was clear.

Then came the unexpected: a phone call asking me to come to a meeting with U.S. Senator Tom Eagleton, the most powerful Democratic elected official in the state. It would be held in the home of his area administrator, who happened to be my back-yard neighbor. Clearly this was intended to be a very private meeting. I knew enough to take someone with me, my state sen-ate campaign manager Jody Newman. It was a clear February day, and I remember walking slowly to my neighbor's house past familiar backyards, knowing something special was brewing.

When we walked into the house, we discovered not just Eagleton but also Louis Susman, a top Democratic fund-raiser and attorney for August (Gussie) Busch, CEO of Anheuser-Busch. After some social niceties about refreshments and the weather, Eagleton and Susman got down to business. They informed us that they and other party leaders had decided to back someone else for the senate nomination, a man named Burleigh Arnold, who was the current Democratic national com-mitteeman from Missouri, as well as a Jefferson City banker and lobbyist. Although he had never sought a popular elected office, they said he could raise more money to give Danforth a stronger race. They said I could not. Running a credible race would require millions. Would I be able to appeal to big donors? After all, from the public viewpoint, I was nothing but a suburban housewife. Perhaps I'd like to consider running for secretary of state some time? Was it my imagination, or did they put special emphasis on the word "secretary"?

Jody and I were stunned. Running for U.S. Senate was a stretch for a state senator, but the Eagleton and Susman comments were a dismissal of nearly twenty years in public life: eight years a city council member, two years a state transportation commissioner, six years in the state senate, plus national leadership in several policy areas. And there were the ten years in television, and my current weekly commentary on a network radio station. Nothing but a suburban housewife? There were people all over the state who had worked with me on ground-breaking legislation to reform nursing homes, improve the tax code, and tighten drunk driving laws. Yes, there would be the usual labeling because I was pro-choice and had sponsored the Equal Rights Amendment, but otherwise my views were no different from Senator Eagleton's. I felt I had paid my political dues. How could I be rejected in favor of a bank lobbyist?

Inwardly I was churning with anger, but I managed somehow to hold back any emotional explosion. Jody and I needed to talk. We walked out, returning to my house in silence in a world that suddenly had turned wintry. We sat down in the dining room, our old state senate campaign headquarters, and we started to consider the options. Clearly I had been naïve in thinking Democratic Party leaders would let a woman pursue the nomination even if no one else who was credible seemed to want it. I had just been dismissed by my own party's leaders. Did we have the ability to defy them? If I ran in the primary, I would face a candidate funded and supported by the Democratic Party establishment. In contrast, we would have to start from scratch to raise money and build an organization.

Running statewide is enormously difficult even in a small state, and Missouri is large, the eighteenth largest in land area, with 68,898 square miles, and the sixteenth largest by population with more than 5 million residents, of whom 3 million are registered voters. Missouri also is quite conservative, with vestiges of southern culture plus the fundamentalist Ozarks and the vast farmlands across its northern half that often politically outweigh the bigger urban centers. It was daunting to think of covering that territory without the ready-made support of local party officials. I had no staff. My husband Jim would be supportive of whatever I decided, but as a newspaper editor, he wasn't in a position to help. There were voters out there who would respond if we could reach them, but could we do that on our own?

Deciding whether or not to run for U.S. Senate was the toughest decision in my political life. Only years later did I see its broader significance: If a woman with an established public record could be dismissed so arbitrarily, what woman in this country ever would run for U.S. Senate? At the time I was just angry. The two men had remarked, pityingly, that I surely didn't want to be humiliated by an embarrassing loss. The true humiliation was their demeaning evaluation of me as a politician and public official.

We called two women friends in Kansas City, at the opposite end of the state from St. Louis, who had just started a political consulting firm. They shared our indignation and offered to help. It could be a team effort, with Jody as campaign manager. It might not have been rational, but the four of us thought we might just pull it off. We decided to plunge ahead to seek the nomination against Eagleton's candidate, setting in motion forces that some would later say had a permanent impact on women's politics in America, including the way women's candidacies are financed. Of course, there was no way at the time to foresee what would happen.

Word of the Eagleton dismissal leaked out—not from us, I hasten to say. A banner story on the front page of *The St. Louis Globe–Democrat* shouted: "Eagleton Privately Asked Sen.Woods: Stay Out of Race."[1] A wonderful thing had happened; a women's network no one knew existed had gone to work. Fourteen women elected officials, all but one of the Democratic women in the legislature, signed a letter to Senator Eagleton expressing indignation that they had not been consulted about such a drastic step as telling me not to run. "We [women] are often overlooked when party leaders convene to determine the best direction for Democrats. We resent this exclusion and all of us are particularly stung by this most recent example. . . ."

When the letter was given to the press, the story became big news.[2] *The Kansas City Times* editorialized: "What appears to be happening among some leaders is more than a hesitancy about Mrs. Woods' position on [social] issues. Her supporters can name male politicians who have views similar to hers. What one can read between the lines is some old-fashioned sentiment, shared

by many male political leaders, that a woman cannot win."[3]
Suddenly a race that had drawn little interest because of its seeming futility was worth covering.

Missouri media reported as major news how women were standing up for women against the political power structure. They didn't understand that a women's support system had been developing in Missouri since the early 1970s. It was no accident that the letter to Eagleton was written by State Representative Sue Shear and St. Louis County Councilwoman Betty Van Uum, among the first women supported by the new Missouri Women's Political Caucus. Women who made it into elected office in the 1970s understood the importance of sisterhood. For better or worse, my U.S. Senate candidacy of the early 1980s had become a cause.

In 1982, this support from formal and informal women's networks meant volunteers and publicity but not much money. Women still didn't feel empowered to write checks for political candidates. How could we run for U.S. Senate in eight months, from a dead start, with inadequate resources? By running a disciplined campaign. Eventually there were nine men and one other woman in the primary. While the other candidates battled to win the August primary, we set a seamless strategy toward November. Our posture would be utter confidence of victory. It was particularly important to project strength because the assumption behind rejection of a woman candidate was that she would be weak.

Even small decisions became important. Would our campaign buttons say: "Harriett," "Senator Woods," or "Woods"? We decided on "Senator Woods," accurate because I was a state senator but also conveying status and experience, important for a woman planning to face a powerful U.S. senator.

As to message, we could draw a nice contrast between my record helping ordinary people and a wealthy incumbent out of touch with his constituents. He wore imported Gucci shoes while Missouri shoe workers were unemployed. We stuck to one message: "Harriett Woods cares about ordinary working people. She and her husband have raised three sons on an average working income; she has a record of public service to the people of Missouri. And she is angry that the American dream no longer is possible for many people." I repeated that theme to the point of nausea. Months later, when *The Washington Post* asked how I could win the general election, I said: "I am going to continue to emphasize that I am closer to people. My husband and I have raised three children on a very average income. We understand what it means to pay bills, send our children to public schools, worry about retirement income. At the same time, I have a public record people can look at."[4] I could say it in my sleep.

Of course, the cold, cruel reality was that very few people in Missouri even knew who I was. My primary opponents were busy trying to tell them, describing me as "too liberal," the automatic tag placed on women who support women's issues. It was this marginalizing identity I once futilely had tried to avoid. There also was ambivalence among older women. I recall the kindly expression of one such woman at a Democratic gathering in northwest Missouri. She took my hand and said: "You seem so nice and smart, but women aren't supposed to be senators." Did she fear her own life would be devalued if some women made different choices?

No one knew me in Washington either. A trip there was a humbling experience. The only things that interested funders was the controversy about Senator Eagleton, a known personality. Without money for a professional poll or a slick presentation, we were ignored. Our only support came from the American Nurses Association (ANA) and the Women's Campaign Fund (WCF) whose PACs made early commitments, and the NWPC and the NARAL, which provided some funds, but even more important, a place to go to sit down and make calls. The ANA hosted a gathering of the leading political women in Washington. They expressed enthusiasm, but few of them wrote checks.

We needed national publicity to generate more contributions, but the Missouri race wasn't of special interest to the national press—except to women reporters who were fighting their own battles for advancement and recognition. Few in the nation's capital paid any attention until a full page feature story on the Missouri senate race ran on the front of *The Washington Post* Style Section. A young woman reporter names Elizabeth Bumiller wrote it.[5] It was good for her career as well as mine when the story played so prominently. Another boost came from National Public Radio which had a cluster of talented women who were becoming household names, Nina Totenberg, Cokie Roberts, Linda Wertheimer and Susan Stamberg. Their presence made a huge difference in covering races like mine.

Campaigning was a humbling experience. Here are early observations on my performance recorded by an experienced political observer: "Doesn't work a crowd well. Needs more applause lines. Needs to loosen up—be more assertive. Needs to remember to campaign all the time." We all have to start somewhere. The pols also said we couldn't raise money. Proving them wrong was the toughest challenge. Experienced campaigners warned that no one could run for U.S. Senate without being able to look a potential donor in the eye and say "I need $1,000." I still hated asking for money and had to be pushed by the staff. It would take a long time to forget a lifetime's training that asking for money for oneself was unseemly and to understand instead that it was giving people an opportunity to invest in their convictions.

My concerns were broad: income disparities, the health of the social security system, and social policies. Focusing on women hadn't been my priority; but the Eagleton incident made gender identity strategic. Our first direct mailing featured a caricature of the proverbial backroom politician smoking a big, fat cigar. The printed message that told the story of my rejection was headlined, "The good ole boys do it again." It brought an amazing response from across the country. Traditional political donors spurned me. Most donations were $5 and $10 from people who probably never had given before.

The bigger checks came from working women, the new professionals who were just beginning to move into positions that gave them respectable salaries. In California, Barbara Boxer, aspiring to enter Congress, put on a fund-raising lunch for women at $100 a head and feared no one would come, but they did. In Texas, Ann Richards, running for state treasurer, got pledges by telephone of $1,000 each from 200 women in the course of one day. Our version was to reward women who gave $1,000 with original lithographs; 75 signed on, some on the installment plan. There also was a $350 check that came from a woman in northeast Missouri with this note: "Lots of luck dear. Girls can do everything."

My candidacy was a learning experience for everyone. What should a woman running for major office look like? Men are automatically in uniform when they put on suit and tie. Women create their image in what they choose to wear. Campaign staff replaced my jumbled wardrobe with a couple of pastel silk suits and a variety of blouses. I added a denim skirt and cotton shirt for the country. How should a woman behave? The worst expectation was that a female candidate wouldn't know how to play the game. That was partially fulfilled when we told urban political clubs we didn't have enough money to pay them for primary election-day activities. One black committeeman was so threatening that I finally offered him $50. He spread word around St. Louis that he had been insulted by a cheap white woman.

There also was a first experience with overt antiSemitism. I had assumed my husband's name, Woods, in good 1950s practice, and I never had been known by anything else during the years in elected office. Suddenly, an ultra-conservative rural Missouri paper began referring to me as "Harriett Friedman Woods." I always have been proud of my maiden name; it is my father's and I am proud of him, as I am of my mother, whose maiden name was Wise. But it was pretty clear that this paper wasn't interested in my heritage except to suggest to any suspicious readers that there was something alien about me. There aren't many Jews in rural Missouri.

On the other hand, there was a wonderful feeling developing with the voters themselves. Beginning in May, three months before the August primary, newspaper polls showed me running almost 3 to 1 ahead of Eagleton candidate Burleigh Arnold who was even running behind another, relatively unknown candidate. A handful of also-rans had insignificant numbers. We had to overcome a lot of early skepticism; an Associated Press reporter following the campaign through rural areas said I won over men with "dynamic speeches."[6] As for the women, "the ladies just flock to her like bees," a local editor reported. "Mrs. Woods has a way of getting down to the nitty-gritty." One day we traveled 250 miles, covering eight counties, with rallies and court-house tours in every one. People kept me going, a growing coalition of working people, the elderly, consumers, farmers, teachers, women, minorities, and independents.

I remember stump speaking at a fish fry on a creek bank in a sparsely populated county in the most remote corner of the state. A young girl called to me as I was leaving, and I turned back to talk to her. It was our only stop in that area, so on election night we were pleased and surprised to learn we had carried the county. We later heard that folks there decided that if I took time to talk to a child, I'd also have time for them.

At campaign stops, I told them how my father came to America as an immigrant boy and grew up to give speeches about America. They met my husband Jim, born and bred in central Missouri's Little Dixie, who hated public speaking but loved the home cooking at the carry-in suppers that were the heart of country political rallies. It helped that the men knew my son Pete as a former Missouri quarterback who had been drafted by the pros and that he took a semester off from law school to become a campaign coordinator in the eastern half of the state.

He valiantly substituted to whitewash a fence in Hannibal during a Tom Sawyer celebration and took a very urban Jody on a learning swing through southeast Missouri. That included a mandatory stop at Lambert's "Throwed Rolls" restaurant where the owner literally throws the rolls at the customers. When Jody ordered hot tea, an unusual request in that territory, he accompanied the tosses to her with the jovial remark: "For the little lady with the hot tea!" Jody rarely ventured out of the metropolitan area again.

We won the August primary overwhelmingly, 2 to 1 over party favorite Arnold, and 46 percent of the vote against the field. We had raised $250,000 from 4,000 contributors. We also carried 80 of the state's 114 counties. When we filed, the power brokers said we couldn't raise the money to wage a credible campaign. They said we couldn't win outstate. We proved them wrong on both counts. We had outworked the opposition with the help of an avalanche of enthusiastic volunteers and a disciplined strategy: We stayed with a consistent message, used every available dollar for media, and focused on our Republican general election opponent.

There was great satisfaction in the respectful remarks of male party leaders who had opposed us. "Mrs. Woods ran a magnificent campaign," Lou Susman said. "She proved a lot of people wrong." State Party Chair Pat Lea added: "She's made believers out of a lot of people that rural America is not opposed to a woman, a liberal [on social issues], or a candidate who is pro-choice on abortion."

The primary victory received national publicity under headlines that always mentioned gender, like "Woman Wins Senate Primary." "For the first time in American politics, women are on the brink of becoming an important independent power,"[7] one reporter wrote. She cited the three women including myself nominated for Senate, plus two for governor, adding that many women now active in politics cut their teeth in the ERA campaign "and swore they would never suffer such a defeat again." A spokesperson for the Women's Campaign Fund said: "The theme for the 1980s is women in power." Ann Lewis, then political director of the national Democratic Party, commented: "There is a real appeal in a candidate . . . who comes from outside the institutional leadership. . . . People believe of a woman candidate that she understands what their lives are like."[8]

Victory in the primary was sweet, but the general election still was a Cinderella race against the odds. Jody reminded the staff: "We must take a nontraditional campaign approach due to a limited budget. This means that we cannot afford yard signs, billboards, direct mailings, phone banks, and newspaper advertisements." Every dollar would go toward radio and television. We still were weighed down by a host of gender myths.

It's assumed that women candidates are compassionate and caring—even when they're not—but not tough "enough." My reputation was built on trying to help people—the elderly, the mentally ill, children, working people. To some, that's a soft image. In 1982 we were still in the cold war era when arguing for cuts in military expenditures fed the perception that women were softies. A decade later, Dianne Feinstein of California ran a successful campaign for U.S. Senate on the theme "tough *and* caring" (the underlining was part of the slogan). Of course, by then the Berlin Wall had fallen.

Many commentators didn't think any woman would be able to stand up to debate an experienced U.S. senator like Danforth. At least my height, at five feet, eight and a half inches, kept me from being dwarfed at side-by-side podiums. So many topics are fair game in a Senate race. Reason dictated that I prepare by framing fairly simple answers to the most likely questions. Instead, I spent hours I didn't really have studying the most obscure points so that I would not be found wanting! Is it peculiarly female to want to be totally prepared for every challenge? It was a victory when reporters judged that I had held my own.

In late June, 45 percent of voters polled said they never had heard of Harriett Woods, with Danforth favored 62 to 26 percent and 12 percent undecided. By early August, after the primary victory, it was 52 to 35 favoring Danforth with 13 percent undecided. But by mid-October, only 8 percent said they had never heard of me, and the score was 51 percent Danforth to 43 percent Woods. Among likely voters, the race had tightened to 47 percent Danforth to 46 percent Woods.

A model of risk taking was behind those final figures. From the time of the primary, our campaign had been using smoke and mirrors to stretch dollars; television and radio were run on alternate weeks hoping that people would think they'd seen or heard the commercials even when they hadn't. But at that rate of exposure, there was little chance to win. Jody recommended that we gamble—take every cent we had and concentrate it all in a single solid week of media, trying to hit the week before the next major newspaper poll. If we guessed right, the concentrated exposure would raise our poll numbers and attract the money we needed for the final weeks. Of course, a bad guess could doom the campaign. We decided to go for it. After all, the whole campaign had been a leap of faith. Indeed, so had my whole political career.

As events turned out, we guessed right—our commercials were timed perfectly for the polls, the numbers went up to show us in a dead heat, the news spread around the country, and money came in. Everyone loves a potential winner. We eventually raised $1 million in the general election period, but $546,000 of it came during the last two weeks, which meant we never had enough money sufficiently early to build momentum. And it still was just half as much money as my opponent raised. The late surge in donations also proved a bittersweet success because the sudden jump in poll numbers shocked Republicans into action. The Danforth campaign had complacently written me off. Now they cut hard-hitting negative ads for the last weekend of the campaign, portraying Harriett Woods as a fuzzy, somewhat sinister liberal. The ads were very effective, raising just enough doubts with people who couldn't really know me well after a brief campaign.

There were some humorous sidelights to this roller coaster ending. Before our new poll numbers came out, we were impressed when two well-known national political reporters suddenly began to cover the campaign, even tagging along for the smallest of small-town parades. Then we realized they were just using the campaign for an expense-paid trip to see the St. Louis Cardinals play in the World Series. There was a measure of revenge when one of their patronizing stories appeared just as our race became the hottest U.S. Senate contest in the country.

There is another story from the final days that will always leave some questions. With less than a week to go, we started airing a very simple commercial in which I looked straight into the camera and stated my support for the right of a woman to make her own decision about abortion, in consultation with her doctor, her minister, her family. No one in the country running for major office had ever run such a commercial before. At the time, the word "abortion" was not said on television. Conventional wisdom was that being pro-choice was a tremendous negative in Missouri and that the less said on the subject, the better.

We ran the ad with the advice and help of our excellent consultants, Joe White for media and Tubby Harrison for polling. Harrison said his analysis showed that this statement of principle on abortion, while risky, could swing to our side undecided independent women voters. It also would let me state my own views accurately, knowing that the anti-choice contingent would be out in force with their poisonous flyers. And it demonstrated to voters that I would be direct and honest with them, not just another politician.

There's a lot of interest now in targeting so-called soccer moms or working women, or other special female voters, but Harrison was ahead of others in 1982 in identifying a swing vote among women on reproductive rights. We didn't keep the commercial on the air long enough to see if he was right. There was an explosion from male labor leaders who said the spot would lose the votes of their blue-collar pro-life members—who hadn't been too thrilled to support a woman in any case. Should we keep it on the air? We had no money for polls to test response to the ad. We later learned that the Danforth campaign had day-by-day tracking polls that gave them an information advantage. We decided to wait for the next public newspaper poll on the Friday before the election. If we were even or ahead, we'd yank the commercial to avoid the risk of losing any votes. If we were behind, we'd keep the abortion spot on the air to gamble on winning the extra votes we needed.

On Friday, the newspaper poll showed me leading the race by a couple of points. We pulled the abortion spot. It was the one instance in the campaign when we decided to play it safe.

On election evening, based on early returns, national television commentators were predicting my victory. Former President and Mrs. Carter called with congratulations. Barbara Walters wanted a morning interview. It was heady stuff. Yet our own analysis of mid-day returns gave us less confidence. The count dragged on and by midnight or so, the outcome seemed clear. Danforth was gracious in his televised victory statement, saying: "Oh, man, was that ever tough! I couldn't believe what a tough race this was."[9] The final count was 784,494 to 756,943. I got 49.1 percent of the vote, losing by 27,500 votes out of 1.5 million.

The 1982 Missouri Senate race was one of the first modern women's campaigns. Not only was there a woman candidate but also a female campaign manager—at a time when women never were hired for key campaign positions. Writing in *Working Woman* a year later, Peggy Simpson wrote that the campaign became "a symbol of all that is right, and all that is wrong about today's tough political process and women." The campaign inspired other women to become candidates and officeholders themselves. Our difficulty in attracting early money prompted new initiatives, including EMILY's List, to raise money for women candidates. And Democratic women activists, furious because the male establishment never had fully supported me, began to strategize about putting a woman on the national Democratic ticket in 1984.

What made the difference between winning and losing? Obviously, money, but there are too many factors in a major campaign to tell. It's tough running against an incumbent. Some would say we couldn't have come as close as we did if Danforth had run a better campaign, and others were convinced that a progressive woman just couldn't win in 1982 in a conservative state like Missouri. But even our severest critics agreed that it was an extraordinary effort. We proved women can compete on the same basis as men, that women will write checks, that candidates do better when they stand up on their convictions, and that ordinary people do make a difference.

In the end, what mattered for women was this: I lost, but women didn't.

8

Leveraging Power

I want you to see that power is not a bad thing.
But having the power and not using it is a total waste.

—Former Texas Governor Ann Richards, speaking to college students, 1998

The 1982 election may have been a turning point for political women. It certainly was for me. Nationally, there was a new determination to turn defeat into victory and to leverage whatever power women had to achieve a major breakthrough in the next election. For me, the highly publicized Senate race had created a new public life, drawing me into national activities involving women, the Democratic Party, and a woman vice-presidential candidate. In the next year, I would be stumping to create a risk capital fund for women candidates and appearing on national television as part of the response to President Reagan's State of the Union message. It seemed that I now had personal power to leverage. It was head-spinning stuff.

None of this could have been predicted immediately after the election. The press conference held by political women's groups in Washington on November 4, 1982, was not a happy occasion. One news story carried the headline "Women Took a Beating;" another quoted one of the women: "We all considered wearing black."[1] When final returns were in, all the women running for governor or senator had lost their races. I had been rushed to Washington for a different, celebratory press conference with pro-choice candidates. Having lost, I found it a little embarrassing, but apparently even moral victories were welcome. And I owed the abortion rights group a great deal for their early support of my campaign.

But the overall mood was grim. A conservative national administration was threatening women's past legislative gains, and the deadline for ratifying the ERA was passing. The movement needed a lift. What is remarkable is that women provided it—not just a lift, but a historic breakthrough—and they did it by leveraging the perceived power of their votes. In the gloomy aftermath of the election, political women looking for solace had found it in the recent dramatic increases in the number of women voting, plus a change in the pattern of those votes that could be interpreted usefully to manipulate male political leaders.

The facts were these: Women were 52 percent of the electorate and had been voting in somewhat greater numbers than men for years, but in 1980, for the first time ever, women had begun turning out to vote at a higher rate than men did. That greatly increased the number spread.[2] Now in 1982, women's greater participation rate translated into 4.3 million more votes cast by women than by men.[3] In addition, the trend to voting Democratic, first noted in 1980, was confirmed in 1982. Although Reagan had won a majority of votes from both men and women, fewer women supported him, and about 5 percent more women than men voted Democratic in congressional races.[4] Their votes were credited with electing several new Democratic governors. This was what women had begun calling the "gender gap" and what they thought could be used as leverage.

A woman leader asserted: "We are at the cutting edge of new perceptions of women as voters and candidates."[5] And a woman reporter wrote: "After two years of debating whether the 'gender gap' would carry over to other races and issues [than Reagan's election in 1980], most strategists now consider it an accepted fact of political life. . . . The 1982 elections offered proof that women voters can be an independent, pivotal force."[6]

To be accurate, the *gender gap* is simply the difference between the way men and women vote. It can mean a lot or very little depending on how votes are cast. In 1993, it served the purposes of angry and frustrated political women to grab the idea of a distinctive women's vote as a powerful tool to advance their cause. If male politicians were impressed by the large female turnout and believed that they needed to appeal to women voters in order to win, perhaps they also would believe that the best way to attract those voters would be to put a woman on the ticket—the presidential ticket.

Just before the election, *Newsweek* had carried the buoyant feature "Women in Politics" ballyhooing the record number running for office and pointing to a larger role being played by women both as candidates and behind-the-scenes officials.[7] That may have prompted the Democratic Party to ask me to tape a discussion with Governor Bob Kerrey of Nebraska that was used in the official televised response to President Reagan's State of the Union message. They wanted to showcase a woman among Democratic officials, and the media had turned the Missouri senate race into a symbol of women's thwarted political ambitions.[8] I was this year's flavor.

Pamela Harriman, glamorous Washington political hostess and wife of millionaire Averill Harriman, former governor of New York, invited me to be on her PAC board that was dedicated to achieving a Democratic senate. Her Georgetown home provided a wonderful place to stay, complete with original French impressionist paintings and memorabilia of her earlier marriage to Randolph Churchill and her husband's time as ambassador to England.

As a younger woman in Great Britain and France, Mrs. Harriman was credited with using feminine wiles to build relationships with powerful men. In Washington, she was determined to achieve her own power base. She held political salons featuring discussions with intellectuals and political leaders, and staged fundraisers for candidates like me that won her deserved gratitude. Averill Harriman's wealth, and her skillful management of men, made her a formidable figure without ever holding a public office herself. It was a revelation. Within a few years, she would become Ambassador to France, the first woman to hold this prized position.

In April 1983, 170 prominent women from forty-five states signed a letter to all Democratic presidential candidates warning them they couldn't count on women's votes unless they gave high priority to issues important to women. I was invited to be a signer. The letter warned Democrats not to be complacent about the current gender gap. Women will vote for Democrats, we said,

only if there is commitment by Democrats to issues such as pay
equity, equal rights, and family and children's policies. "As a
majority of the electorate, we women have it in our power to
choose the next president of the United States as well as the
Democratic Party's nominee for that office."[9]

In truth, women vote for as many different reasons as men,
and Democratic women were hardly about to vote for Ronald
Reagan, but we really believed women voters could make the difference in the 1984 election, and it was worth the effort at intimidation because the men were so easily impressed.

Five of the hottest Democratic prospects seeking to face
Reagan in 1984 showed up to be grilled at the National Women's
Political Caucus convention in San Antonio, Texas, on July 10,
1983: Senators Alan Cranston of California, Gary Hart of
Colorado, John Glenn of Ohio, and Ernest Hollings of South
Carolina, and former Vice President Walter Mondale. The Caucus
asked me to serve as moderator.

The *New York Times* described the event as a "bidding war" for
women's support. Senator Cranston said he would actively consider a woman vice president and cited Harriett Woods as "an
American leader who would make a great vice president." (I
smiled modestly.) Mondale said *his* list would include
Congresswomen Patsy Mink of Hawaii and Bella Abzug of New
York, both of whom happened to be questioners.[10] All the men
pledged that they would use federal funds as leverage to pressure
states that failed to ratify the Equal Rights Amendment—and also
to guarantee abortion rights.

One almost felt sorry as they struggled for relevancy. Senator
Hollings apologized for the campaign brochures he had brought
to the convention headlined "the thinking man's candidate."
Senator Glenn stumbled by referring to "man and wife" when
the preferred language was "husband and wife." (I hadn't
thought about that myself.) Gary Hart got into the most trouble
when he refused to stop talking and ignored time signals to end
his remarks. NWPC Chair Kathy Wilson said he exhibited an
"attitude of disregard" toward women.[11]

Whatever their stumbles, it was clear that these male politicians were taking the potential impact of women's votes very
seriously indeed. That was not true back home in the Missouri
senate. Very little had changed there. The members couldn't care

less that I had run for the U.S. Senate. They did worry that I might run for governor. A woman governor? The president pro tem made sure he gave me a minor committee chairmanship, playing a familiar game. But as always, there were important issues that were being neglected, such as the health threats of asbestos in old buildings, poisonous dioxin left on people's property, and the need for pay equity for women state employees. These became my focus for the final two years in the senate.

I also was searching for a way to solve the problem that had confronted the campaign and that continued to discourage so many women candidates: the lack of early risk capital. During the NWPC convention in Houston, a number of women—Ann Richards, Barbara Boxer, and others—talked about a way that each of us could call key donors when a promising new woman candidate appeared. The few PACs that donated to women required a time-consuming approval process. I began talking up the idea of a quick-response fund, with captains who could call 10 to 15 allies who would write $500 or $1,000 checks. That way the new candidate wouldn't be facing the skeptical questions about her ability to raise money or be turned down because she couldn't finance an early poll.

There was another approach. Jody had moved to Washington to work in the Mondale campaign, and a group of us gathered in her apartment to brainstorm starting a fund. We only talked, but thankfully one of us took action: a quiet philanthropist named Ellen Malcolm. By 1984, she had launched EMILY's List (early money is like yeast; it makes the dough rise). It would become the most important vehicle for funding major races of pro-choice Democratic women, although not always providing the risk money we had sought.

Amid all the politics, there was my personal life to get back in order. All three sons were off with their own careers, but Jim needed some attention, starting with a wife who would be at home for a while. That meant I needed to ponder my political future. The Senate race had changed everything. There were many people who now looked to me for leadership. Should I keep going? National publicity already had led to a serious proposal to run for president ("some woman needs to do it"), but that sounded beyond our abilities. What about governor? It would be an open seat and the office certainly represented power. We needed to explode gender myths about serving as governor; too few women were trying for the position.

The executive title carries the kind of masculine stereotyping that make it difficult for women to compete;[12] a governor is considered an authority figure, with expected qualities like decisiveness, aggressiveness, and rationality that are thought of as male, in contrast to such qualities as caring, efficiency, and independence that are thought of as female. When a woman becomes governor, as did Ann Richards of Texas or Christine Todd Whitman in New Jersey, there are constant reminders of gender in the way the media covers their performance, whether it relates to who they appoint or who is executed. Women politicians carry their sex as a modifier.

However, I had always said that I wouldn't just run for the next open position. I didn't want to be governor partly because I didn't want to be stuck in the state capital dealing with Missouri's good old boys and partly because I still wanted to be a U.S. senator. We decided that the best way to get there would be to run for lieutenant governor (a separate race from the governor's in Missouri), and then, with a statewide win, we would be ready to run for the next opening for U.S. Senate in 1988. That was a presidential year when there should be a bigger Democratic turnout than we had in the 1982 off-year. The one thing that worried me was the appearance of weakness in deferring on the chief executive position, the suggestion that a woman couldn't run for governor.

The press conference announcing my decision was one of the most embarrassing moments in my life. I told reporters: "A strong argument for [governor] was that for too long women have been relegated to secondary political roles. Certainly, I believe I am qualified to be governor." But lieutenant governor was "the one office that offers the freedom and flexibility—the time—to meet with people, to hear their ideas, to develop answers to issues in a continuing partnership with the people of Missouri."[13] It sounded ridiculous even to me, but I didn't think I could announce that I was running for lieutenant governor just to position myself for U.S. Senate. Commentators had a field day. Some called it a big let-down, but others winked at the strategy, observing that no one in her right mind could really want the lieutenant governor's job for itself, when the only regular duty was presiding over a state senate that preferred to run itself.

Meanwhile, outside my knowledge, a campaign to put a woman on the Democratic presidential ticket was unfolding at the national level. An ad hoc group of a half dozen savvy Democratic women calling themselves the "A Team" decided they were tired of the guys saying they would pick a woman running mate and never doing it. This time, they would make sure someone did.[14] As ammunition, they had all the data about the women's vote, including the gender gap, which was being carefully promoted by women's organizations.[15] Former NOW President Eleanor Smeal issued a press release saying: "Reagan can be defeated on the women's vote alone." Years later, authors Linda Paget and Glenna Matthews would write that "Smeal preferred a strategy based exclusively on the numerical strength of women's votes, not their issue preferences" because that served NOW's organizational needs.[16] In fairness, many women activists genuinely believed that women were motivated to vote on so-called feminist issues. They desperately wanted to believe in a women's voting bloc. All that mattered to the advocates in 1984 was convincing male politicians that a woman on the ticket would bring them votes. This was women's perceived political power; it's what they had to use for leverage.

They also needed to recruit the right woman. That wouldn't be easy; female prospects with the expected qualifications were hard to find. There was only one woman governor in the whole country, Democrat Martha Layne Collins of Kentucky, but she had just recently been elected. There were no Democratic women U.S. Senators. Mayor Dianne Feinstein of San Francisco had executive stature heading a large city but not a lot of national status. One of the thirteen Democratic congresswomen, Lindy Boggs of Louisiana, had been mentioned in the press because "men politicians do not find her threatening—often an essential for women who are breaking barriers."[17] There were others whose names could excite more interest, like Barbara Jordan, Pat Schroeder, and Barbara Mikulski, who were willing to cooperate for the sake of the project.

The team finally settled on Congresswoman Geraldine Ferraro for very practical reasons. Ferraro was a favorite of House

Speaker Tip O'Neill, and she seemed to have the ideal profile to balance a national ticket: She was an Italian American from a populous state and a mother, and she was married to a business-man. She had been a teacher who took time to start a family, then went back to law school, started her career as a prosecuting attor-ney, and ran for Congress in 1972 at a time when getting elected as a woman required being both courageous and tough. Ferraro definitely had the reputation for both qualities in the House, but she was politic enough to have made herself an effective insider.

In a setting described in the book *Running As a Woman*, the team took Ferraro to a Chinese restaurant and planted fortune cookies with special messages like "You will win big in '84" and "You will meet a man in San Francisco [site for the convention] and travel with him."[18] Ferraro was skeptical but agreed to be considered as a way to advance the concept of a female vice pres-ident and with the understanding that the goal was to get the strongest ticket to beat Reagan. It was important not to let it appear that a woman was being chosen as a result of special-interest pressure rather than merit.

Ferraro successfully lobbied to be named chair of the platform committee for the July party convention, feeling this position would dramatize her strengths on domestic issues and her negoti-ating skills with those of differing views. The strategy group decided to surround her with supportive players. That's when I became involved, being recommended to fill a spot as a vice chair of the platform committee. Everyone got into the act. A question-naire was circulated to all known presidential candidates by a women's presidential project made up of such well-known femi-nists as Gloria Steinem, Coretta Scott King, and Mary Tyler Moore; and a number of prominent Democratic governors added their endorsement of the idea of a woman for vice president.

On May 4, Speaker O'Neill endorsed Ferraro. On June 4, *Time* magazine put Feinstein and Ferraro on the cover for a story titled "Why Not a Woman?". Barbara Walters interviewed Ferraro on her program *20/20*. Pressure was building on Mondale, the expected nominee. He had asked for a diverse list of possible run-ning mates to include women, but many, including Ferraro, thought this was only to make political points. She said she didn't believe any man would name a female running mate until he was in real trouble, at least 15 points down in the polls. When

Mondale appeared at the NOW convention in late June, he was met with such signs as "Woman Veep Now" and "Fritz and a Ms." He was upset, concerned that all the pressure would make him look like a pushover for "special interests."

In early July, twenty-three prominent Democratic women flew to Minnesota to meet with Mondale and make a final case for a woman on the ticket. Around the same time, the NWPC released a survey showing that 79 percent of the convention delegates thought a woman vice president would be a plus; only 9 percent said it would be a negative. There was a lot of leveraging going on. Mondale's staff had been given a detailed memo showing how a woman running mate could help him win. He knew that he wasn't the first to consider a woman; it was reported that Gerald Ford had considered Anne Armstrong as a running mate in 1976; but the initiative in 1984 clearly was a much more serious and concerted effort.

Both Feinstein and Ferraro were interviewed in Minnesota by Mondale. Ferraro said she felt she did poorly. She also was angry about leaks from Mondale's staff she felt were designed to sidetrack her, and she was ready to withdraw her name.[19] When she arrived in San Francisco for the convention on July 11, she called her husband John Zaccaro to verify his feelings in case an offer really came. She writes: "As I look back on that conversation now, I wonder whether it was fair. Did John really have a choice? Could he have said no? I question whether I was telling him what might be about to happen to us just so that he'd know or whether I was making sure he'd never be able to say I hadn't asked his opinion."[20] This was soul-searching any married woman candidate could understand, a reflection of the special strains women candidates experience.

Ferraro had said it would take a double-digit deficit for a man to make a woman his running mate. "And on the morning I flew to my vice-presidential interview, that's just what the spread was: fifteen points."[21] Mondale called her to offer the nomination not long after she had talked to her husband. The announcement of Ferraro's selection set off a frenzy, especially at the daily women's Caucuses held at the Democratic Convention, in the St. Francis Hotel. We replaced the stickers calling for a "Woman VP Now" with ones saying "Yea Ferraro!" Strategizing began immediately to get her elected (along with what'shisname).

It was astonishing how far political women had come in the last decade, and even since the last election. Women had been named Democratic Convention chair, chief executive officer, as well as platform committee chair for the convention itself. A woman was political director of the Democratic National Committee. A woman was mayor of San Francisco, the host city. Perhaps more importantly, after a long, hard struggle, a rule requiring 50 percent female delegates has been adopted in 1980, and that meant that half the delegates in 1984 were women. That too was power that could be leveraged. There even was a press conference to encourage women to donate money to candidates. One candidate described receiving checks through the new EMILY's List with a note attached saying: "I didn't give money early enough to Harriett Woods, and I don't want to make the same mistake again."

Republican women also were pressuring for more visibility. They were angry because Muriel Siebert, a broker and former superintendent of banking in New York, had received little money or party support in a bid to oppose Democratic Senator Daniel Patrick Moynihan. She told a GOP luncheon, "If things don't change pretty quickly and dramatically, the Republican Party can count on the same degree of support from women that it has come to expect from blacks." Secretary of Transportation Elizabeth Dole was named to head a coordinating council on women in the Reagan administration, and efforts were stepped up to send more women to the party convention in Dallas: They were 47 percent of the delegates in 1984, compared to 29 percent in 1980.[22] However, moderates felt themselves outnumbered.

Republicans didn't talk about a women's voting bloc; when it came campaign time, they shrewdly broke the women's vote into many small subcategories, by special interests and social and economic factors, to target with different messages. They would claim this helped them win women's votes.

Of course, women had been courted before and then let down. All the talk about women's votes, and even a woman nominee, still left us a long way from holding real power. We needed to enjoy the attention while we could. There was an exhilarating feeling in San Francisco that women mattered; it must have sent off a scent. Film producer James Brooks came nosing around the convention to pick up clues for portraying the strong and independent-thinking female television producer who would be the central figure in the film *Broadcast News*. We had breakfast together, but it was hard to pay much attention to a film director's problems when real events were so much more exciting.

We were waiting for one moment, the official nomination. Everyone understood that Ferraro's appearance on the podium as the nominee would make history. Many male delegates had given their convention floor passes to women and the convention hall crowd at the expected hour was overwhelmingly female. When Ferraro appeared high above us, dressed in white, with the distinctive flip of her haircut, a big smile and a wide wave, all our pent-up emotion was released in a burst of cheers, shouts, applause, and tears. Above everything, we could hear the sustained high-pitched cries of "Gerr-ee, Gerr-ee, Gerr-ee." At that moment, Gerry Ferraro embodied all of us. She was the heroine who had broken a seemingly impenetrable glass ceiling. She might not be running for president, but she soon could be just a heartbeat away. We had worked so long to get a woman into such a position of power. Now we hoped that all of our dreams would be fulfilled.

Ferraro understood this, just as I understood the role I was playing in Missouri. She later wrote that she was determined not to let us down. Of course, she had no idea what was coming. Those who go first, take the hits. The press soon was writing not about Ferraro's ideas but about her short-sleeved dresses. They described an awkwardness in Mondale and Ferraro being together on the campaign as a man and a woman. Should they touch? Ferraro called it "silliness." Pat Schroeder said: "It's stupid. All this focus on her haircuts, hemlines, manners and how many pearls she has really trivializes Gerry's candidacy. It's an affront to all women."

Back home in the lieutenant governor contest, there was a different target practice, with letters to the editor labeling me "the darling of chic feminists, movie stars, pro-abortionists and other leftists from coast-to-coast." The Republican state chair said: "California has its Jane [Fonda], New York has its Bella [Abzug] and Missouri has its Harriett." One could laugh except, as Madeleine Kunin noted in 1982, during her first (losing) battle for governor: "It's always dangerous territory if you are viewed as a woman's candidate or as a feminist."

The problem was that a chasm still existed between the perceptions of male and female roles. Men still were perceived as authority figures with a unique ability to get support in power positions from voters, who it was assumed wanted strong (male) leadership. Women were stereotyped as caring and compassionate, unlikely to be able to master issues like foreign policy, and best placed in supportive (female) roles. No one in the Mondale camp seemed to know what to do with a woman running mate. According to press reports, the Mondale staff alternated between describing her as a "Queens housewife" and too "strident." The staff resisted her efforts to reach out to women voters and sidelined her to secondary media markets.

But all of this was overshadowed by the media explosion when she revealed that her husband had refused to release his tax returns. Immediately the question became: What was he hiding? Eventually Zaccaro did release his records, and Ferraro held a press conference that answered every question about the couple's personal and business finances, but the incident dramatized the greater attention that would be received by a male spouse in a society where men still were presumed to be the dominant figure in a marriage. His finances were still more important.

And then there was the remark George Bush made to a group of longshoremen after he and Ferraro participated in the debate for vice-presidential candidates: "We tried to kick a little ass last night." One of his advisers would say later that it hit just the right tone with men who liked the idea of keeping women in their place.

In Missouri, there were men who felt the same way about me in the race for lieutenant governor. My chief opponent in the primary was a male legislator who was a well-known turkey caller. I gritted my teeth when he livened our debates with samples of his skill, winning great applause from the audiences. The next thing I expected was for him to whip off his jacket and flex his muscles. It gave me nightmares that he would win a rural landslide. (I beat him handily.) Then without any warning, Senator Eagleton suddenly announced in the middle of the campaign that he would not run again in 1986, raising the obvious question of whether I would quit as lieutenant governor in two years and run for his seat. At a minimum, the timing of the announcement showed indifference to the impact on my prospects. Commentators said it put me into a quandary, with opponents demanding a pledge to serve the full four years as lieutenant governor. I came up with such fatuous responses as: "No one politically ever locks any doors."

My general election opponent was the well-known author of a successful tax limitation initiative, and no pushover. We set up a statewide organization, building on the network of friendships and support from the U.S. Senate race. This was especially important as it became increasingly obvious the Mondale-Ferraro ticket was in trouble. I remained on call for the national party, and I remember desperately trying to keep the crowd occupied in an airplane hangar at Columbia, Missouri, while waiting for a circling plane to land with Gerry Ferraro. She was up there, equally desperate, trying to prepare answers for media reports that her father had Mafia connections. It wasn't true; it was just another example of the media using the role of a male relative to judge a woman candidate

The experience of running for Senate stood me in good stead in handling both political roles that year, my own race and national representation. We leveraged the power that had been built through the risk taking of 1982. Five statewide offices were up for grabs in 1984: governor, lieutenant governor, secretary of state, treasurer, and attorney general. I was the only woman and the only pro-choice candidate. When the votes were counted, I also was the only Democrat who won. Across the country, Madeleine Kunin also won, becoming Vermont's first woman governor, and Arlene Violet of Rhode Island was elected the first female state attorney general in the country. But Gerry Ferraro and Walter Mondale were defeated in an electoral landslide. There would be no female president-in-waiting.

What had happened to the much-touted women's vote? I had agreed to coordinate the Women's Vote Project in our area. We registered women everywhere—at grocery stores, malls, and exercise clubs. In November, a record 54.5 million women were reported as voting nationwide, compared to 47.4 million men. That was a turnout of 60.8 percent of eligible women voters, compared to 59 percent of men.[23] Large numbers, but not a large victory for Mondale. Ronald Reagan won among men 62 to 37 percent. He also won among women 54 to 44 percent.[24] That difference in the relative spread was a gender gap,[25] a male gender gap that benefited Reagan. Putting a woman on the presidential ticket could not get the needed votes of women who preferred Reagan to Mondale.

Women voters still showed their preference for Democrats in U.S. House races by 3 percentage points, so the general trend of 1980 and 1982 continued aside from the presidential race. Women's votes were credited with assuring the election of three Democratic senators, as well as Governor Kunin. In the final analysis, women, like men, had based their votes on a variety of factors, including their pocketbook, their family, their job, their health, their values, and their personal feelings about the candidates.

It was inaccurate to suggest that women could deliver some kind of bloc vote for a woman running for vice president on a ticket headed by a man, but it wasn't a mistake to fight to get a woman as a vice-presidential nominee, even in a losing election. As NWPC Chair Kathy Wilson said after the election: "We in the women's movement have never won anything without pressing, fighting. This year we fought to elevate women's status in national politics . . . [and] we helped make women matter."[26]

Women were empowered by Ferraro's nomination. Every woman who walked into a voting booth in 1984 and saw Ferraro's name was forever changed. Daughters held high above the crowds by their fathers to see a powerful woman would remember when they grew up. Someone had to be first, Ferraro wrote. "My candidacy says America believes in equality. And the time for that equality is now."[27]

Looking back, it's clear there was some deception in the statement I made when I declared my candidacy for lieutenant governor of Missouri, I was indeed planning to use a victory for the lieutenant governor's office as a stepping stone to U.S. senator. However, in and of itself, the successful campaign for lieutenant governor ultimately broke a barrier and helped other women to become winners. There surely was some exaggeration in the claims women made that helped convince Mondale to select Ferraro, but her campaign forever changed our sense of how a potential president looks, sounds, and acts. We leveraged the power that we had in the difficult struggle to win positions traditionally held by men so we could demonstrate that those positions could function as well, or better, with different gender leadership.

It has been observed that women entering masculine positions face two unhappy choices. Either they can conform to gender expectations, try to act female and perpetuate stereotypes, or they can "do masculine leadership" and try to imitate masculine styles.[28] Ferraro did something else. She demonstrated strength and courage under the most adverse circumstances while remaining her own person. She proved she had the intelligence and strength to be president. And that has hastened the day when a woman will sit in the Oval Office.

9

Playing the Game

The question for [Dianne Feinstein
and Ann Richards] was, to what lengths
were they willing to go to win? The question
for the public was, would it allow these women to
use the same political tools men are allowed to use?

—**Celia Morris,** *Storming the Statehouse*

In the entire United States in 1985, there were only sixty-eight women in major elected positions—twenty-five in Congress and forty-three scattered across the country as statewide elected executives, including two governors, five lieutenant governors, ten treasurers, and seventeen secretaries of state. That was double the number there had been in 1970, thanks to the new breed of women running for office, but it still represented a pitiful potential for women being seen in positions of public authority. We could talk about our goals for high office, but at this rate, we didn't have much chance to play the game.

That made it doubly important to be effective when we were players. It soon became clear how important the visibility of a woman lieutenant governor was to young girls in Missouri. When school classes filed into the senate galleries, they looked down on a sea of dark suits, but they also saw a woman presiding, pounding the gavel and recognizing speakers. The girls wanted to have their pictures taken with the woman lieutenant governor and have her as the commencement speaker at their high schools where no woman had spoken before. They saw me as a powerful feminine figure standing tall on the podium.

The truth of the situation was something else; the senators had long since stripped any real power from the presiding officer function of the lieutenant governor. They wanted to run things themselves. One of my male predecessors literally had been carried from the chambers when he tried to assert himself. The senators jealously guarded their prerogatives. They also still held their gender biases. On one occasion, when the president pro tem was losing control of the floor, he angrily attacked me for "looking at him that way." (I *was* pretty disgusted.) He clearly wouldn't have so referred to a man's "look," but there wasn't much alternative to listening to his tirade. A couple of male senators came up to the podium to express their sympathy. For an instant, I understood the attraction of having a male protector to fight one's battles. But just for an instant.

The experience of being isolated within male institutions was so commonplace that political women had organized Caucuses for mutual support within legislatures all across the country. Those of us in statewide positions had our own organization, called Women Executives in State Government (WESG). We held workshops to build skills and help each other develop resources, but what we enjoyed most was sharing war stories. In 1986, I had one of my own. Missouri was one of a handful of states with separate elections for governor and lieutenant governor; that could result in the top two executive positions representing different parties. It had happened in Missouri in 1984. Governor John Ashcroft and I definitely were the odd couple: one a progressive Democrat and the other an extremely conservative Republican.

Shortly after we were sworn in, the governor asked for a meeting. His attorney was present. The governor said he would like my agreement to end the practice of the lieutenant governor's serving as acting governor whenever the governor leaves the state. The Missouri Constitution dictates this practice, stating that on "absence from the state or other disability of the governor, the powers, duties and emoluments of the governor shall devolve upon the lieutenant governor." This is separate and in addition to the provision for replacing the governor upon death, conviction, impeachment, or resignation. Modern communication and speed of travel probably make the first provision unnecessary, but it's seen as a safeguard in case of natural disaster or other emergency. And it's the law.

The governor's request suggested that he was uncomfortable leaving the state in my hands. I declined, and I assured him there would be no abuse of executive power in his absence. It worried me that giving up the backup role so casually would be a sign of weakness, particularly damaging to a woman politician, the first elected statewide. But what to do? The governor really held all the cards. He could just ignore me and take his trips. A court case would be a waste of taxpayer money. The only other recourse would be to hold a press conference to say the governor was defying the constitution and try to get public sympathy. But would the public really care?

Despite our differing parties, it was important to maintain good relationships between our executive offices but not to be pushed around. The governor had left the state once without notifying anyone. It couldn't happen again. I hired an attorney to prepare an analysis supporting current law and delivered it to the governor. If he failed to contact our office again, we'd go to the press, risky as that would be. We learned of an upcoming trip, and we prepared a press release. I held my breath. In the early hours of the morning, a letter from the governor spelling out his travel plans was slipped under our door. The crisis was over.

When I told this story at the next meeting of the WESG, there was spontaneous applause. I saw it as an exercise in political gamesmanship; the other women saw it as a gender victory in a world where women too often get pushed around. Rethinking the event, I wondered whether gender had been the dominant factor. It's true there was a principle of law involved, but why be confrontational when there rarely was any activity in the governor's absence that was worth fighting about? But, like the WESG women who applauded, I had experienced slights that had undermined my effectiveness and had made me both extra sensitive and more combative. Collaboration and respect made more sense than confrontation, but we had reached the point as women where we expected our good behavior to be reciprocated.

It turned out that there was plenty to do as lieutenant governor, even without the governor's cooperation. The lieutenant governor's office coordinated volunteerism in the state and also served as ombudsman to receive citizen concerns, so administrator Mary Schantz had her hands full. We added a hotline for state employees to make suggestions for eliminating waste and efficiency, and we held hearings around the state to encourage small-business development in smaller cities. I took the lead in pushing for more state contracts for women and minority businesses. And then there was the question of a second race for the U.S. Senate.

In an article in *The New York Times Magazine*, December 30, 1984, assessing the impact of Geraldine Ferraro's loss on women's political future, Maureen Dowd wrote that a few days after my election as lieutenant governor, "a group of women, unbeknownst to [Woods], got together in a private meeting in Washington to begin planning her Senate campaign for 1986."[1] There were changes since 1982, Dowd wrote, when I lost "after squeezing money out of a national party which was skeptical that a woman could win. Now, she [Harriett Woods] . . . talks about improvements in the political mood. 'The fact that I was the first woman elected statewide in Missouri [Woods said] did not even make the headlines this time.'"

It was remarkable what a difference even two years had made. The idea of a woman running for Senate had been a sensation in 1982; in 1986, it was expected. In a newspaper article headlined "Women's campaigns come into their own," Ruth B. Mandel, director of the CAWP, described the increased sophistication of women's campaigns in 1986 as "15 years of hard work paying off."[2] In 1982, raising large sums from women had been a heroic endeavor; in 1986, the article noted, the $3 million raised by Woods by mid-October (before the 1986 election) placed that campaign second among all Senate candidates. EMILY's List helped; so did women writing checks in their new positions as attorneys, accountants, and business executives. But women were raising money from all sources. The good news, one male consultant said, " is that women are now winning according to the same rules men did."

It is noteworthy that in 1986, we didn't question whether that was really such good news.

So many women were running that there were fourteen state and national races in which women were running against one another, with two female candidates competing for governor of Nebraska and two for U.S. Senate in Maryland. There also were a number of come-back races. An article in *USA Today* described women who had won higher office in 1984 after losing earlier bids—Governor Kunin, Rhode Island Attorney General Arlene Violet, Congresswoman Helen Bentley, and me: "Many are middle-aged veterans of local government or service work." NWPC Chair Kathy Wilson remarked: "A common trait of these women is tenacity, a real persistence in the face of incredible odds. They are undaunted."[3]

In a speech before the NWPC annual convention in Atlanta that year, I said: "I will run [for Senate] if I can make a difference, if there are things that we can do together that will change the way people are treated in this world."[4] To be truthful, nothing could stop me from running. There's no doubt the 1984 statewide win had given me new confidence to fulfill an old ambition. Sounding "every inch a candidate," according to a reporter covering the speech, I praised the special qualities that women bring to public dialogue. "If the qualities of love and compassion and cooperation and candor and patience are feminine, then we're proud of it. What we have to offer is exactly what this country needs. . . . We're the mainstream. We're the wives and workers and the child-raisers and the caretakers and the educators and at last the public decisionmakers, because more than half of the voters are women." And referring to politicians searching for the mainstream, "Why do they keep looking? Here we are."

It seems strange in retrospect that our second Senate campaign had so little in common with that message. Our biggest concern at the beginning was that the guys would once again try to preempt the nomination, perhaps with Congressman Richard Gephardt who had increasing national visibility. We leaked our own poll that showed me with the strongest favorability rating and name recognition of any Democratic politician in the state. All other major candidates, including Gephardt, soon declined to run. (He would run for president in 1988, with me serving as one of his national co-chairs.) In 1985, almost two years before the 1986 election, Jody Newman again became my campaign manager. All we did the first year was raise money. This time, we were determined to have the best campaign that money could buy.

In 1982, I had been dismissed as a barefoot Cinderella. In 1986, I was a statewide elected official on the priority list of national Democratic donors and expected to compete with the big boys. The campaign eventually raised $4.25 million, more than any other woman's campaign ever had raised. Staff didn't have to push me; I would stay at the phone, asking strangers for $500 and $1,000 until the daily quota was met. The need to raise such huge sums still appalled me, but this was the way the game had to be played. I had lost the first time for want of timely funds; that wouldn't happen again because of any failure on the candidate's part.

Our impressive total reflected large amounts received in response to letters targeting supporters of different causes. We had built an astonishing base of 10,000 out-of-state donors in the 1982 race. Emotional appeals produce results, but it costs a lot to send out a direct mailing, and the average contribution is smaller per contact than the typical donation to an event. That means the net profit available from a direct mailing to spend by the campaign is a lot less than appears from the big figures.

My first Senate campaign had established that there was a new donor base for women candidates through direct-mail appeals; this now was standard procedure for most Democratic women's campaigns, but it produced a large number of smaller contributions. My opponent, former two-time governor Christopher "Kit" Bond, like other established male Republicans, could raise more money with fewer and bigger contributions by drawing on deep pockets of corporate interests, and their executives and families. Both of us pulled in PAC money, mine from labor and environmental groups, his from utilities and corporate interests. Raising money was a competitive business.

One reason we needed so much money was to pay top price for consultants. We expected a rough campaign and decided we should choose a Washington insider this time, someone with a reputation as a tough in-fighter. It turned out to be a terrible fit. Bob Squier had a macho style without a clue about feminine candidates and their strengths. Of course, there hadn't been many. It worried me that I would appear in his commercials as simply a man in skirts, so we set up a quiet get-acquainted lunch to help him get a sense of the candidate. He spent the whole time talking about himself. Perhaps women are more concerned

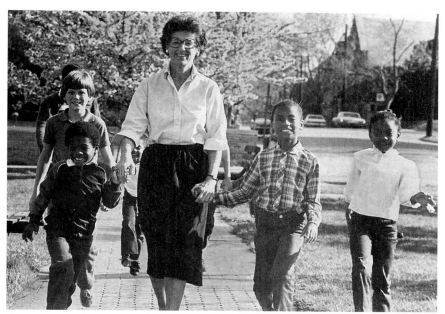

It was community causes, such as ending racial discrimination and achieving social justice, that drew women into politics in the 1960s and 1970s. Photo courtesy of the author.

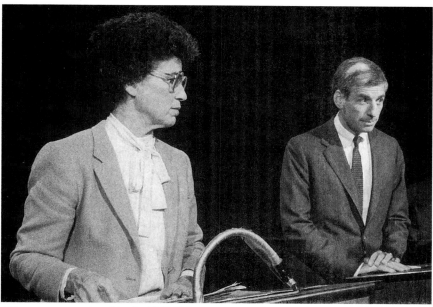

When women protested in the 1982 U.S. Senate race, the campaign attracted national attention as a symbol of women's political progress. Here is a televised debate with Sen. Jack Danforth from that race. It was unusual to see a woman candidate debating a male U.S. Senator. Photo by The Kansas City Star.

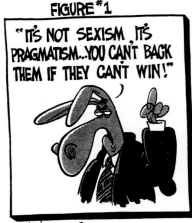

Cartoon by Lee Judge/The Kansas City Star.

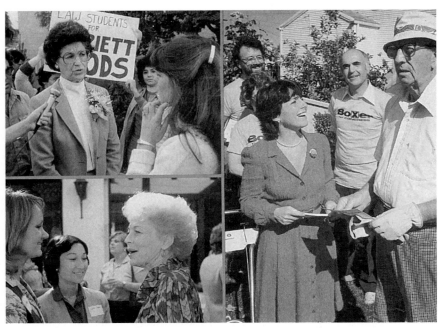

Stung by the defeat of the ERA, women are off and running for office—overcoming hurdles rarely encountered by men (clockwise from top: Harriett Woods in Missouri, Barbara Boxer in California, and Ann Richards in Texas), November 1982. Photo copyright © 1982 Newsweek, Inc. All rights reserved. Reprinted by permission.

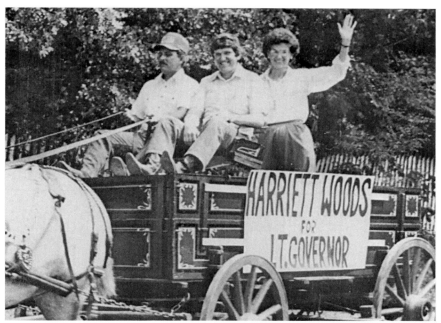

Riding in a parade in outstate Missouri. Photo courtesy of the author.

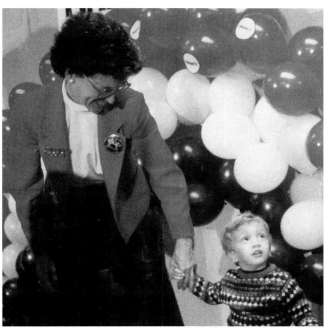

Celebrating victory in the lieutenant governor's race in 1984 with first grandchild, two-year-old James. Photo courtesy of the author.

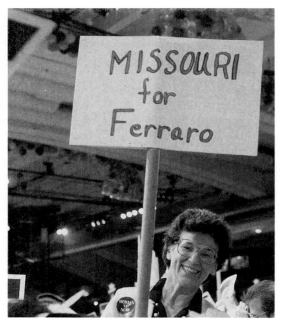

Euphoria on the floor of the Democratic convention in 1984 as Geraldine Ferraro accepted the nomination for vice president. Photo courtesy of the author.

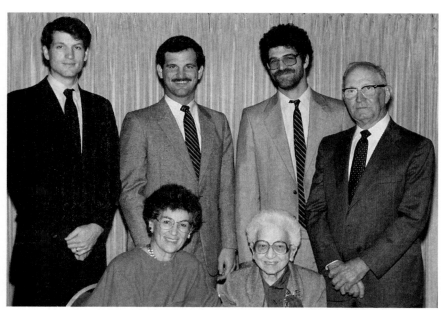

Sons Andy, Pete, Chris, and husband, Jim, with my mother, Ruth Wise Friedman. Photo courtesy of the author.

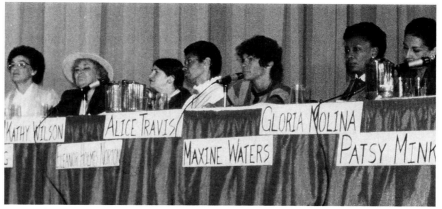

Caucus leaders interrogate male candidates seeking women's support in the 1984 presidental election. Photo courtesy of the National Women's Political Caucus.

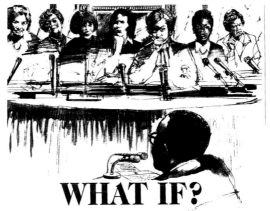

WHAT IF?

What if 14 women, instead of 14 men, had sat on the Senate Judiciary Committee during the confirmation hearings of Clarence Thomas?

Sound unfair? Just as unfair as fourteen men and no women.

What if even **half** the Senators had been women? Women are, after all, more than half the population. Maybe, just maybe, women's voices would have been heard. Maybe the experiences and concerns of women would not have been so quickly dismissed or ridiculed. And maybe all of America would have benefited.

The behavior and performance of the United States Senate during the Clarence Thomas confirmation hearings demonstrated a stark truth: women are tragically under-represented politically. As long as men make up 98% of the U.S. Senate and 93% of the U.S. House of Representatives, women's voices can be ignored, their experiences and concerns trivialized.

The need for women in public office has never been more obvious. Or essential.

Men control the White House, the Congress, the courthouse and the statehouse. Men have political power over women's lives. It's time that women help make the rules, create the policies, and pass the laws about sexual harassment, day care, affordable health care, and hundreds of decisions that affect American families every day.

The National Women's Political Caucus is determined to even

the odds. To hear the voices of women echo in the halls of power.

If you're angry about what you've witnessed in the United States Senate, don't just raise your fist, raise your pen. Join us. The goal of the National Women's Political Caucus is to **increase the number of women elected and appointed to public office. We're the only national bi-partisan grassroots organization working across this country to recruit, train and elect women into office at all levels of government.**

Turn your anger into action. Join us.

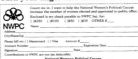

Count me in. I want to help the National Women's Political Caucus increase the number of women elected and appointed to public office. Enclosed is my check payable to NWPC Inc. for:
( )$250   ( )$100   ( )$50   ( )$35   OTHER $____
Name _____
Address _____
City/State/Zip _____
Please bill my ( ) Mastercard ( ) Visa   Amount $____
Account Number _____ Expiration Date _____
Signature _____ Date _____
Contributions to NWPC are not tax deductible.
National Women's Political Caucus
1275 K Street, N.W., Suite 750, Washington, D.C. 20005

Paid for by the National Women's Political Caucus

This full-page ad in the national edition of the New York Times, *October 25, 1991, in response to the Clarence Thomas–Anita Hill hearings, helped launch the "Year of the Woman." Photo courtesy of the National Women's Political Caucus.*

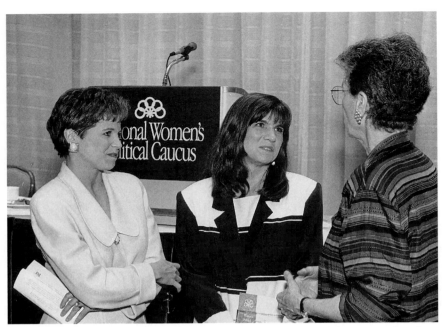

Women in media and politics have been mutually supportive (from left, NBC's Today Show anchor Katie Couric, former New York Times *columnist Anna Quindlan, and me), 1992. Photo courtesy of the National Women's Political Caucus.*

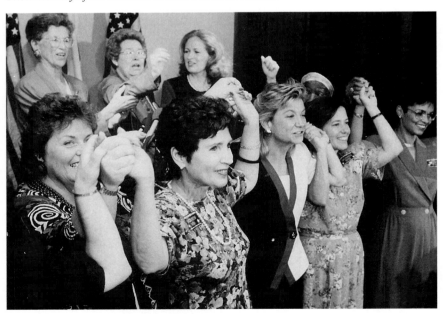

Our press conference at the 1992 Republican convention in support of Republican women candidates included U.S. Rep. Connie Morella, Maryland, and U.S. Rep. Susan Molinari, New York, second and third from left, front row. Photo courtesy of the National Women's Political Caucus.

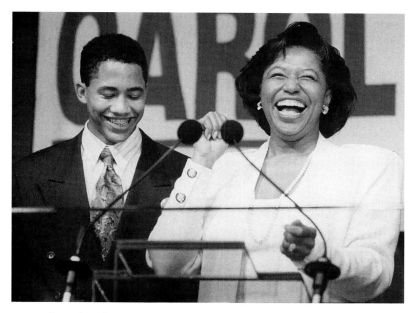

A record number of women were elected in 1992, creating banner news everywhere. Carol Moseley Braun, shown here with her son, was the first African American woman elected to the U.S. Senate. Photo copyright © 1999, USA Today. *Reprinted with permission.*

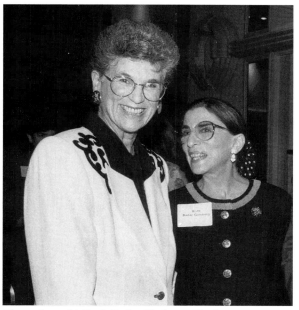

The author with Ruth Bader Ginsburg. Ginsburg accompanied her husband, Martin, who received an award from NWPC at the "Good Guys" fundraiser in 1993. Photo courtesy of the National Women's Political Caucus.

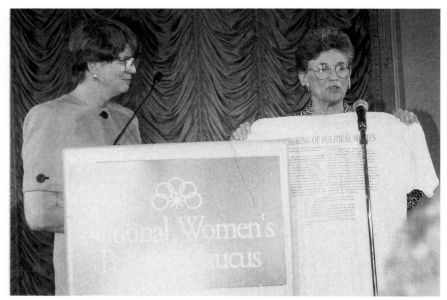

First woman Attorney General, Janet Reno, is saluted at the women's political caucus convention, 1993. Photo courtesy of the National Women's Political Caucus.

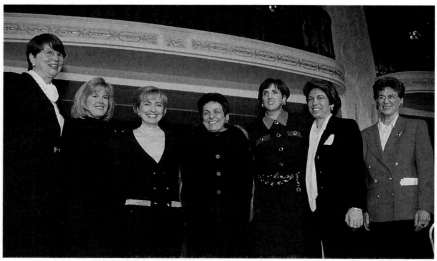

Attorney General Janet Reno, Tipper Gore, Hillary Rodham Clinton, Secretary of Health and Human Services Donna Shalala, EPA Administrator Carol Browner, President's Council of Economic Advisers Chairman Laura D'Andrea Tyson, and myself at the salute to women appointees in the Clinton Administration, February 1994. Photo courtesy of the National Women's Political Caucus.

about relationships, but relationships are critical in campaigns, not just for routine decisions but because of the need for trust in time of crisis. We would learn that lesson soon.

The Senate then was 53 to 47 Republican, but a couple of Republican retirements and a strong Democratic field raised the hopes of the Democratic Senatorial Campaign Committee, led by a vigorous Senator George Mitchell of Maine. My race was seen as winnable, and a steady stream of senators came to help with fund-raisers. I particularly remember a joint appearance by Senators Jay Rockefeller and Bill Bradley, twin gangling giants, who were a smash hit with quips about the current political scene. They also were very good troopers who forgave me for tangling their long legs together in a tiny private plane and risking their lives, and any hope of a Democratic majority, as we spiraled up and down through bad weather into the downtown Kansas City airport.

National Democratic fund-raisers liked the idea of having two viable female Senate candidates; Congresswoman Barbara Mikulski of Maryland also was running. The usual routine at events was for each candidate to speak briefly about his or her race, in as optimistic a tone as possible. I never mentioned that my opponent led in early polls, was expected to have much more money, that President Reagan's ratings were the highest they had ever been in Missouri, and my opponent could trump my visiting senators by bringing in the president (he came three times).

Still, I felt good about the race. There was at least one issue we could build on where Reagan's low ratings created an advantage—the current farm crisis. Missouri agriculture was in deep trouble in 1985 with massive farm foreclosures and the calling of loans. Farmers who had been encouraged to stretch their credit to expand production were having trouble making payments because crop prices and markets had collapsed. Analysts were predicting we would lose one in five of our owner-operated farms, the worst agricultural disaster since the 1930s. With collapse of the farm economy could go many small businesses, local banks, and support for schools and communities. I recommended intervention to extend credit; Republicans were for the status quo.

It's impossible to discuss the 1986 race without telling the story of the "crying farmer" commercial; it became the most publicized part of our campaign. It showed me harshly denouncing farm foreclosures as I talked to a farmer crying about his farm being foreclosed by an insurance company on whose board Kit Bond served as director. Squier turned the footage into a three-part commercial, like a soap opera, complete with "to be continued" tag lines. Part one introduced me harshly denouncing foreclosures; part three showed the crying farmer, together with the message about Bond. When Squier previewed it, I told him he might win an award, but I would lose the election. It was an unpleasant first impression of me for voters. Squier assured me it was a "silver bullet" that would be used only late in the campaign after other commercials had established me with voters, and if it didn't work, I could fire him.

In late spring 1986 Bond had pulled ahead as a result of running a heavy schedule of commercials. Our pollsters, Hickman-Maslin, insisted we needed to act quickly to pull down Bond's ratings and that the farm commercials were the strongest message Squier had prepared. We resisted. Voters needed to get comfortable with me first; it was too early for such a negative attack. We debated long distance; they were too busy to come to Missouri. Ultimately, they wore us down. What was the point of having all these high-priced consultants if I didn't listen to them?

Weeping families may be commonplace on the news today, but a crying farmer was controversial in a political commercial, and a reporter sought him out. After being badgered with questions, the family said that Squier had not informed them that the spots would be used as part of a political attack. The wife told the reporter: "I kinda felt like we had been used." The Bond campaign seized the quote and ran a commercial attacking me for exploiting the farmer. The "crying farmer" suddenly became a liability rather than a weapon.

Voters often see women candidates as different, as more honest and not playing the usual political games. We're seen as outsiders who are less likely to be corrupted or get caught in any shenanigans. This generalized image is part of the advantage that balances the automatic no votes against us as too weak and unassertive. If anything happens to puncture the image, it can mean a disproportionate loss in support. The commercials did indeed pull down Bond's ratings, but they pulled mine down as well. All the years of building a reputation as the high-minded campaigner for truth and good government, of asserting my identity as not just another politician, were going down the drain. I fired Squier.

Campaign manager Jody Newman commented: "There used to be a theory that men couldn't attack women. However, in this election it's almost that women can't attack men because the women get classified as bitchy or shrill." The pollsters quit in protest over fellow consultant Squier's firing and placed a story in *The Washington Post* blaming the campaign. They were more concerned about saving face with the crowd inside the Beltway than doing damage to a candidate. Of course there was the usual suggestion that the problem was a woman-run campaign.

We quickly replaced the consultants and went back on the offensive, and by fall at least one poll showed us running even, but the incident had shaken the campaign's confidence. Decisions seemed even more difficult to make. What was more important was the impact on our message. We had hoped to use the farm issue as symbolic of Bond's lack of concern for working Missourians; loss of credibility over the "crying farmer" ads made that a lot harder. We never found a cutting-edge issue to replace it. The economy was healthier, and the pocketbook issues that draw a contrast between candidates didn't rouse the voters in the urban areas as they had in 1982.

Ultimately it became a battle about character: Harriett Woods as a person of integrity, fighting for the people and getting things done; or Kit Bond as a former governor who knew the people of Missouri. The battleground was paid television, and despite our record efforts, he had far more money to buy ads. This time I made my statement of principle about abortion and kept it on the air, but it no longer was earth-shaking to do so. Antiabortion groups had bought $100,000 worth of television time in the state to pound the opposite message. Many people applauded a candidate who looked the voters in the eye and said what she believed, but it couldn't decide the election.

We had a wonderful staff and dedicated volunteers and ran a vigorous campaign, but in the end, we each got our votes, and I got fewer of them. I lost 777,612 to 699,624. This time, I outpolled my opponent among women 56 to 44 percent, but lost with men, 43 to 57 percent.

The worst part isn't losing; it's losing your true self in the battle. Before we started, I said that I wouldn't mind a defeat as long as we felt we had done our best. We ended up feeling we hadn't done our best. I felt we had played someone else's game instead of our own. There was a constant tension between what I wanted to be and what I had to be. I had let myself be packaged by fancy consultants and had lost my bearings. There's no point to second-guessing. We stimulated important debate on issues like education, health care, taxation, federal spending, personal liberties, and personal choice that mattered to many people. One commentator said he just didn't think it was possible for a liberal Democrat to beat a well-packaged WASP governor in a conservative state like Missouri in a nonpresidential year. Only one politician said it was because the campaign had been run by too many women. At least we had made that much progress.

In retrospect, a few gender incidents did offer bizarre humor. There was an organization called the Hollywood Women's Political Committee that wielded real power through fund-raising. On a California fund-raising trip, a key member, songwriter Marilyn Bergman, set up an informal lunch at her house with Barbra Streisand and Jane Fonda. It turned into a support session for Streisand who came rushing in late, distraught over the problems she was having with a director who didn't understand a woman's response to childhood abuse. (The movie was released as *Nuts.*) We spent most of the time reassuring Barbra Streisand, although I had a feeling she could more than hold her own. Then Streisand and Fonda generously wrote $1,000 checks for my campaign.

When Republicans saw the Fonda contribution listed in our financial report, they sent out a mailing that said: "When Missouri boys were making the ultimate sacrifice for America, Jane Fonda was touring North Vietnam. . . . These are the kind of people Harriett Woods represents." Leaflets were distributed in rural areas with a picture of Fonda in Vietnam on one side and me on the other, labeled "Hanoi Harriett." When questioned, Bond said: "People of Missouri are concerned about her point of view and the viewpoints of the feminist groups, the Hollywood liberal groups and the people who are raising the money." I countered that voters should be more concerned about the money Bond was getting from oil and insurance companies and out-of-state banks.

The St. Louis Globe–Democrat, the morning paper I once worked for as a reporter, hired a conservative political gossip columnist (apparently none of their regular reporters wanted to do the story) to expose my sinister Hollywood connections. A three-part front-page series recounted my 1983 trip to Hollywood for a dinner party at Frances and Norman Lear's house and a fund-raiser for a woman mayor that was held at the home of Jane Fonda and then-husband Tom Hayden. Hayden was a member of the California State Assembly at the time, but he was identified in the story as a "former student radical."

The story probably didn't matter much to voters, but it cost me a trip to Barbra Streisand's ranch. That was the year that she agreed to help Democratic Senate candidates by giving a concert, her first live performance in years. All the candidates attended except me. We were too worried that there would be photographs that would become further distractions to the campaign.

You know the campaign is over when you come downstairs and have to pick up your own briefcase. Jim knew it was over when I stayed home and cooked dinner. As always, he had maintained an even balance through the madness. There was only one emergency in all my campaigns that he couldn't handle—the storm-caused leak that ruined a large section of our kitchen wallpaper. He tracked me down by phone. Taking care of such things was my job, even if I was in the middle of a U.S. Senate campaign. A friend who runs an interior design firm stepped in, selecting new wallpaper and hiring a contractor without my involvement. Of course, the new wallpaper didn't match the cabinets and we eventually had to redo the whole kitchen.

A lost campaign is a little like a death; there's a need for grieving, to mourn what was good, to regret what failed, and then to move on. Some of those close to me worried that I wasn't grieving enough, and they sat down one on one, to try to talk about it. But endless self-analysis never has been my way. It was very clear in the final week that we were likely to lose; indeed, I fought on long after others in the campaign really had given up. There was comfort in consoling letters from strangers: "Thank you for . . . the integrity and directness with which you offered the voters a clear alternative." "I've never been involved in politics before, other than voting, but now I'd like to very much." "Thank you for being you."

And the defeat hadn't kept the Democrats from regaining control of the U.S. Senate. Barbara Mikulski had won her race, becoming the first Democratic woman elected to the Senate in her own right. A large chunk of her financial support had come from women. I had lost the game, but there was satisfaction that she had won.

The long struggle that began with my 1982 race had paid off, even if not for me.

10

New Challenges

Shall we pause now and turn our back upon the
road that lies ahead? Shall we call this the promised
land? Or, shall we continue on our way? For "each age
is a dream that is dying, or one that is coming to birth."

**—President Franklin Delano Roosevelt,
Second Inaugural Address, January 20, 1937**

Women in politics have to remind themselves constantly that
the ultimate goal isn't just winning higher and higher positions; it's meeting challenges to improve the quality of life for
everyone. So when there is a defeat, like mine for the U.S.
Senate, it's important to look for new opportunities to keep the
juices flowing. We must keep on trying to change the structures
and institutions that make our lives so difficult. One thing about
taking on new challenges: You never can tell where they'll lead.
In my case, ultimately, it was Washington, D.C.

Despite the weakness of the lieutenant governor's office and
the discouragement of the Senate loss, there was a measure of
power that had been built up in all the campaigns and years in
public office. There is power just in having a title. The nature of
celebrity is that people have an idea you're important and will
listen to you even when they're not quite sure who you are.
What I needed was a worthwhile way to use that power, and it
arrived in the form of homelessness.

In the late 1980s, there was a rising tide of homelessness, a new economic kind that included an increasing number of women and children. Neither traditional shelters nor government agencies were prepared. In one rural Missouri county, a destitute woman seeking food assistance for her children was told that if she didn't find a place to live within five days, her children would be taken away. She couldn't find housing she could afford so never went back for the help she needed.

This was a cause worth addressing in the remaining days as lieutenant governor, something that restored a sense of purpose after the election loss. Homelessness was a crisis that required both short- and long-term strategies and involved issues that had engaged me for most of my life—issues of social justice, more responsive government, and fairness. Added to that was a sense of responsibility for women. Homelessness underscored the need to look at the economy from a gender perspective, something women economists had been advocating for more than a decade.

While some of us had focused on women's political progress, other women were founding policy centers that worked on legal and economic issues affecting women's daily lives.[1] Out of these studies came a special term, the "feminization of poverty," to describe the impact on women of a lifetime of lower wages, inadequate or absent pensions, and the burden of child care without sufficient support. In 1989, only 51 percent of the women due child support received the full amount; 25 percent received nothing. Women were statistically the fastest-growing poverty group in the country: three-fifths of all poor adults and nearly three-fourths of the elderly poor.[2]

The public didn't like to hear about poverty and was only a little more interested in women's problems at the other end of the economic pipeline. The term "glass ceiling" was first popularized in 1986 when *The Wall Street Journal* described "an invisible—but impenetrable—barrier between women and the executive suite, preventing them from reaching the highest levels of the business world regardless of their accomplishments and merits."[3] Without anyone noticing, women had been moving into the economic mainstream at a phenomenal rate. From 1978 to 1988, the number of women in management positions more than doubled, from 2.5 to 5.6 million, becoming 39 percent of all executive, administrative, and managerial positions.[4]

This was the good news, but women made up less than 5 percent of senior managers, and the number wasn't growing at a rate that seemed appropriate given other progress.[5] The assumption had been that the gap would be closed with the passage of time, as more women moved up the executive ladder, but it didn't seem to be happening. There was growing frustration among middle-management women with the unresponsiveness of the corporate culture itself.

When Catalyst, an organization devoted to the progress of women in corporations, asked 1,251 female managers how they got into their positions, they said they had consistently exceeded expectations, developed a style with which male managers were comfortable (one mentioned talking about sports), networked with important colleagues, and found influential mentors. The factors holding them back, they said, were male preconceptions of women and the exclusion of women from informal communication networks, plus a lack of significant general management or line experience. Catalyst concluded, "Gender is a powerful determinant of career experience." Women work harder and still too often go unrewarded.

Twenty years after the contemporary women's movement began to assert itself politically, it was clear that just opening doors wasn't enough. Many women still lived and worked in circumstances that gave them very few options. Poverty, racial and ethnic separation, limited training, poor health, and heavy family responsibilities all played out differently for women, yet most couldn't conceive of speaking out, or becoming leaders, because it took all their energies just to survive. It was our job to help them find their voices. I needed to get involved.

Over the next few years, I began to work with community organizers who were developing programs to empower poor women. We also initiated summit meetings of all area women's organizations and many individuals to explore how women could use their new strengths to make social structures more responsive to their needs.

Those of us in public office had known from the beginning that gender affects every aspect of our society. Sometimes there is gender bias, as reflected in the questions to Geraldine Ferraro asking whether she would be able to "push the red button," or in the assumption that a woman professor shouldn't be tenured because she might take time to have a baby. In other cases, there's gender discouragement, as when a Citadel military academy turns away a qualified Shannon Faulkner.

The homeless crisis was a good example of the dangerous consequences of gender insensitivity. A national study in 1992 would estimate that single women headed 80 percent of homeless families.[6] A third of the 30,000 Missouri homeless in the 1980s were children. In other words, those on the street weren't just the addicted and the mentally ill. Many were families unable to pay rent or mortgage because of a changing economy that offered few jobs for those lacking education or special skills. Others had lost out in the farm recession. But because public officials were locked in conventional gender expectations for street people, they hadn't taken appropriate action.

Agencies accustomed to housing male drifters in dormitory settings were unprepared for single mothers with two or three children under the age of five. Most shelters were set up only to provide beds at night; what were these women to do with their children during the day? A lack of transportation might mean no medical care, or no school.[7] In a gym converted to a shelter, I discovered a small boy lying on a cot who had been discharged from a hospital the day before after a hernia operation. As lieutenant governor, I began visiting local shelters all over the state, using my official status to draw media attention to the problem.

The governor showed no interest; in fact, he had cut several hundred thousand dollars for homeless interventions from the proposed state budget. So our office took the lead. Following the pattern of the past, we began by convening those most involved, in this case the service providers such as local shelters, service agencies, and community coalitions. About thirty of them became part of the Lieutenant Governor's Task Force with two goals: to address the current performance of state agencies responding to the homeless and to propose a statewide strategy that would deal with prevention.

Department heads who didn't respond to calls from beleaguered local service providers were more obliging about coming to a meeting at the lieutenant governor's office. After they had heard the concerns of those affected, they were responsive to the idea of creating a cabinet council, including education, social services, health, and mental health, to coordinate responses to the crisis. Meanwhile task force members hammered out ideas for change, and after four months they gave the governor, department heads, and the media a report analyzing the problem, with specific recommendations for action.

We also supported new initiatives that were beginning at the community level, such as day shelters for women and transition housing for families in crisis. My responsibilities included communicating with the public, writing commentaries, and giving speeches. Did the fact that I was a woman official have any bearing on my actions, my interest, or follow-through? Perhaps. It was clear to me that the homeless were simply the most visible evidence of failed economic and social policies. They were the ones who had fallen through holes in the promised safety net; the ones who lacked community mental health and alcohol treatment services; the ones who couldn't find affordable housing; the ones who had been defined out of eligibility for health, welfare, and job programs in order to save a few budget dollars.

Homelessness wasn't a temporary crisis to be solved by finding beds for people found sleeping on grates. America's homeless didn't need more emergency shelters; they needed alternatives.

This wasn't the only challenge that had our attention. Other women also needed alternatives. A risk-taking homemaker named Ann Ross had an idea for selling quality paper products and party materials. No bank would lend her any money to open a store. The first commercial landlord she approached tried to increase the rent because she was a woman. Finally she took all her personal savings, $4,600, and signed a lease for a year. She purchased an old cash register, painted some used shelves, hired three friends, and opened her first store. Other women entrepreneurs gave her advice, and she survived her mistakes to become so successful that she eventually opened two more stores.

Women like this didn't want handouts. They wanted fewer roadblocks based on their sex and a respect for businesswomen that would make their risk taking less difficult. In 1970, women owned less than 5 percent of America's businesses. From 1977 to 1985, women-owned sole proprietorships nearly doubled from 1.9 to 3.7 million. By 1987, women owned 30 percent of small businesses. By 1990, there would be 5.3 million women-owned small proprietorships, the fastest-growing sector of small business.[8]

Most of these women didn't think of themselves as feminists, yet the changes they initiated were intricately linked with the whole women's movement and the kind of challenges being taken by elected and appointed women in government. They needed to learn their history. It was a woman, Congresswoman Leonor Sullivan of Missouri, who chaired the subcommittee that developed legislation in 1972 to eliminate discrimination preventing women from getting credit in their own names. It was the new women's think tanks that provided witnesses and suggested language for the bill. It was the Congressional Caucus for Women's Issues that pursued goals such as improving federal contracting opportunities for women-owned businesses.

What interested me was that these entrepreneurial women entering a predominantly male business world were following patterns very similar to women who had entered male-dominated legislatures. They were creating their own support organizations[9]; they were exploring obligations for community problem solving; and they were taking responsibility for the needs of other women. Many seemed to do business in a way different from male competitors, in spite of—or perhaps because of—juggling so many responsibilities as homemakers and mothers along with the exhausting demands of running businesses.

Raydean Acevedo, founder and CEO of RMCI, a national environmental engineering firm, invested heavily in the education and training of her three hundred employees, most of whom were women. She commented: "Giving back is as much a part of business as looking forward at cash-flow projections." Muriel ("Mickie") Siebert, president of a securities investment firm, donates half her commissions to charity and says, "I have always felt that with success as a business woman comes obligation. I see it as a way of paying back." Cheryl Womack, CEO of VCW, Inc., a Kansas City-based insurance business, established an on-site daycare center that she says "has paid for itself many times over by reduced absenteeism, better employee morale and peace of mind."[10]

Ann Doody, president of Techline Madison, in Madison, Wisconsin, gives every employee who has a baby a fax machine as a shower gift. They can use the option of working from home. "I remember having huge conflicts over daycare issues or sick kid issues or snow day issues," she says, recalling when she worked for others. Now that she's boss of a successful national firm, she says: "We celebrate babies and then we work around them." She says that gender has everything to do with how she runs her company.[11]

The toughest challenge women were facing going into the business world wasn't competitiveness or even individual toughness; women were competing everywhere and succeeding on their merits. The toughest struggle was finding a way to keep the best of themselves even as they achieved success. These women were strong in their insistence on empowering others and inspiring confidence and cooperation even among those with whom they disagreed. The women I observed understood that when you get power, you don't pull up the ladder behind you and that when you break a barrier, you don't forget all those who may not have strength to try.

According to a 1996 report on women's business enterprise: "Anecdotal evidence suggests that women-owned businesses are more likely to offer flex-time, child care, and other family-friendly practices than U.S. businesses generally."[12] It quoted a study of women's enterprises to say that "women-owned businesses become the training grounds for female employees to leave and launch their own businesses, which creates an ever-widening circle of women hiring women to solve problems that affect women. . . . Through business ownership women are becoming the role models they never had."

In the early years as an elected official, women audiences were primarily homemakers or civic activists. What linked us then were community challenges and an understanding that we had little individual power as women. We developed ideas and lobbied men as a way of getting things done. Now as women moved into decisionmaking positions in the economic mainstream, the challenges were different, and it was important that they continue to care about community and maintain their own values. I found myself giving the same speech over and over: "It's impressive how far we have come, but women won't be able to reach major goals in industry until we get rid of the outdated obstacle course. . . . The power structure has remained unchanged . . . and those key positions control civic affairs, internal personnel practices, and major political decisions."

Our challenges had to include changing institutions and attitudes. The Ford Foundation reported that during the 1970s only six-tenths of 1 percent of all philanthropic dollars went to women and girls. In 1989, another report concluded that "from national health research grants to local community support for Boy Scouts and Girl Scouts, women get less and are perceived to be less important." In 1990, the gap between the amount received by the YMCA and YWCA was $39 million. As late as 1992, Girl Scouts would be receiving $31.1 million less in United Way grants than Boy Scouts.[13]

But looking at a different side of the issue, the report pointed out that women give less in donations and that the disparity between men and women goes deeper than a differential in wealth. It was important that women who gain power think carefully about how they use it.

All this new activity had me thinking very hard about my own future. The contacts with women in the private sector, combined with the renewed involvement with issues of housing, race, and the elderly, suggested that there were challenges to be met from outside public office. Perhaps it was time to leave government for an entirely different life.

The suggestion upset others; it was hard to explain to all those who saw me as their advocate. There were so few women in major power positions that there was great pressure on each of us not to give one up. Besides, I really enjoyed the power, the opportunity to leverage change, and to make government work for ordinary people. But what had drawn me to seek election in the 1960s was the chance to address significant social problems, not just have a title, and I wasn't sure that those challenges would be there in my present position. Perhaps the last Senate loss had affected me more than I wanted to admit. Political friends suggested that I should try for the Senate again, running in a presidential election year for a change; a number of men had succeeded only after three tries for the Senate. Was it worth spending another two years doing nothing but raising money in order to find out if I could do the same?

I no longer felt the desire I would need to do that or to inspire a campaign, the kind of drive that had sent me running up and down front steps a dozen years earlier. Yes, there were power perks that went with being a U.S. Senator, but after climbing twice to the Senate campaign mountain top and looking over the other side, it was clear that the Senate in Washington wasn't much different from the one in Missouri; it was just another male clubhouse. It was time to move on.

We wanted to handle the announcement in a way that wouldn't reflect some kind of feminine weakness. We had the worrisome example of the way the media had responded to Pat Schroeder. She had launched a campaign for president in June 1987 that created both excitement and anxiety in the women's community. There was concern that she had entered a crowded field too late to raise the millions necessary to compete effectively. It was when she reached that conclusion herself and held a press conference to announce her withdrawal that the trouble occurred.

"I rarely show emotion in public," Schroeder would write. "When I reached the crucial part of my speech and said I would not be running for president, the crowd groaned. . . . My heart sank, and I began to cry. I went on with my speech, but it was my tears not my words that got the publicity."[14] Schroeder handled the media reaction with aplomb, wryly noting that male politicians had been praised for showing honest emotion, but in St. Louis, we cringed, knowing those tears would be used to perpetuate the myth of women's emotional instability. It still wasn't safe for a woman leader to show any weakness.

That certainly was true in Missouri, where as the only statewide Democratic elected official, it should have been automatic for me to head the Missouri delegation to the Democratic National Convention in Atlanta in 1998, if only as a final salute. Indeed, a healthy majority of the delegates ultimately selected me to chair the delegation, but the likelihood of my retirement from office made me vulnerable. Without the prospect of holding a major office, I no longer had power to intimidate. Another candidate ran for delegation chair, forcing me into time-consuming negotiation to put together the necessary votes. It was just one more signal from those who weren't comfortable with a woman in control, even if the control extended mainly to deciding who would get passes to the floor of a Democratic convention.

In January 1988, we held the press conference announcing the decision not to run for reelection as lieutenant governor or for any other office. In February, I gave a major speech to assembled community and business leaders in St. Louis, challenging them to address the issue of homelessness and affordable housing. In fall

1988, I became a Fellow at the Institute for Politics at the Kennedy School of Government at Harvard University, leading a weekly seminar called "Getting Inside When You're Outside— Women in Leadership" and ruminating about the future. The following February, in 1989, I officially became president of the Institute for Policy Leadership at the University of Missouri–St. Louis, a new think tank and leadership training institute.

Over the next two years, the institute gradually developed the Regional Housing Alliance to coordinate all the complicated efforts involved in producing more affordable housing. Deputy Director Debra Moore spent endless hours massaging the initiative until it eventually was spun off to work with local community development organizations, funders, builders, foundations, investors, and government.

We also brought Missouri legislators together across lines of party, power, and urban-rural status to develop alternative ways to get public business accomplished in legislative bodies. It was a first move toward changing the structures in society, structures that have become increasingly unattractive to women, indeed to all legislators as well as the public. Despite initial skepticism, the legislators surprised themselves by reaching consensus on a number of proposed improvements that they presented to the Speaker of the House—who actually implemented some of them. In another session, we applied conflict resolution strategies to adopting a state budget.

Was any of this gender related? In one of her innovative books on corporate management practices, Harvard economist Rosabeth Moss Kanter credited women for modeling a new style of power sharing among workers and management and predicted it would produce better results for business. It really didn't matter to me what the source was of a different approach; our democratic institutions were not properly serving the public interest and needed to be reformed.

It would take men and women working together to do it, just as it would take committed collaboration to construct more family friendly policies for the workplace. But there weren't enough women in policy positions to assure an adequate representation, and it still would take a special effort to get them there. It was another challenge. At about that time there were several calls asking whether I'd consider running for president of the National

Women's Political Caucus. The urgent tone of the calls suggested the organization was in trouble, but frankly, heading an all-woman organization was very low on my priority list.

Two people made me think again. One was Betty Van Uum, who by then was an assistant to the chancellor at the university. She appealed to my ego and my sense of responsibility for women. She said: "Women need a national spokesperson. You can make a difference." The other person was my former campaign manager, Jody Newman. She called to say that she was getting restless in Florida where she had moved and was thinking about getting a job in Washington, D.C.

I asked her to meet me at the NWPC offices in Washington. This might be the right challenge after all. Maybe we should just take a look.

11

Organization Women

We put women in their place . . . for a change!

—Publication of the National Women's Political Caucus

In 1991, the offices of the National Women's Political Caucus were located on the edge of the high-rent district on K Street, newest address of Washington lobbyists and lawyers. The outside of the building was impressive; inside, the office was in chaos. The small NWPC staff was frantically preparing for the annual convention just weeks away, but that didn't explain the halls and closets stuffed with boxes and papers. A cursory review of financial records was downright scary. There were multiple bank accounts, mysterious debts, and no cash flow. I could see why the current president had decided not to run again. Could this organization survive?

Jody Newman was with me on this inspection visit and asked the current executive director her own questions about operations while I looked around, becoming more and more discouraged. As we were waiting at the elevator after leaving, I turned to Jody and said: "It may be too big a headache to straighten that place out." I was surprised when she responded: "You know; it would be fun to take on the challenge of making it work." If Jody were willing to come in as partner, I thought, it might be worth considering. She could take on the administrative chaos while I concentrated on political issues and organization building.

There was some soul-searching as we left the building. It was possible that I was a little intimidated by the idea of taking on a national office in Washington, D.C. For me, this always had been the town where there was no place to sit down. Whenever I came to testify before a congressional committee or to talk to a member of Congress, I always seemed to be walking endless hard marble corridors, with no place to perch except someone's ante-room. There was a power symbolism; I didn't feel I belonged. There were so few women with power here. The NWPC would give me a seat, but real power was another question.

There were some tradeoffs to consider. The NWPC is multi-partisan and that meant I'd not only have to give up my institute at the university but also all partisan Democratic activities, including the Coalition for Democratic Values (CDV), a new orga-nization created by Senator Howard Metzenbaum of Ohio in order to strengthen the Democratic Party's progressive tradition. Senator Metzenbaum happened to be my mother's cousin, and in conversation with him, I had agreed to be CDV vice president. It was a real kick joining leading senators like Ted Kennedy, Tom Harkin, Paul Simon, and Metzenbaum giving rousing speeches on opportunity, fairness, individual rights, and social justice. There were so few opportunities to offer a countervoice to the current conservative trend.

It would be difficult switching from that broad political visioning to focusing just on women, a gender concentration I'd always tried to avoid. There was one compelling argument to take it on: It was Caucus members who had given me my first boost into significant public office and who continued to do the same for women all over the country. If I really meant what I had been saying to everyone about accelerating the flow of women into power positions, then revitalizing the NWPC was one way to do it. As for the NWPC's multipartisanship, there were Repub-licans I preferred to some of the Democrats in Congress and the Missouri General Assembly.

It was a big leap to assume leadership of a national organiza-tion, but most major accomplishments involved risk; in this case all that was at stake were my time and reputation. If the goal was worthwhile, and it was, then so was the risk. It's true there were practical problems in moving to Washington and a strange new world, but there also was tremendous opportunity. We hadn't walked far out of the building before my enthusiasm was revived. I needed to talk to Jim. I flew back to St. Louis for a couple weeks of soul-searching and then began calling key members of the NWPC all over the country to ask for their support. When the only other candidate withdrew, the way was clear for my election in July at the NWPC's annual convention in Washington.

The delegates at the convention seemed enthusiastic, but there was a warning sign of internal disorder when the old leadership tried to block hiring Jody as executive director. I needed Jody. It's important to understand one's own strengths and weaknesses. Jody is an administrator. She had the really tough assignments: getting the office cleaned up, straightening out the bookkeeping and computer systems, putting together staff, and tracking bank accounts and loans to save us from going broke. My mission was to reinvigorate the NWPC and attract membership, media, and money so that we could be more effective in our basic mission of recruiting, training, and supporting more women for public office. I was the visible outside spokesperson; Jody was the inside administrator.

The first few weeks of this new life were filled with appointments to renew acquaintances in Washington, plus strategy meetings to turn our plans into action. It would take time to learn the territory. Congresswomen offered enthusiastic greetings, saying over and over how much they needed help to increase their current number (just 27 women out of 435 House members and 2 women out of 100 senators). How could that be when there seemed to be a huge number of organizations here? Perhaps there were others that like the NWPC had lost the vitality that marked the early days of the women's movement.

Women's organizations had been on a roller coaster ride since the middle of the century. In the 1950s, they had been an attractive refuge for women isolated in a male society; in the early 1960s, they were a launching pad for women moving out to tackle great causes; in the 1970s, they brought women together to ratify the Equal Rights Amendment; but in the 1980s, they turned defensive against a conservative political tide. Their membership reflected these changes. The numbers rose very gradually through the 1960s, went up more rapidly after 1970, and remained high through 1982, the last year for ERA ratification. Then, membership began to drop, quite sharply for most groups.[1]

Media and public interest in the women's movement peaked in 1975, in the burst of enthusiasm over likely ratification of the ERA,[2] but there was another factor in the ups and downs in membership numbers. The very success of the older mainstream groups in helping to open up opportunities for women in business and the professions robbed them of members and leadership. "Career women simply do not have time nor the need for a volunteer organization," a local AAUW leader told a state officer, while informing her of the "painful and difficult" decision to suspend chapter activity in Durham, North Carolina, in 1975.[3] I had seen the same process occurring with the Caucus in the St. Louis area. Women who once were the leadership had moved on to professional careers and were not being replaced.

One-third of American women had jobs outside the home in the 1960s; the figure was nearly 50 percent by 1980. Women volunteers, "whose work was once prized because there was no one else to perform it, may now question the value of their unpaid labor in a society in which status is equated with salary," noted AAUW General Director Pauline Tompkins.[4] The new professional women often chose to give whatever volunteer time they had to associations in their professional discipline rather than to the traditional women's groups. Or they simply lost interest.

There was an upward membership spurt at the end of the 1980s, prompted by concern for reproductive rights and the *Webster* decision by the Supreme Court, but the writing was on the wall. "Changes in women's work patterns and social roles had profound implications for the fate of American voluntary associations, including women's organizations."[5] In order to thrive, not just to survive, the organizations would have to adapt to women's changing lifestyles, and they would have to offer compelling reasons for involvement. I knew that would be particularly difficult for the NWPC because it was focused on politics, and traditionally many women had been reluctant to get involved in anything they considered confrontational.

The original purpose of the National Women's Political Caucus had been very compelling. It was to establish the "representation of women in all levels of government, in both elective and appointive office, in numbers proportionate to our percentage in the population."[6] That's how Congresswoman Bella Abzug summed it up in a proud speech to the House on July 13, 1971, two days after the Caucus was organized. She described the Caucus as a "new political force" and said it would start moving womanpower out of the talking stage and into practical politics.[7]

"At the time the Caucus was born, women as a group were not a political factor of any importance. The issue of how many women were serving in political leadership roles had not scratched the public consciousness. No one, in fact, monitored or knew how many women there were in public office nationwide. The representation of women at national party conventions was of interest only to a small group of reformers. . . . There were no national campaign funds for women candidates and no one was lobbying for the appointment of women to public office. The Caucus was the leader in changing all of this."[8] The Caucus can justly claim credit for creating women as a political-interest group, founding member Rona Feit concluded.

Traditional women's organizations like the AAUW, the LWV, and the BPW were just awakening to the need to become politically active. It was "a turning point" for the AAUW when members voted to endorse the ERA as a top priority at its 1971 convention.[9] By contrast, the new Caucus adopted a 20-point program focused on eliminating racism, sexism, violence, and poverty by electing women. We want to get women "out of the purity that has . . . afflicted [them] in the League of Women Voters, and . . . out of the rhetoric and carrying on that have afflicted [them] in the women's movement," Caucus co-founder Betty Friedan declared at the founding session.[10]

Bella Abzug emphasized a strong commitment to changing the direction of society. Gloria Steinem told the founding members, "We don't want to elect Uncle Toms who are themselves imitating men, and who, once in power, only serve to keep their sisters down,"[11] and Mississippi civil rights leader Fannie Lou Hamer issued a plea for unity among blacks, youth, and women: "Hooking up these minorities and we'd become one hell of a majority."

The initial NWPC steering committee was a model of diversity and broad experience.[12] It reflected women's participation in the advocacy of the 1960s. Abzug said women were "in the forefront of the peace movement, the civil rights and equal rights movement, the environment and consumer movements, the child care movement, the movement to reclaim our cities and communities for human beings," but not in public office. "We have to put our organizing ability and energy to work to thrust women into political power at *all* levels of government, by running for city council or the school board or the state legislature."[13]

In the next few years, Caucus chapters were initiated in almost every state by an amazing variety of women, many of whom had no previous connection with the organized women's movement.[14] That certainly was true in Missouri in 1972 where women like me who had been busy with our own civic lives and somewhat put off by the rhetoric of other feminist groups welcomed an organization with the practical goal of getting women elected. The Caucus appealed to me because of its nuts-and-bolts approach, tied to principles in which I believed.

The first demonstration that a new kind of women's organization was on the scene occurred at the 1972 Democratic National Convention in Miami. Only days after the Caucus was founded, Congresswoman Abzug had written a letter to party leaders, serving notice that women were half the population and should be half the convention delegates. The Caucus would challenge any state delegation that didn't reflect fair gender representation. The NWPC set up a separate foundation to recruit and train women delegates, helping assure that women were a record 40 percent of those attending. When the convention opened, daily Caucuses were held to bring women together and provide them training.

The first confrontation was a floor fight challenging the seating of the South Carolina delegation, which was three to one male. The fight was lost due to defection by delegates pledged to presidential candidate George McGovern, prompting considerable bitterness among the women. The next battle occurred when the platform committee refused to include a plank on abortion. Women took that to the floor also. The debate divided "sister against sister with Bella Abzug taking off on [actress] Shirley Maclaine"[15] whom McGovern had named as his women's liaison, to the great annoyance of the feminists.

The women lost that fight too, but they extracted a painful revenge. They nominated Frances "Sissy" Farenthold, a Texas legislator and former gubernatorial candidate, for vice president against McGovern's choice, Senator Thomas F. Eagleton of Missouri. Eagleton won handily, but the lengthy battle, complete with state roll call, pushed McGovern's acceptance speech back to 2:28 a.m., dropping his television audience from 17,400,000 homes to 3,600,000.[16] For McGovern, it was a political catastrophe. Most of the Caucus women supported McGovern and should have been concerned, but they left the convention exhilarated. They had proved they couldn't be ignored.

"When the convention broke up, women power 1972 was real," political historian Theodore White would write.[17] This was a different kind of women's organization, ready to use whatever muscle it had. By 1976, leaders of the women's movement were invited to sit down with Jimmy Carter before the convention to negotiate an agreement about appointments. They also won his commitment of support for the ERA. Columnist Ellen Goodman wrote: "When the NWPC was founded, it consisted of some 'names,' a good press, and a grassroots feeling labeled sisterhood. Today, the Democratic women have learned the ropes, the Robert's rules of order, and the arts and crafts of political numbers."[18] By 1980, the battle for mandatory 50 percent representation in party leadership was won.

Republican Caucus women had been active also. At the Republican Convention in 1972, women were 30 percent of the delegates, a big increase over 17 percent at the 1968 event. Led by NWPC policy council member Jill Ruckelshaus, they helped win approval of Rule 32, instructing each state to work for equal representation for male and female convention delegates. In order to maintain pressure, the Republicans and the Democrats formed separate task forces within the multipartisan NWPC through which to work on party issues. The general Caucus activities continued to be multipartisan, but the existence of the party task forces underscored the political character of the new organization, in contrast to traditional women's groups, which remained nervous about any partisan activity at all.

The Caucus grew throughout the 1970s and 1980s, reflecting increased political activity in the women's movement. NWPC leaders spoke out on current issues, lobbied Congress on gender-related legislation, joined marches, held fund-raisers, set up a coalition for women's presidential appointments, ran a project to help ratify the ERA, taught political skills, organized delegates at party conventions, and most of all, supported women for political office. The Caucus prided itself on the political and racial diversity in its leadership, and on grassroots control. That may explain the improbable decision to designate as board of directors a national steering committee elected proportionately from all the chapters, producing a board of 100 to 150 members that could change from meeting to meeting, depending upon local elections. The administrative committee was smaller, but its membership was tangled in requirements for race, ethnicity, party, and geography. Within a decade one founder had written about the Caucus, "For all its strengths, . . . it remains overextended, undermanaged, underorganized and underfunded."[19]

That description still applied in 1991, although in twenty years, the NWPC had come a long way. Its endorsement was highly sought by women candidates. Vigorous past chairs like Millie Jeffrey, Kathy Wilson, and Irene Natividad had made the Caucus name respected as a voice for political women, but there was constant turnover of leadership, and the rather narrow membership base of political activists didn't supply enough dues money to finance ambitious goals. The Caucus was capable of great things, but it was virtually ungovernable.

A weekend meeting of our national steering committee (NSC) in early fall 1991 was a painful revelation. It had been scheduled by the previous leaders in a rotting hotel in Miami Beach, Florida that had yet to be rehabilitated. Amid complaints about malfunctioning plumbing, I tried to deal with vicious political battles over committee appointments while at the same time desperately fending off a resolution favoring silicone breast inserts that we lacked information to debate intelligently. No one wanted to hear about the organization's financial crisis or face the need for structural change.

For the preceding two years, the NWPC meetings had followed a feel-good philosophy, starting late, letting the agenda get controlled by whatever voices were the loudest. This was misunderstood as grassroots participation. We started a new regime, beginning on time and crisply following an agenda to conclusion. The rank and filed loved it, but a handful of the old guard complained about everything, even progress. I was learning more than I had ever wanted to know about running a women's organization. It was hard to maintain a sense of humor.

As an organization president, there was more to do in Washington than time to do it, in large part because of all the meetings. Washington was chock full of meetings: between, among, and with everyone, members of Congress, the administration, lobbyists, consultants, associations, businesses, unions, and agencies. Every legislative and policy crisis required meetings of whatever groups saw themselves as speaking for affected constituencies around the country. In 1991, the Congressional Caucus for Women's Issues listed a hundred organizations with primary interest in women's issues, from the Association for Women in Science to the National Women's Party. There were fifty-five names on just the core fax list of organizations concerned with reproductive rights.

As a newcomer, I dutifully attended each coalition to which the NWPC belonged in order to stay informed, but I was mystified as to why some of these groups even existed or why more hadn't consolidated. Eventually I stopped going. Somehow those who had the least to contribute always had the most to say. There were several respected organizations that had built a reputation for effective research and lobbying, but they were rarely seen at the meetings. I realized that if the NWPC was going to survive, we needed to establish priorities and use time and resources well.

As an alternative to large meetings, I tried lunching with individual leaders of the larger groups. People were friendly, but there was a competitive tension. Everyone was trying to raise money; everyone wanted to be the most visible; everyone wanted to be closest to power. Washington wasn't going to be the warmest of towns.

Most of the women I met seemed far removed from the heartland where my political life had been spent. They were oriented to making decisions at the seat of power. Listening at meetings, the participants didn't sound like a cross section of women in the country: their language was full of technical lingo that required translation, and their presumptions about positions that should be taken seemed unfounded. Who said women wanted a separate party? Or even, sad to say, that they wanted to push once again for an Equal Rights Amendment? Only a few groups had grassroots membership to express opinions. Building a coalition among us too often meant summarizing all of our demands, creating a laundry list that would turn off most women who read it One such list had nearly forty items, from protections for organizing in the workplace to implementation of women's rights internationally.

These were intelligent women, diligent in advocating their causes, but neither they nor the various organizations they represented seemed able to mobilize women behind the talk. That was the movement's weakness. Congressional sponsors periodically complained that they needed more public pressure in order to prevail. It was a viewpoint I understood from earlier days as a state legislator. Barring a major emotional event, like the Anita Hill case, it was difficult to get an intimidating citizen effort unleashed, for daycare or fair pay.

It became an advantage that, like a member of Congress, I was commuting back and forth to St. Louis every weekend because I could talk to people there and get their thinking. Jim had been adamant about staying in St. Louis. He had retired from *The St. Louis Post-Dispatch* and enjoyed puttering around the house and yard, playing golf with friends, and keeping up with family. It made for hectic weekends at home, but it meant I had no responsibilities but work during the week in D.C. I came to the office early and stayed late, occasionally stopping by a fund-raiser after work to show support for an endorsed candidate. It was a pattern similar to the years in the legislature, and I enjoyed it.

My primary concern was that the NWPC seemed to have lost its distinctive identity as the organization that recruited, trained, and supported women for public office. In D.C. we were lumped together with groups the media arbitrarily labeled "feminist," like NOW, or else with pro-choice groups like NARAL and Planned Parenthood. There was nothing wrong with the association, but unless we performed our own distinct function, we had no business taking up space. We needed to establish ourselves as *the* expert on political women. That also would help us reach out to broader audiences, such as business women, Hispanics, African Americans, and young women, to regain the respect and enthusiasm that our founders had commanded. We had diversity in leadership, but it wasn't reflected in numbers in our base.

I was sitting in my office one day a few weeks after taking office, thinking about this challenge when the receptionist announced unexpected visitors: two executives of McDonnell Douglas, a St. Louis defense contractor. That got my attention. McDonnell Douglas never had supported me in my U.S. Senate races and always had funded my opponents. It never had shown the slightest interest in political women. What could they be doing here? Send them back to my office, by all means, I said.

The two men explained that they needed my help. It seemed that the "iron triangle" that traditionally took care of military expenditures (defense contractor/Pentagon/armed services committee) no longer could guarantee success. With budgetary considerations overtaking cold war concerns, defense projects were being given tougher screening through the appropriation process. McDonnell Douglas needed approval for a project from the House Appropriations Committee, and there were women on that committee. Their stereotypical view told them that women would be against defense expenditure so would I help them get an appointment with Congresswoman Barbara Boxer?

Inwardly I could hardly stop laughing; outwardly I inquired politely why they hadn't asked one of their women executives to contact the congresswoman. That brought expressions of bewilderment, as if they were thinking: "What women executives?" or maybe: "Do women executives make such phone calls?" Clearly they needed more help than a phone call to a congresswoman.

I told them I would be happy to assist a St. Louis firm by contacting Congresswoman Boxer's office, but there was something else we could do for them. We could conduct a workshop to make sure whatever women executives they did have would learn how to impact public policy. If these women didn't know how to play the game, their company was losing "bottom-line" benefits from their employees; the women were losing traction on their career paths; and we were losing the potential impact of their political muscle. I didn't mention that such a workshop might also help the NWPC connect with more mainstream women who might become members, candidates, and donors.

Mac, as the company then was known in St. Louis, consisted of a bunch of engineers, so it took eighteen months to prepare the training to everyone's satisfaction. They even paid for focus groups comparing the attitudes of male and female executives.

We learned that neither men nor women were enthusiastic about political office but that there were some differences by sex. When asked directly by the facilitator what they would do if they *were* interested in running for election, the men projected confidence. They indicated that they would just go see some political or business leader or ask friends for help. The women were filled with doubts and excuses. They said they didn't know how to run for office, that they didn't have time, or that—in effect—they "needed permission" (from a boss, a husband, society).

It's dangerous to generalize from focus groups, but the women's answers did ring a bell. Women said they came to our campaign training because other training programs didn't deal with gender issues that cost them confidence, such as concerns about media and raising money. We understood that the same sense of isolation could exist for women inside a corporation or a large law firm. A woman was less likely to find a male mentor who would throw an arm over her shoulder, urging her to come along to the political fund-raiser, the kind of mentoring young men often received. Women still were trying to advance by out-working everyone else, then becoming frustrated when a male "rainmaker," who had been mentored into important connections that benefited the firm, was given the promotion they felt they deserved. When they had less power, potentially, so did we.

The training we eventually offered Mac women (and later offered women at other corporations) helped them understand that politics is all about relationships. Women legislators, members of civic boards, and local elected officials shared their experiences with the Mac participants, pointing out how the contacts they made had benefited their careers, strengthened their companies, and added to the well-being of the community. Inevitably the Mac women began to talk about their own frustrations within a company almost totally dominated by men. They proposed strategies for supporting one another, and they discussed how power connections outside the company could add value to their lives.

One of the women talked about becoming a candidate for school board. Most significant of all, through a Caucus connection, a participant who was a tax attorney was appointed by the governor to be director of revenue for the state of Missouri. It was the kind of lateral power move usually exercised by men and a timely example of how women's networking can make a very real difference.

Even as we started planning the first corporate training that fall, we were only a year away from the 1992 general election. In early October, the three electorally oriented women's organizations, the NWPC, EMILY's List, and the Women's Campaign Fund, held a press conference to announce a historic joint effort called "Operation W.I.N." (Winning in the Nineties). We released a poll to show that pro-choice women were the best candidates for both parties, doing better than male or anti-choice counterparts, and we jointly pledged to raise $7 million to support women in 1992 races.

The good news in the survey was that voters viewed women as populist outsiders who could effect change. The bad news was that voters still assumed women were less likely to win, even if they were voting for them. "Women still have to prove to their party, the press, and even to the very voters who support them that they can run and win," the poll concluded.[20]

We clearly had a major challenge as an organization. Jody was performing miracles with the Caucus office. Systems had been reorganized; debts retired; mailings produced—we were on our way to sound financial condition. But what about our credibility as a promoter of women candidates? What about the NWPC's visibility as a political voice? What about the task of raising major funds and—most of all—what about getting more women elected? Those were *my* responsibilities. It looked as if it would be a very long haul. There was nothing I had observed at all those meetings of women's organizations that made it seem likely they would do anything to produce more candidates. Despite all our hard work in the NWPC upgrading training workshops and encouraging candidates, it looked as if 1992 was a very iffy year. Electing more women was just not society's top priority.

Who could have foreseen the impact of an event called the Hill–Thomas hearings?

12

Anita Hill

The Anita Hill hearing may be the first time
in the history of the country that popular culture
focused on women's experience in prime time for three days.

—Gloria Steinem

Long after the hearings were over, they were credited with causing all sorts of public events, including the election of new women U.S. senators and sensational sexual misconduct charges in the armed services. Did Anita Hill foresee the firestorm that would result when she came forward to testify? She certainly knew that she was taking a risk. "It would have been more comfortable to remain silent," she said. She told the press she came forward only after great anguish and that she was driven by a sense of public responsibility.

The discomfort of recounting an experience of sexual harassment weighed against her concern for other women in the workplace. The confirmation of a Supreme Court justice was at stake, and a fellow African American at that. By choosing to tell her story, she inserted herself into a bitter national political battle. The result was a clash of strong personalities with conflicting credibility and a muddy political battle that soiled the reputation of the Senate and many of its members; at least two would write books to explain their conduct. The hearing also had an extraordinary impact on women's perceptions of their political power, and on women's organizations themselves.

At the heart of it all was a slim young law professor from Oklahoma who charged that Appellate Court Judge Clarence Thomas, a nominee for the Supreme Court, had engaged in sexual misconduct toward her while he was her boss ten years before at the Equal Employment Opportunities Commission (EEOC). She offered sensational detail, citing Thomas's reference in talks with her to the penis, breast size, and pubic hair. The hearings developed a soap opera flavor that had the American public riveted to its television sets. More were watching the Hill–Thomas hearings on the final Sunday than sporting events.

Anita Hill's willingness to talk candidly about sexual harassment in so public a setting served as a release for countless women who had suffered their own versions of sexual humiliation in silence. Sexual abuse of women, whether on social dates or in the workplace, usually was ignored or even made the subject of jokes. Without the consciousness developed by Anita Hill's testimony, it's unlikely the Air Force women in the Tailhook case would have come forward less than a year later to charge naval aviators with sexual misconduct during a convention. Or that the Navy would have given serious attention to the charges, eventually penalizing a top officer. It's unlikely that the Senate would have taken any action a year later in the sexual harassment case involving Senator Robert Packwood if senators hadn't feared repeating the political damage they experienced with Anita Hill.

A sea of change occurred in the private sector where women suddenly felt empowered to speak up. The number of sexual harassment claims filed with the EEOC went up 50 percent in 1992, right after the hearings, and roughly doubled over the next couple of years. As a result of public reaction to Anita Hill's testimony, worried corporations began to conduct employee training, looking for ways to handle and prevent such incidents. Public service announcements about sexual harassment ran on television.

In an insightful commentary on the impact of the Hill case on the whole issue of race, gender, and ethnicity in the judicial system, Judith Resnik, a professor of law, said that the pressure that forced the Senate committee to give Hill a hearing "was evidence of women's newfound powers."[1] Women represented formidable voting numbers. But she added that the "minimal role women played in the subsequent proceedings (which in many ways did not deserve the appellation 'hearing')" underscored the limitations of those powers in the late twentieth century. Senators only recently had begun asking judicial nominees their views about women's legal rights. The Clarence Thomas case would demonstrate again that the confirmation process itself traditionally was insensitive if not downright hostile to women.

The very first press conference in which I participated after becoming president of the National Women's Political Caucus concerned a still-semiobscure federal appeals court judge named Clarence Thomas. Timing is everything. I had been elected in mid-July 1991 at a convention that also went on record opposing Thomas's nomination to the Supreme Court on the basis of writings and speeches that appeared hostile to women's rights. His confirmation hearings began in September. It was quite an introduction to Washington politics.

I clearly remember a couple of weeks after my election taking a taxi from the airport directly to a meeting about Thomas called by the Leadership Conference on Civil Rights (LCCR) at its headquarters, then in an old mansion on Massachusetts Avenue. The NWPC was a member of the LCCR Executive Committee and the executive director, Ralph Neas, had been a fellow with me at the Kennedy School.

There was overwhelming consensus to oppose the nomination based on Thomas's written opinions and other statements he had made indicating he favored removing guarantees of minority rights and current government remedies to protect them. Abortion rights spokespersons were particularly alarmed. I cautiously raised my hand. "There's something else. Thomas has expressed strong belief in natural law, and experience in the Missouri Senate indicates this could be a disaster for women." I described the debate in which state senators had refused to make women equally liable for support under the Missouri criminal code because natural (religious) law ordains that only a male can wield authority as head of household. These same senators had fought fiercely to crush ratification of the Equal Rights Amendment in 1977 when, as a freshman senator, I had been its chief sponsor. They truly believed in a patriarchy, and natural law was their authority.

Shortly thereafter, I found myself in the press conference called to announce LCCR's opposition to Thomas. The reporters didn't seem terribly impressed with the point on natural law, which admittedly was hard to explain, but there was mild interest in my connection with Missouri, scene of Thomas's early career, as well as in the idea that the NWPC presented a woman's viewpoint. The LCCR felt it was important to include some representation from women's groups that had been very vocal in turning aside the nomination of Supreme Court nominee Robert Bork. The only other women's group at the press conference was the American Association of University Women (AAUW).

There were plenty of women's organizations, but their roles were not very well defined in the public mind. In my presidential acceptance speech for the NWPC, I had said that the NWPC needed to emphasize its unique mission of supporting women for elected and appointed office and respect the special functions performed by other women's groups. Instead of competing, we should complement and coordinate. Women's groups must be like shingles on a roof, overlapping one another to create a strong support system.

We certainly were overlapping shingles at the Senate Judiciary Committee hearings on the Thomas nomination. The committee chair, Democrat Joseph Biden of Delaware, insisted the hearings would be a model of fairness. Witnesses would be divided equally pro and con. In order to precisely balance with conservative voices, spokespersons for progressive and mainstream women were squeezed onto one panel on September 20, the very last day of the hearings: Eleanor Smeal of The Feminist Majority; Molly Yard of NOW; Anne Bryant of the AAUW; Helen Neuborne of the NOW Legal Defense and Education Fund; Byllye Avery of the National Black Women's Health Project; and me, for the NWPC. The senators wanted to get the hearings over as fast as possible; Majority Leader George Mitchell had pledged an early floor vote.

The other women made the case against Thomas on privacy rights and on writings that showed a lack of respect for women's equality and health concerns. My role was to cite the statistics on women in Congress: only 29 women out of 435 House members, just 2 among 100 senators (none on the committee). "You see," I said, "women get elected one, by one, by one, by one, just the way that Clarence Thomas would have them get relief from job discrimination. . . . Without adequate representation, women must petition for their rights before committees like this, and before the courts. That makes Judge Thomas pretty important."

We considered this a vital point. History is full of examples of laws that discriminate against minorities and women that were passed by legislative bodies in which they were not fully represented. They often turn to the courts, and they need to be assured that they will be treated fairly there. Our democracy, with its system of checks and balances, works only if everyone has fair access to every part of the system.

In 1991, there were just 49 women (7 percent) among 740 sitting life-tenured judges, and four of the thirteen federal appellate courts had no women judges at all.[2] In addition, of the "1,050 administrative law judges [working] in the Social Security Administration, dealing with claims of wrongfully terminated welfare and disability benefits, fewer than 5 percent were women."[3] At the state level, only 9 percent of more than 28,000 judges were women.[4] With women's voices so poorly represented in the judiciary, it was important to know the viewpoint of male appointees regarding women's legal rights.

The senators lectured us on making abortion a litmus test, with several insisting we should accept Thomas's denial of any viewpoint on that issue. Thomas had stunned many of us, and the media, by claiming he had never discussed the *Roe v. Wade* decision legalizing abortion at any time in his life and therefore had no opinion to express. He ducked questions related to abortion by committee members "at least seventy times in the next few days," despite citation of remarks from speeches he had made to conservative groups indicating a viewpoint.[5] When we tried to point out that our policy concerns ranged far beyond abortion, several senators made clear that as far as they were concerned, abortion was women's only issue, and they were tired of it.

This was specially ironic because Sandra Day O'Connor, the first woman nominated to serve on the Supreme Court, had been closely questioned in her confirmation hearings "about abortion, women in combat, and her efforts as a state legislator to obtain equal pay for women. . . . A subtext of suspicion lurked, as if she might do special favors for members of her own sex. . . . In contrast, . . . male nominees have not been examined about their possible partiality toward their own gender."[6]

The White House strategy was to emphasize Thomas's rise from humble beginnings and to have him avoid answering any questions that might stir controversy.[7] His evasiveness cost him the vote of at least one conservative southern Democrat who had been expected to give him support. This has the appearance of a "confirmation conversion," commented Democratic Senator Howell Heflin of Alabama. He said that Thomas's writings and speeches suggested he "might be part of the right-wing extemist movement."[8] "I support a conservative court. However, I am not for an extremist right-wing court that would turn back progress made against racial discrimination as well as the progress that has been made for human rights and freedoms in recent years."

Senator Paul Simon of Illinois faulted Thomas "for tailoring his testimony for the hearings, rather than frankly stating his views,"[9] and Senator Biden said, "Throughout his testimony, Judge Thomas gave us many responses—but too few real answers."[10] There also were concerns about the judge's credentials. Erwin N. Griswold, former solicitor general for both Presidents Johnson and Nixon, and a Republican law professor at Harvard University, testified that Thomas lacked legal ability and experience. There is "no reason [to approve] a presidential nominee who has not yet demonstrated any clear intellectual or professional distinction," he said. Confirming someone like this to the Supreme Court who "could serve for forty years, until the year 2030" was "an awesome risk."[11]

It was forgotten in the later controversy that the Thomas nomination was in trouble long before the Anita Hill issue arose. It originally was expected to breeze through the committee, but the committee split 7 to 7 along party lines, with just one Democrat, Dennis DeConcini of Arizona, favoring Thomas and preventing a negative vote. Members then voted 13 to 1 to send the nomination to the floor without a recommendation. The full Senate vote was scheduled for Tuesday, October 8, and word was that Thomas would be confirmed 58 to 42.

On Friday, October 4, two different reporters, Nina Totenberg of National Public Radio and Tim Phelps of *Newsday,* separately were pursuing rumors that a young law professor from Oklahoma named Anita Hill had said she had been sexually harassed by Thomas some years ago. The story had reached the public over the weekend and had become a sensation by Monday when Anita Hill herself held a press conference confirming the charges. The press said that the Senate committee had been aware of the sexual harassment accusation but hadn't considered the subject to be serious enough to extend their hearings. Would the Senate now be willing to delay its scheduled confirmation vote to investigate the charges?

A tidal wave of phone calls from irate women washed over the capitol, swamping switchboards. Senator Simon reported Illinois Bell said that on one day, 57,780 callers tried to get through on the phone lines to the Chicago offices for himself and Senator Alan Dixon. "Even the launching of a war in the Middle East did not evoke that kind of response."[12] *The New York Times* quoted Senator Christopher Dodd's staff: "We're just flooded; we've gotten over a thousand calls."

The NWPC office was inundated as well. I telephoned Senate Majority Leader George Mitchell, an acquaintance from the Senate race, and said: "Senator, don't let anyone tell you that this outcry is the result of organized lobbying. This is spontaneous. These are women who tell us they've never responded before to a political event. They are angry."

"I think the whole thing makes us look very bad," commented Democrat Senator Bob Kerry of Nebraska; and Republican Senator Arlen Specter of Pennsylvania, a member of the committee, said: "The Senate itself is on trial." Senator Barbara Mikulski of Maryland, one of only two women members, expressed women's feelings exactly: "What disturbs me as much as the allegations themselves is that the Senate appears not to take the charge of sexual harassment seriously. . . . To any victim of sexual harassment or sexual abuse or sexual violence either in the street or even in her own home, the message is nobody's going to take you seriously, not even the United States Senate."[13]

Thomas supporters wanted no delay. Senator John Danforth of Missouri, Clarence Thomas's mentor and sponsor, argued fiercely that the nominee denied the Hill charges and he believed him. *The New York Times* quoted me calling the Senate a "men's club": "John Danforth is a Yale man who can stand up and say, according to the rules of this club, 'I've asked the gentleman if he committed the crime and he said no. He's a friend of mine. He's a gentleman. And we should take his word.' That's the way it always was in this club."

Seven congresswomen marched across the courtyard to the Senate to demand a reopening of the hearings, producing marvelous news photos of determined women asserting themselves.[14] The senators refused to see them. These pictures were used effectively in the 1992 campaigns a few months later to help elect women to the Senate. Somehow the confirmation battle was becoming a contest between male politicians and women. The senators were nervously aware of an undefined "women's vote" and certainly didn't want to antagonize it. Faced with this public response, Danforth no longer was sure he had the votes to confirm and announced that Thomas actually wanted a further hearing to clear his name.[15]

The Bush White House had retreated, but not without winning important concessions. Biden agreed to constraints "that all but sealed Hill's fate"[16]: Although some Democratic senators argued it would take weeks to prepare for and properly conduct an investigation, Biden set the hearings to start that very Friday, in three days, and he also agreed that Thomas could open the hearings to tell his side and then close them in rebuttal after Hill's testimony. That would let him dominate television exposure. "Joe bent over too far to accommodate the Republicans, who were going to get Thomas on the Court come hell or high water," commented Senator Metzenbaum, another Democratic committee member.[17]

The White House had mounted an all-out campaign to assure the nomination, including spinning emotionally charged life stories of the nominee as a poor black who had risen on his merits, busing black church members from the South to line the corridors leading to the hearing room, and setting up a coordinated hearing strategy with certain Republican senators designated to cross-examine Hill. The tactics were familiar to women who found their own lives subject to scrutiny when they brought sex-related charges. Senator Danforth led a relentless effort to destroy Anita Hill's credibility, an effort that became the subject of a belated confession in his post-hearing book.[18]

Republican Senator Alan Simpson, a Thomas supporter, warned in a speech on the Senate floor: "She will be injured and destroyed and belittled and hounded and harassed, real harassment, different from the sexual kind, just plain old Washington variety harassment which is pretty unique in itself."[19]

Anita Hill was an amateur in this world. She didn't even have legal counsel forty-eight hours before the hearing. A combination of fellow women law professors and Washington attorneys rallied around to help prepare testimony, decide on witnesses, and try to counter the negative campaign about her character. The civil rights community didn't know Hill but saw an opportunity to defeat Thomas and offered support. However, the usual political machinery of the capitol seemed awkwardly silent. Democrats apparently were intimidated by Republican accusations that someone on the committee had leaked information about Anita Hill's charges. As so often happened, concern about process trumped attention to content.

No one, aside from Senator Mikulski, seemed well informed about sexual harassment, and she wasn't on the Judiciary Committee. No woman was. Could sex harassment really be a crime, the senators were asking, particularly after ten years? These questions were a swing back to the 1970s when sexually experienced women were often assumed to have consented to unwanted sex. It wasn't until 1986 that the Supreme Court ruled that sexual harassment is a form of job discrimination that prevents a worker from enjoying equal employment opportunity. It doesn't require actual physical contact; it can involve rude remarks, negative stereotyping, and offensive written or graphic material that create a "hostile environment" for the alleged victim. Sexual harassment involves a power relationship, so it is not at all unusual for a victim to feel powerless to take action (particularly, as in the Thomas case, if the person accused is head of the very agency, the EEOC, that enforces discrimination law).

We found ourselves clandestinely funneling legal research on sexual harassment to Democratic contacts on the Judiciary Committee staff. The situation was ridiculous. Republican senators were openly working with Thomas, but Democratic senators were being "objective." It was impossible to know the truth about Anita Hill's charges at this stage, but it was very important for women everywhere that the charges be treated seriously and that there be expert witnesses to clarify the issue of sexual harassment. That was never allowed.

The Senate Caucus Room in the Russell Building is an impressive space, and the scene of many historic events. It was completed in 1909 as the meeting place for party Caucuses to elect officers and conduct other business. It is large, capable of seating three hundred people, and classically decorated, with elegant chandeliers and Corinthian columns. A number of famous Senate investigations have been conducted here—the sinking of the *Titanic*, the Teapot Dome scandal, Pearl Harbor, the Kefauver Crime Committee, the Vietnam War, and Watergate.

For the Thomas hearings, the room was set up with a long table for the senators across its width at one end, with access behind it to doors through which senators and staff could go in and out. There was a smaller facing table for witnesses, then preferred seating for the press, and finally, chairs for observers lined up theater style extending to the back of the room. The overflow leaned among the columns that lined the length of the room.

During the first stage of the hearings, the room had been reasonably full; now it was a madhouse. A Senate doorkeeper admitted people through the public entrance using an approved list (and his own winking order). It was a good idea to make friends with the doorkeeper. There was special frustration for me knowing that Thomas was Senator Danforth's protégé. Those who knew about the close race against Danforth would approach and say: "Oh Harriett, if you had just beaten Danforth, we wouldn't have to worry about Clarence Thomas." That didn't add to my good humor.

Outside the hearing room, a bank of microphones and cameras was jammed into an alcove. At every break in the hearing, there was a mass dash to the microphones, with fierce elbowing to be the first to "spin" the events from inside for or against Thomas. Meanwhile the print reporters grabbed recognized spokespersons, or were grabbed in turn by staff of those wanting to comment.

There was a certain pecking order in media attention, beginning with senators. Few reporters knew me, but the NWPC's communication director, Pat Reilly, would steer them in my direction, or I would shamelessly join someone being interviewed. Senator Danforth and I occasionally crossed paths racing to the microphones. He was playing the same game but with greater prerogatives. It was "Hi, Jack" and "Hi, Harriett" until he outfoxed me one time after I politely waved him ahead by substituting a woman to praise Thomas's character. Never again.

It's difficult to convey the pain and fascination sitting in that hearing room. Thomas was a strong, emotional witness, denying any act of harassment and shrewdly issuing an angry warning to the chair that he wouldn't tolerate any questions that intruded on his privacy. In contrast, Hill's appearance was cool, dignified, and emotionally controlled as she described Thomas's unwanted talk to her about sex and pornography, including the shocking reference to a Coke can and pubic hair. The only rebuttal Thomas needed to make when he appeared afterward was his accusation that he was the victim of a "high-tech lynching." "Listeners in effect were given the choice of either siding with racism or siding with Judge Thomas."[20] That intimidated liberal senators like Metzenbaum, Kennedy, Leahy, and Simon, as well as a southern senator like Heflin.

The Democrats already "were in almost total disarray,"[21] "None of us on the Democratic side looked good," Senator Simon would write in a book prompted by the hearings.[22] Cowed by Thomas's cries of racism and by the controversy over the leak (of the Hill story to the press), the Democrats basically caved in, never engaging in any tough questioning of Thomas.[23]

Instead, it was the alleged victim who was attacked by the Republicans. Senator Specter cross-examined Hill about statements she had never seen or heard before from men who alleged she was prone to sexual fantasies. He asked questions proposing that her charges against Thomas were part of a conspiracy by "advocacy groups" or that she had been romantically spurned. It was suggested that she had a psychological problem or was suffering from "erotomania." The Republicans couldn't figure out a motive for Hill coming forward so they attacked her character.

Senator Simpson, in an imitation of Joe McCarthy's tactics in the 1950s related to alleged Communists, declared: "I am getting stuff over the transom about Professor Hill. I have letters hanging out of my pockets. I have got faxes, I have got statements from her former law professors, from people that knew her, statements from Tulsa, Oklahoma, saying, watch out for this woman. But nobody's got the guts to say that, because it gets all tangled up in this sexual harassment crap."[24] His evidence was judged too unbelievable to use, even by the Republicans. Simpson would become head of the Institute for Politics at the J. F. Kennedy

School of Politics at Harvard after his retirement from the Senate in 1996.

Hill herself would write later that these attacks were based on a typical readiness to believe the man in harassment cases. "Women who accuse men, particularly powerful men, of harassment are often confronted with the reality of the men's sense that they are more important than women, as a group. Consequently, the man's word is often lent more credence than that of his accuser or even observers."[25] Senators were publicly declaring that no harassment had taken place because Clarence Thomas was such a fine man that the charges were unbelievable. Senator Hatch even suggested that educated, professional women like Anita Hill couldn't be sexually harassed.

The hearings were pressed to a conclusion within three days, with Republicans successfully dragging out questioning of Thomas's witnesses to use up time and prevent the appearance of another woman who also claimed Thomas spoke to her improperly. Would her testimony have mattered? Clarence Thomas ultimately was confirmed as a Supreme Court justice 52 to 48. That was more negative votes than any successful nominee for the Court ever had received. At least six senators had switched their votes as a result of the second hearing. "The fact that six men were moved in seven days should be understood as a moment of empowerment," Professor Resnik wrote.[26]

It's questionable whether Hill's charges would have held up under the precise requirements of sexual harassment law, but they were very pertinent to questions of character in a hearing on a Supreme Court nominee, and despite all that she went through, Anita Hill did succeed in telling her story. When it was over, she returned to teaching in Oklahoma, but her life would never be the same, and neither would women's politics.

Professor Hill made only rare public appearances in the next year. One of her first was in November at a conference for women state legislators in San Diego sponsored by the Center for the American Woman and Politics. She was greeted by deafening cheers and a pink blizzard as elected women of both parties leaped to their feet, swirling their pink napkins overhead in a spontaneous show of support. It was a portent of what was to come. "The hearing combined a variety of potentially volatile elements—gender, race, power, sex, and yes, politics—which when combined and subjected to the glare of television caused a mild explosion," Hill would say in her book.[27]

It was a big explosion. Although national polls showed that the public believed Clarence Thomas, Anita Hill had become a potent symbol of courage for women. It would be a mistake to see her as unique. There had been other heroines in recent history who took risks that translated into progress for women. Twenty years earlier, Jo Carol LaFleur, banished from a Cleveland public school classroom because she was pregnant, fought all the way to the Supreme Court to win a decision that protects a woman's right to continue to teach when pregnant, subject only to her individual capacity to work. Ida May Phillips, a waitress in Florida with seven children, saw her application for a higher-paying factory job arbitrarily rejected because she was a woman with preschool-age children. She sued under Title VII of the Civil Rights Act and, after losing in the lower courts, carried the case to the Supreme Court, which in ruling in her favor, established that there must be equal opportunity in employment regardless of gender.

Each of these women—and others over time who have brought complaints to bosses or cases to the courts—had to make lonely decisions with little support, exposing themselves to public attack, as happened with Hill. They never thought of themselves as leaders, just human beings seeking justice.

In the spring before the hearings, members of the NWPC's Capitol Hill Caucus, most of whom were on the staffs of members of Congress, had asked members to adopt policies for their offices that defined sexual harassment policies. This was necessary because Congress had exempted itself from regulations to protect employees that were imposed on all other employers. Only 200 of the 635 members signed up. Immediately after the Hill–Thomas hearings, Chapter Chair Jean Dugan noted a sudden surge of returns and commented, "Members [of Congress] are rushing to go on record against sexual harassment." Congress later would finally enact employment rules that provided legal recourse for its staff.

Millions of Americans had watched the Hill–Thomas hearings. They reached differing conclusions about who was telling the truth, but public opinion surveys showed a clear consensus that the senators had performed abominably. Kennedy, Simpson,

Simon, Specter, Leahy—all issued apologies for some aspect of their conduct. John Danforth quoted his own administrative assistant in his book who told him after he had made one of the charges against Anita Hill, "You were about as far in the gutter as I can ever remember seeing you."[28] One woman told Senator Simon, "The television show *Designing Women* did more to defend Anita Hill than the United States Senate did."[29]

For years the NWPC had recited sad statistics revealing the low percentage of women in public office and what that cost all of society. Suddenly the powerful image of an all-male committee grilling Anita Hill with so little sensitivity made clear the connection between who gets elected and the likelihood that women will get fair treatment under the law. Many women understood for the first time what it meant that Congress was mostly male. Seeing the Hill–Thomas hearings on television got the message across to people who never knew or cared or paid attention to politics that the committee was all white men, and *they just didn't get it.*

After watching the confirmation vote, I rashly told a *Washington Post* reporter that "we are going to fire up, and if necessary . . . find a woman to run against every one of these guys." I appeared on *Crossfire*, defending Hill but also scoring Democratic senators "who fell over on their fannies." This dismay at the continuing insensitivity to women's concerns finally exploded on a *Nightline* Special Edition that was televised immediately after Thomas's confirmation.

The *Nightline* forum was held in the Hart Senate Office Building. I attended in good faith, by invitation, and listened carefully to instructions. Questioners would be recognized in rotation from various microphones. Of course it was fixed. In order to assure a lively show, Ted Koppel and his producers had arranged in advance for certain people to be speakers. This isn't unusual on such shows, but I didn't catch on until Ralph Nader was led to a microphone. What did he have to do with the hearings? There hadn't been a single woman led to the microphones yet!

The next time someone walked away from a microphone, I darted behind it. The closest floor manager looked unhappy but couldn't very well drag me away publicly. Grabbing the mike didn't mean getting to use it; Koppel wouldn't recognize me. I stood there stubbornly for a solid hour, getting more and more tired, until it was so embarrassing that he finally called my name.

You just don't get it either, I said to Koppel, in controlled fury. "This is about women and you don't even have women speaking." He was treating this as the usual insider Washington political game, all about who did what to whom, rather than seeing the broader repercussions on public policy—for example, the way sexual harassment would be affected. Something more had to be expressed: This was about male arrogance of power; it was about insensitivity to women's life experiences; it was about needed changes in the workplace and an EEOC that failed to enforce the law.

Once finished, I felt a little sheepish. As a former television producer myself, I understood *Nightline*'s desire to control the program. But at least one woman had her say. The next day, there were calls from all over the country as people found the NWPC's phone number and voiced support. "Powerful," "very eloquent," "Thank you." "Koppel was disrespectful of women"; "It was the best statement." We loved every response, including the occasional negative ones. The focus had been put back on women and power where it belonged. We knew the hearings had hit a hot button among women, but this emotion needed to be translated into action, specifically to help elect women. How to do that?

We decided to run a full-page ad in the national edition of *The New York Times*. The problem was that it would cost $50,000—just for the space, let alone production costs. We were floored; we didn't have that much money. The reality was we were just beginning to dig the NWPC out of a financial mess. We couldn't possibly pay for an ad, yet it had to be placed immediately to have any real impact. People cared right now; we had to help them make a difference. It was time for risk taking.

Executive Director Jody Newman was asked to find someone to design an ad while I got on the phone to raise money to pay for it. The calls went to women who had been high donors in my U.S. Senate campaigns. We raised $30,000 quickly and decided to gamble for the rest. The result was a famous ad headlined "*What If*," designed by Mandy Grunwald, then a relatively unknown member of Frank Greer's campaign consulting firm but later famous for proposing the innovative media style that helped Bill Clinton win the presidency. The ad's opening lines read: "What if fourteen women, instead of fourteen men had sat on the Senate Judiciary Committee during the confirmation hearings of Clarence Thomas? . . . Sound unfair? Just as unfair as fourteen men and no women."

What caught the eye was a sketch across the top of the ad showing fourteen diverse women at a committee table thoughtfully contemplating a male witness, who even from the back had a striking similarity to Clarence Thomas. That resemblance worried me so much that I had to be persuaded not to change the drawing. The ad copy pointed out that men made up 98 percent of the Senate and 93 percent of the House. It called attention to the behavior of the Senate during the confirmation hearings, and it concluded: "If you're angry about what you've witnessed in the United States Senate, don't just raise your fist, raise your pen. . . ." Below was a coupon soliciting contributions, with these words: "Turn your anger into action. Join us."

Almost as important to the NWPC as the money was the fact that the ad distinguished us as the organization that put women into public office. The response more than paid for the ad; we raised $80,000. Reprints were equally effective in direct-mail fund-raising. Now we had resources to launch an all-out effort to recruit, train, and support women for 1992. We had accomplished the ultimate object, energizing the public to make the connection between Anita Hill and electing women in the upcoming election year.

It was an election year that would earn the media label "The Year of the Woman."

13

The Year of the Woman

It's still a little early to say the Senate is
going to start its day singing, "I am Woman."

**—Lynn Martin, former congresswoman
and U.S. Senate candidate from Illinois**

The media called it "The Year of the Woman." But that wasn't really accurate. It was actually a year of opportunity that was seized by well-qualified women candidates and their committed supporters. It's true that a record number of women were elected. The number in the U.S. House rose from twenty-eight to forty-seven, and the number in the Senate, from two to six. But it wasn't as if the American public woke up on election morning and said: "Let's elect women." Those who succeeded earned their victories the hard way, through difficult decisions, painful fund-raising, good strategy—and plenty of risk taking. Their victories were a payoff for twenty years' effort by a whole movement.

We had begun the election year initiative with the ad in *The New York Times,* knowing we needed to get more money and volunteers. We increased our schedule of training sessions for candidates and we encouraged all the credible candidates who appeared. Normally, we put candidates through a tough screening that was as much about how much money they had raised as their qualifications. Now we needed risk takers willing to seize the opportunities where there were openings for major office. We sensed that we just needed one or two unexpected victories to ignite the whole country.

The first one came in Illinois. Chicago and St. Louis newspapers had quoted our impulsive promise to run a woman against Senator Alan Dixon, a Democrat who had voted for Thomas and who now was up for reelection in Illinois. The notion of challenging an incumbent would have been wishful thinking, except for a breakfast in Chicago during the Hill–Thomas hearings where key local political women told me there were real prospects for a viable woman Senate candidate in Illinois. They specifically mentioned Carol Moseley Braun, a former state legislator who was currently the Cook County recorder of deeds.

In the furor after the Hill–Thomas hearings, she actually filed, and the NWPC made an immediate commitment to the campaign. I went to Chicago to help her raise money and get publicity. My honest expectations may have slipped out at the fund-raising lunch where I said: "If she doesn't make it this time, you'll be making a sound investment for the future!" Other women's groups refused to oppose the Democratic incumbent by supporting a candidate who appeared to have such a low chance of success. But we had experienced chicken-and-egg defeatism in my campaigns. If Braun (she would change this to Moseley-Braun after her election to the Senate) was willing to take a risk against the odds, then the time to help her was early when she really needed it.

Her story was familiar. As a young mother and attorney, she had taken leadership in local efforts to preserve Jackson Park. Appreciative neighbors in Chicago's liberal Hyde Park area pushed her into running for an open seat in the Illinois House in 1978. She won and launched a highly successful legislative career. Moseley-Braun later said that she ran that first time because of those who said, "Whites wouldn't vote for me because I was black and nobody would vote for me because I was a woman. And that was all I needed."[1] She campaigned hard, and "blacks voted for me, whites voted for me, men voted for me and I won."

She maintained a liberal voting record in the Illinois House, and after 10 years was asked to run for Cook County recorder of deeds by Harold Washington, Chicago's first black mayor. Moseley-Braun was a mesmerizing campaigner, with a stirring speaking style and an electric smile. Still, she was vastly underfunded in 1992 compared to her Senate primary opponents. It also was assumed that as a black, she would have trouble getting support from conservative downstate Democrats. It was definitely an upset when she won the primary.

We took credit for the white suburban women who crossed political lines to vote for her because of Anita Hill, but *Time* magazine wrote: "Braun, a strong supporter of abortion rights, owed her victory less to women's anger than the arrogance and myopia of her rivals. Both Dixon and challenger Al Hofeld, a lawyer, found Braun so insignificant—perhaps because she was a woman, perhaps because she was black—that they ignored her. While they knocked each other out, she finished first with 38 percent of the vote." Her general election opponent, conservative Republican Richard Williamson, quickly reversed his longstanding opposition to abortion,[2] but he was a weak candidate. Money and attention came pouring in to Moseley-Braun, attracted by the certainty of the first black woman to be elected to the U.S. Senate.

Her primary victory had exactly the galvanizing impact for which we had been hoping. In Pennsylvania, a civic leader named Lynn Yeakel, reading the Illinois results, filed for U.S. Senate, hoping to defeat Republican Senator Arlen Specter, one of the fiercest interrogators of Anita Hill during the hearings. It was another long-shot primary, against the sitting lieutenant governor. This time, leaders of all the political women's groups hastened to the scene. Just one month after Moseley-Braun's victory, Yeakel won the Democratic nomination, becoming the latest in a string of "stealth women candidates," women who weren't well known but had the qualities for success. This was a year for the outsider, and women were seen as the ultimate outsiders—even when they were inside.

If Illinois and Pennsylvania were the first gusts of change, California was the tornado. Two women, former Mayor Dianne Feinstein and Congresswoman Barbara Boxer, were running for separate U.S. Senate seats, despite nay-sayers who said electing two progressive women in the same state in the same election was impossible. Skeptics insisted the country wasn't ready; they would hurt one another's chances. They underestimated voters who were quite capable of evaluating the candidates on their quite different personalities, not simply as women. Both won. So did an incredible sixteen non-incumbent women who then were nominees to the U.S. House. Exit polls showed 75 percent of Feinstein's voters and 63 percent of Boxer's felt that the Senate should have rejected Clarence Thomas.[3] It was just one factor, but it seemed to crystallize voter discontent.

Finally, in Washington State, a feisty state senator (and Caucus leader) named Patty Murray ran for Senate as "just a mom in tennis shoes" (originally a brush-off label from a male politician). It had seemed an improbable long shot when she filed against incumbent Senator Brock Adams, who was being charged with sexual harassment, but when he decided not to run, she was in the right position and she won the primary. After the Anita Hill hearings, Murray represented just what voters were looking for: an outsider who was close to them and understood their lives.

There also were other stealth candidates whom we supported, women like Marjorie Margolies-Mezvinsky, a former television reporter running for the House in a Republican-leaning Philadelphia suburb; Cynthia McKinney, a black local official in Georgia; Susan Stokes, a Republican businesswoman in Kentucky; and Lynn Woolsey, a divorced former welfare recipient in California. They were all well-qualified House candidates who just hadn't penetrated media consciousness.

Jeannie Austin, co-chair of the Republican National Committee, credited women's success in running effective campaigns to "a changed mind set. . . . Women in the past said we can't raise money or do the things necessary to win. But now they see they can. Women used not to be major donors. It was always their husband or daddy. But now they are responding when women candidates call for help."[4]

As the excitement mounted, donations poured into the candidate support groups. EMILY's List would raise an incredible $6 million during this election cycle, compared to $1.5 million collected for women candidates in 1990, making it the largest PAC in the nation. It offered women a familiar approach; they joined it rather like a club, paying $100 a year dues with a commitment to donate $100 apiece each election cycle to at least two recommended candidates. Members received information on candidates and checked off those to whom their money would go. Oregon congressional candidate Elizabeth Furse reported receiving $43,000 after being mentioned in just one EMILY's List mailing.

A Republican counterpart called the "WISH List," was organized in 1992 by Glenda Greenwald, former publisher of *Michigan Woman* magazine. It would raise more than $400,000 in 1992 from women, using the same contribution formula.[5] The bipartisan Women's Campaign Fun, raising money through events and mailings, would give more than $1 million to pro-choice candidates in 1992, and the NWPC's own PAC donated a half million, raised through direct-mail solicitation and member contributions.

Women candidates also were proving to be effective fundraisers on their own. In 1988, women nominees for the U.S. Senate raised $2.9 million. In 1992, in a report as of September, they raised more than $28 million.[6] Even allowing for an increase in candidates, that was an astonishing surge that challenged the myth about women finding it hard to raise money.

We were determined to spread the message to ever-broader audiences of women. We decided to approach the mass-circulation magazines. They were published in New York so that's where we went, Communications Director Pat Reilly and myself, visiting editors of major publications like *Working Woman, Working Mother, Vogue, Glamour, Good Housekeeping, Elle, Ladies' Home Journal,* and *Lear's.* With the exception of *Glamour* and *Working Woman,* they had reputations of absolute hostility to anything political. Their editors had decided that readers wanted fashion, recipes, sex, child care, romance, and how-to's. It was a kind of 1950s world.

We used the interest aroused by Anita Hill to pitch to them the potential for good stories about women candidates. Some were warmly interested, others were arrogant, but the trip was rather fun. It showed me that we all needed to be more connected. We even discussed some future joint forums in New York. Reilly later fed them ideas to fit specific editorial interests that would work with deadlines that are weeks before the publication date, keeping in mind the varying primary dates. Eventually a number of articles appeared.

Meanwhile our political director produced fact sheets about candidates that reporters could rely on in developing stories. This was good for the NWPC because we came to be viewed as the authoritative source for information on political women, and it also was good for political women because reporters were more likely to run stories when they could get swift, reliable data. We also held press briefings with media decision-makers like Hal Bruno of ABC, Dotty Lynch of CBS, and Tom Hannon of CNN. "The Year of the Woman" had become a legitimate story, and everyone was interested.

There were a record 213 women candidates for the House at the end of April, compared to 171 two years previously.[7] The final total nominated for the fall, after primary votes, would be 106 for the House, a huge jump from 70 in 1990, with 11 nominees for the U.S. Senate, up from 8 the year before.[8] In April, the NWPC held a highly successful candidate training program in Washington that was covered by print and television media. Our trainers gave women from across the country such practical advice as: Don't say "I feel that I am quite capable; just say, I *am* capable."[9] *The Washington Post* headlined its story, "Politics' New Wave of Women; With Voters Ready for a Change, Candidates Make their Move."

We did *not* participate that April in a NOW-sponsored march for reproductive rights. Indeed, I was very annoyed that it was held. Toward the end of 1991, Patricia Ireland, the new president of NOW, had stopped by for an introductory visit. It was more than a gracious get-acquainted call. She informed me there would be a massive march sponsored by NOW in Washington the next April around the theme of reproductive rights and invited the NWPC to be a co-sponsor. When I demurred, questioning the timing of such a demonstration, she told me all the other women's groups were joining in.

NOW had a proud history of pressing actions and lawsuits to break the back of sex discrimination in all its forms. But it was crystal clear to me that such a march was not where women should be putting their energies in an election year. We needed to recruit, train, and support women for office, taking advantage of voter discontent and women's anger in 1992. The NWPC was absolutely committed to reproductive rights, but the last thing we needed was to see our candidates waving from a Washington march, looking like single-issue advocates, when they had to go home and get elected on issues like health care and the economy.

After consulting with the NWPC's leadership, I wrote a letter to Ireland expressing just those thoughts and declining to be a co-sponsor.[10] We can do more to advance reproductive rights, the letter said, "by using our resources to elect pro-choice women to state and federal legislatures." We wanted women on candidate phone banks, not on buses headed for Washington, D.C. Leaders of other women's groups said they agreed with me, but only one, the League of Women Voters, declined to be actively involved in the march. The pressure of being loyal to the "sisterhood" was too great. A survey of our local leadership had verified our decision, but I was learning that women leaders in Washington listened to one another more than to women around the country.

There's a rich diversity in women's groups: Some use confrontation to get publicity for issues; others do quiet research that helps pass laws; still others educate members for individual action. To be successful in 1992 we needed to have everyone focused on the election, helping candidates to make connection with women and men voters who were struggling with complicated lives. We just couldn't afford to waste this opportunity. It was particularly annoying to have NOW unilaterally set up the march and theme without any consultation and then expect all women leaders automatically to agree. Not this one.

I wrote a commentary for various newspapers that one of them headlined, "Don't Just Sing, Remake the Choir . . . The powerless half of America must get inside government to affect critical issues."[11] The commentary said women didn't want the strident, outdated style of the past. They needed partners to help them get their voices heard. They needed to get elected. NOW was not happy, but political reporters began calling, giving us the opportunity to emphasize the basic message that women candidates could be big winners in 1992.

We supported the label "The Year of the Woman" because it was a good way to build excitement for women candidates, and by the summer, it seemed 1992 might really deserve the name. Analyzing what was happening, we came up with these factors:

- Women benefited from an antiincumbency mood. They were seen as outsiders. "There's a revolt going on," Patty Murray said. "The old men's club, the establishment... they're going to be just shocked, . . . in November."[12]

- The end of the cold war had changed the agenda from foreign policy and defense to domestic issues, and that favored women candidates.
- A larger number of open seats without incumbents were available because of redistricting and retirements. Many people will not run against incumbents because they have a formidable 95 percent reelection rate.
- There was a pool of women poised for higher office who had qualified themselves within the political system and were ready to seize the opportunities. If the Hill–Thomas hearings had occurred ten years before, it's unlikely the results would have been so striking.
- The Hill–Thomas hearings had a major impact on women. So did the highly publicized rape trials of William Kennedy Smith, who was acquitted, and Mike Tyson, who was convicted. "Millions of women identified with those situations whether or not they believed the particular women involved," commented Ruth Mandel, then director of the Center for the American Woman and Politics. "They identified with the anger of being powerless."[13]
- "The atmospherics are different," according to Mandel, a long-time observer of women candidates. "This may be the first year since I've been watching women in politics that to be seen in your blue suit and red tie is a liability— and that the image of woman is an asset."[14]

However, as we neared time for the two political party conventions in the summer, most of the national media coverage was focused on the presidential race. It was clear that President Bush would be renominated. Bill Clinton was leading among Democrats, but Ross Perot was still a factor, drawing some of the "outsider" attention. Gathering information through party contacts, it became clear that despite all the talk about a "Year of the Woman," not much would be done at either convention to feature women. The Democratic Party, under the direction of Chair Ron Brown, had decided to take control of the daily convention women's meetings that traditionally had been convened by the Caucus and other women's groups, and the Republican Party was virtually excluding moderate women, starting at the delegate-selection level.

Both parties appeared to view women with a mixture of anticipation and dread. Women still were the "other," a mysterious mass that had to be dealt with carefully. Old hands in the Caucus pushed us to make a fuss. On the one hand, party conventions aren't that important anymore. Presidential nominees no longer are decided in exciting roll call votes, and the impact of state primaries has virtually eliminated any last-minute decisions. And only the party faithful really care about what planks are in the party platform. The conventions are basically big promotional events to sell the party's candidates and image to television viewers, but that's exactly what we needed to exploit.

Ten of the eleven women nominated for Senate were Democrats, as were two-thirds of the women running for the U.S. House. We believed that they should get exposure at the Democratic convention in prime time when people at home were most likely to be watching. Party leaders were evasive, saying they already had chosen speakers. In years past, we might have remained frustrated, but in 1992 there were women strategically placed to leverage power on behalf of other women: women like Stephanie Solien (former director of the Women's Campaign Fund) inside the Clinton campaign; Barbara Mikulski speaking for candidates in the Senate; Lynn Cutler, vice chair of the Democratic Party; and then the leaders of our three groups, Ellen Malcolm for EMILY's List, Jane Danowitz for the Women's Campaign Fund, and me for the NWPC. Finally, there was the convention keynote speaker, the dynamic Texas governor, Ann Richards.

To be honest, I wasn't sure anything really would happen. There still were only a handful of us, in a sea of them. On the other hand, women were winning new respect for political savvy, and there was the potential impact of women's votes. In the end, not only were congressional women candidates displayed on the podium in prime television time, but each woman Senate nominee had her own minute on camera, speaking to the greater television audience while standing with her home state delegation. We felt terrific. We had fought a battle for other women, and whatever the measurable impact on voters, we had won.

We also won a struggle to have Bill Clinton address the women's Caucus on Tuesday morning, instead of on Friday, after he was nominated, as was proposed. Women were tired of being treated like supportive handmaidens who are approached only when help is needed. We had made the case that he should appear on Tuesday when all the women candidates were to be showcased and he could help attract television coverage for them, as well as himself. It's important to remember that women weren't terribly enthusiastic about Clinton's candidacy in July 1991. Ross Perot had just withdrawn, and Clinton was trailed by rumors of womanizing. We needed Clinton, but he needed us. I suggested to Clinton's speechwriter that he forget about the usual laundry list of promises and have Clinton speak from the heart.

It turned into one of those unforgettable political moments. The hotel ballroom was jammed; the television cameras were massed; an impressive lineup of women candidates was being applauded on stage; my fellow leaders, Ellen Malcolm and Jane Danowitz, stood with me as I introduced the candidate with all the emotional punch that I could manage. When Clinton entered the room, it erupted. There was an astonishing ovation that I hadn't really expected, and he responded, with a master's touch. He looked intently out at the audience in the ballroom, and through the facing cameras onward to women everywhere, he said: "I am the grandson of a working woman, the son of a single mother, the husband of a working wife . . . I am the father of a daughter who wants to build space stations in the sky." Even the most cynical New Yorkers in the crowd were moved.

Throughout the convention, we did our best to make women part of the media message every day. The Caucus Democratic Task Force distributed stick-on badges with a "Women Win" message. We even set up a joint Women's Election Central in a rodent-ridden hotel across from Madison Square Garden, with Pat Reilly in charge, and the three organization leaders taking turns responding to calls. By the end of the week, we were worn out, having accomplished just about all that was possible for women candidates with our limited resources. I found a seat high up behind the podium to enjoy the convention's final moments: the nomination of the presidential candidate, the showing of the film about "The Man from Hope," followed by Clinton's acceptance speech. Delegates were dancing in the aisles, colorful balloons flooded down from the ceiling, the nominees and their families embraced.

Running from the convention hall to catch the shuttle bus, I tripped on the leg of a metal crowd-control barrier, literally falling flat on my face and was hauled off to a hospital on a stretcher. The ER in a New York City hospital—an interesting way to end the convention. A nice doctor picked most of the sidewalk out of my face, although at the airport the next day, wide-eyed children pointed and exclaimed before their parents shushed them. I wasn't a pretty sight, and there still was the Republican convention ahead.

The Republican convention required different preparation. Months earlier we had brought together representatives of groups that support Republican pro-choice candidates to talk about a common strategy. Moderate Republican women were having a difficult time, as recounted brilliantly by Tanya Mellich in her book *The Republican War Against Women*.[15] The Republican Party once had been the leader in support of women, backing the Equal Rights Amendment as early as 1940. The first woman to chair a major party convention was Republican Mary Louise Smith (a Caucus founder) in 1974. However, the Reagan revolution accelerated an ideological shift to the right. The ERA was removed from the party platform, and antiabortion language put in. By 1992, the rift with moderate women was huge.

Organizations included in our preconvention meetings were Republicans for Choice; Republican Coalition for Choice; Business and Professional Women, USA; the NARAL; the Women's Campaign Fund; and the NWPC's Republican Task Force. It was a reminder that women were a significant factor for Republicans, averaging more than 40 percent of their vote, even though publicity emphasized that women tended to vote Democratic. Those present agreed that the ideological right had preselected most of the convention delegates so there wasn't any point planning a daily women's Caucus.

The NWPC ultimately focused all its energies in Houston on a press conference that showcased a dozen Republican woman candidates who identified themselves as pro-choice. It was the only attention they would get. There was something slightly askew about everything. The Houston Club where we held our press conference had been all male until a few years before, and they had hired special security because we were a women's group. When they realized that the National Republican Coalition for Life was meeting in a room right next door to our press conference, they called the police to keep order.

We existed in some kind of parallel universe to the main events. Our Republican task force cosponsored a pro-choice reception that attracted Republican moderate stars like Massachusetts Governor William Weld. The moderates also held a lunch, but they knew they had no voice inside the convention itself. They called it a "celebration," but it seemed like a death watch to me. I had suggested that George Bush, like Clinton, reach out with an emotional connection to women, but no one had listened. There was a mean spirit hovering over this convention that incorporated most of the backlash and resentment against the changes in women's status achieved by the women's movement during the past twenty years.

Pat Buchanan set the tone with his harsh opening night speech describing "a religious war going on in this country for the soul of America." Mellich wrote that the Houston convention was in the hands of the radical right. "It belonged to Pat Robertson and Jerry Falwell and their exclusionary vision of Christianity. . . . It belonged to the right-to-lifers and Phyllis Schlafly, and to Marilyn Quayle's petulant antifeminism."[16] There was anguish being a pro-choice woman delegate in that hall, she said. "As Buchanan's hatred settled over the convention floor like a miasma, those of us who wore pro-choice Bush buttons were accosted. One man told me I should be ashamed."[17] Mellich had to decide whether to leave the Republican Party. I just decided to go home.

In the final weeks before the election, there was travel all around the country, campaigning for women candidates of both parties in at least a dozen states. There were so many tight races that it was easy to keep the adrenaline flowing. Election night 1992 was an extraordinary feeling. Not only were there the record number of winners for U.S. House and Senate, but at the state level, women also set new records; with this election they held 20 percent of statewide offices, and slightly more than 20 percent of state legislative seats. In Washington State, women were almost 40 percent of the legislature, the highest percentage ever achieved in any state.

In analyzing the results for our postelection press conference, Executive Director Jody Newman came to a significant conclusion: Twenty-two of the twenty-four new women elected to the House had won in open seats. This wasn't a story about women challengers beating male incumbents. Instead, a record number of well-qualified women took advantage of a huge number of open seats created by redistricting, resignation, and retirement, and they ran effective campaigns. Risk taking doesn't mean jumping off cliffs without a safety net. It is important to seize the right opportunities, not just run in any race. It is important to keep women moving up the pipeline. It is important to have confidence that women are winners.

The women who came to Congress in 1993 were the payoff for years of efforts by a great many people. The winners had received record contributions through organizations forged in the women's movement. They emerged out of a transformed society where women now work in almost every occupation, with greater resources and a greater willingness to use them to help other women. And every single new woman elected to Congress in 1992 was an advocate for the agenda that women had been supporting for a generation.

They were the first elected on our watch, and we were very proud.

14

The Difference

We don't want to be queen
for a day. We want to share the power.

—U.S. Representative Pat Schroeder, Colorado

The logical next question was this: What difference did the election really make? During the swearing-in ceremonies, it had been a joy looking down from the galleries to see the bright patches of red, royal blue, and green clothing standing out in the dark expanse of men's suits. Still, aside from wearing different kinds of clothes, what impact would these women have? They had won in part because voters expected women to bring something different to government, as outsiders and agents of change. Yet they still were so few, and they were entering such a hostile environment.

In many ways, the experience of the new women in Congress paralleled mine entering the Missouri Senate fifteen years earlier. There was an initial culture shock moving from a general society where opportunities were opening to women, into a hierarchical institution mired in gender bias. In 1977, it was astounding when a committee chairman had trouble accepting a female vice chair. In 1993, Rep. Henry Hyde of Illinois astounded a new generation by complaining aloud that there were so many women on the floor of the House that it looked like a shopping mall.

Congresswoman Pat Schroeder noted: "They are not saying, 'Oh good, more women.' They are saying, 'Oh God, more trouble.'"[1]

Congress is still being run by the same people, said freshman Susan Molinari, a Republican from New York. "The halls are running with testosterone," added Karen Shepherd, a Democrat from Utah. "Very often on the floor, any debate we have speaks about substance for a short period of time and after that, all day long, it's a question of who's in charge here."[2] The new women were learning that they would have to struggle to exercise the power they thought had been granted to them by voters.

Women still were a decided minority at 11 percent of the Congress, but the publicity from "The Year of the Woman" had raised expectations. Newspaper reporters writing about women swarmed over the national capitol; the Center for the American Woman and Politics (CAWP) conducted a foundation-funded study on women of the 103rd Congress; a freshman congresswoman, Marjorie Margolies-Mezvinsky, wrote a book; and the Congressional Caucus on Women's Issues produced a special report on women's achievements during the session. There seemed to be an urgency to prove whether women in office made a difference.

It was a question that had haunted the women's movement since its beginnings. The Caucus was founded in 1971 not just to equalize gender numbers but to bring about change in society. That assumed the election of women would indeed create change. There were critics who disagreed, pointing out that women don't all vote the same and that they are far outnumbered in office. Still, many in the class of 1992 had run as reformers. Their experiences would make the women of the 103rd an interesting test case to answer the "difference" question.

What worried me, and the Caucus, was that many of the newly elected congresswomen had won close elections in swing districts, and they would be very much at risk in 1994. It would be the voters in those districts who would decide if they liked whatever differences their representatives made and whether they would be reelected. I had warned our members not to be too euphoric after the election. We needed to help newly elected representatives to succeed. The first priority before trying to elect new women in 1994 had to be retaining those who were already there.

With funding from a supporter, we set up some private suppers in the capitol for the new congresswomen, under the bipartisan leadership of Republican Tillie Fowler of Florida and Democrat Margolies-Mezvinsky of Pennsylvania. The idea was to provide speakers and encourage discussion to help them learn the system and become as effective as possible, plus to explore any concerns about the 1994 elections. With two-year terms, members of Congress have to start running almost as soon as the last election is over.

Most of the suppers were held in the Lindy Boggs Room, a small area in the capitol set aside for the women members, where overstuffed couches and mahogany furniture provide a welcoming contrast with the cold marble of the corridors outside. Framed pictures of all the women who have served in Congress hang on the walls. It was a strange feeling to be there, knowing I never would belong by right of election, always an outsider, but now one who was trying to help other women to be insiders.

The first supper was chaotic; the Democratic women arrived late and in emotional upheaval. Party leaders were demanding that they support a Clinton budget reconciliation package that included a tax increase. Only a few had districts that assured reelection; those who didn't were convinced any vote for a tax increase would be used to defeat them, no matter what else they accomplished. The women ran in and out between votes in the chamber, taking time to express resentment over their relative powerlessness. They said the old guard deliberately withheld information, particularly about the intricate rules. "We have to fight hard not be marginalized or marginalize ourselves," said Democrat Anna Eshoo from California.

Despite the difficulty of having to cast crucial votes before they were oriented to their jobs, several of the freshman women had already become leaders in efforts at reform. That included changes in the campaign finance system as well as in Congress itself. "I came here to make a difference," one said. They had my sympathy, remembering how our efforts were squashed in the Missouri Senate. The establishment rarely welcomes reform. Without superior numbers, fairness and efficiency are trumped by power and partisanship.

Listening to the congresswomen's descriptions of the way business was conducted, it was clear that it was hard to work across party lines in the new congress. Members were "whipped" by their leaders to follow the party position, whatever it was.

However, when the NWPC's capitol Caucus reviewed roll call votes, we were pleased to see a dramatic gender difference crossing party lines on a number of high-profile issues. For example, 81 percent of the women in Congress voted for a ban on assault weapons, compared to just 46 percent of the men.[3] The bill barely passed, 216 to 214, which meant women provided the winning margin on something normally not counted as a woman's issue.

A proposal that had begun as a woman's issue, the Family and Medical Leave Act, received support from both male and female members, but there was a revealing gender difference in the numbers, with 87 percent of women voting for passage compared to 58 percent of men.[4] The percentages weren't as high for Republican women as for their Democratic counterparts, but the fact that a spread existed between Republican men and women showed a willingness to vote against party on issues that touched core gender concerns.

On the other hand, women's numbers were still too small to block passage of the Hyde Amendment that prohibited use of federal funds for abortions. Women voted overwhelmingly to defeat it, 77 percent voting against, but it had support from 64 percent of the men, and their greater absolute numbers ensured a majority. If the majority female population in the country had been proportionately represented in Congress, the amendment would have been defeated. A majority of 11 percent women simply cannot beat a majority of 89 percent men, noted Caucus analyst Rachel Leahey. "There is no better reason to continue working to elect 217 women to Congress, a full 50 percent representation."[5]

A major problem was the huge number of subcommittees where most business really is decided. There were 117 subcommittees to be covered, and even 47 women weren't enough. As one staffer commented in the CAWP study, "It really takes . . . a woman there monitoring it . . . I mean it's hard for [a member] to say, 'I'm offering an amendment to cut $200 million from breast cancer.' But they can say, 'On line 19M, strike the figure $500 million and put in the figure $300 million,' and unless somebody is paying attention to what that is, nobody knows."

There never had been enough women to cover the key committees where the most important decisions are made, but in 1993, with some increase in numbers, three congresswomen were named to the House Labor, Health and Human Services Subcommittee of the Appropriations Committee, and three were appointed to Energy and Commerce. The increased leverage they were able to apply in negotiations with their chairs was generally credited with getting appropriation of more than $600 million for breast cancer research programs, as well as funding for breast and cervical cancer prevention programs and ovarian cancer research.[6] Clearly, even a small increase in the number of women had made a difference.

Of course there were a great many issues, like trade, crime, and military affairs and labor, which interested individual women and where the gender issues were less apparent. "I am very interested in looking at the conditions of working women," said Congresswoman Marcy Kaptur, Democrat from Ohio. "Not that I'm not interested in the conditions of working men—I am. But the women's story is generally not told."

Carrie Meek, Democratic congresswoman from Florida, and an African American, argued for social security taxes for household workers, saying: "I was once a domestic worker. My mother was a domestic worker. All my sisters were domestic workers."[7] And Senator Patty Murray rose in debate on the family leave bill to say, "When I was twenty-six years old and an executive secretary in Seattle, I became pregnant with my first child. At that time, even though I was working out of economic necessity, there were no options for working mothers. A family leave policy would have given me the message that in this country, your family is as important as your job." These were differences that only different life experiences could generate.

Senator Carol Moseley-Braun contributed both her race and her sex. She rushed to the floor one day to protest a quick vote that Sen. Jesse Helms of North Carolina had won to protect the Confederate flag as a symbol for the United Daughters of the Confederacy. "The issue," she said, "is whether or not Americans, such as myself, who believe in the promise of this country . . . will have to suffer the indignity of being reminded, time and time again, that at one point in this country's history we were human chattel." I will get this vote reversed, she said, "if I have to stand here until this room freezes over."

"As Moseley-Braun spoke," a reporter wrote, "Sen. Dianne Feinstein of California looked up and saw a tear forming in the corner of her friend's eye. She stood and took Moseley-Braun's hand," saying to her that they would fix it. "The image became a symbol for the women's presence here. . . . It was an instinctive thing,' says Feinstein," and commenting on the surprised reaction to the display of sisterly support, "To this very staid establishment, we add a real note of spontaneity."[8] The Helms amendment was reversed.

The Moseley-Braun story is a reminder that women were bringing variety with their gender. The 1992 election not only had increased the number of women but had made them more broadly representative: 17 percent of the women members were African American, 4 percent, Hispanic and 2 percent, Asian Pacific. A third of the new congresswomen came from either business or education. Two-thirds were married, 11 percent were divorced, 4 percent were widowed, and 83 percent had children.

Those still were small numbers. In Washington State, where women now were 38 percent of the legislature, Democratic Senator Nita Rinehart reported, "There's a wider array of perspectives. . . . When men dominated, there were lots of lawyers and farmers. Now we have more teachers and nurses." Bills mandating insurance coverage for mammography and breast reconstruction wouldn't have been considered before, a representative said. In New Hampshire, Republican Senator Susan McLane observed that women legislators were willing to tackle the gambling interests because we're "a little closer to the [family] purse strings and can envision husbands spending money on gambling rather than bringing home the bacon."[9]

It's unwise to jump to conclusions from anecdotal information, but there was clear evidence that women were having a distinct impact. At the end of the 103rd Congress, in the fall of 1994, the Congressional Women's Caucus boasted passage of a record numbers of measures that benefited women and their families. They cited sixty-six different items, such as improved federal contracting opportunities for women-owned businesses, greater gender-equity efforts in education, the right to safe access to reproductive health clinics, and an expansion of services for domestic violence and sexual assault.

"From the classroom to the workroom, our efforts have produced positive results in women's lives," said Caucus Co-Chair

Olympia Snowe. Men provided votes, but women's voices provided the difference, said Co-Chair Pat Schroeder; this should finally put to rest the question: What difference does having more women in Congress make?[10]

Reporter Kristin Huckshorn took a long look at women in Congress one year after the 1992 election and concluded that they were altering the style of government "with a common-sense approach and a readiness to talk from the heart," but they still lacked the numbers and seniority to foster rapid change.[11] Some male members told reporters that the women brought a different style, that they seemed to build consensus more easily. The women themselves said they just liked to get to the point.

The CAWP study cited, among many examples, the women's success in getting the National Institutes for Health to stop permitting pharmaceutical researchers to conduct clinical trials that excluded women. The congresswomen pointed out the potential damage in women patients' receiving medicines that never had been tested on someone with their biological makeup.

Another example was the concerted pressure from women members in securing passage of the Freedom of Access to Clinic Entrances (FACE) Bill. "It was a female deputy whip who took charge of the whip count, Jolene Unsoeld. The whip counts are such an important part of the process. And she clearly worked so tremendously hard in that. This was more a crusade, . . . not just another boring bill."[12] Senators Kay Bailey Hutchison and Barbara Mikulski led the effort to draft and gain passage of legislation to allow homemakers to establish individual retirement accounts on the same terms as paid workers. And all seven women in the Senate—five Democrats and two Republicans—joined in opposing a deal to allow the admiral held responsible for the Tailhook scandal from retiring from the Navy with the rank and pension of a four-star officer. That viewpoint might not have been heard without them.

The authors of the CAWP study concluded that despite the small numbers and the fact that half were freshmen, "The voices, views and votes of the female Representatives and Senators who served from 1993 to 1995 made themselves heard and felt in legislative debate and in the legislation passed."[13] The study concluded: "Women members made a difference."

As Congresswoman Lynn Woolsey of California said: "We carry the responsibility to women and children—we just do. Because if we don't, it's not going to happen."[14] Even though there are many differences among elected women reflecting party, district, and background, the women of the 103rd Congress did make a gender difference, most notably on the particular votes and issues cited. We wondered how that difference would translate into votes in 1994.

I knew from personal experience that voters don't necessarily pay attention to legislative action and that serving the public doesn't assure election. Women are the majority of the voters, but there is no evidence that they will vote based on gender. As the election of 1994 approached, voters clearly were in a different mood than two years before. They had voted for change in 1992 and were angry because too little had occurred. Now they overwhelmingly disapproved of the job being done by the Congress, currently led by Democrats, as exit polls would confirm.[15] In addition, there was strong male disapproval of President Clinton.[16]

The freshman women's brash efforts at reform had been unsuccessful; for most voters, the women would simply appear to be part of a failed Congress. An aggressive Republican leadership under Congressman Newt Gingrich seized on the discontent to market a set of promises under the label "Contract with America." This particularly appealed to the intense feelings of the nearly 20 percent of the voters who identified themselves as religious right and who could have greater weight in an off-presidential year when fewer voters turn out.

These ideological votes were just part of a backlash against strong women that also had been expressed in 1993 when two women ran for governor in the off-year election. One columnist promptly predicted that 1993 would go down as the "Year of the *Un*-woman" and that both women, Republican Christine Todd Whitman in New Jersey and Democrat Mary Sue Terry in Virginia, would be defeated. He based his conclusion on the recent defeat of a Canadian political party led by a woman. That was evidence, he said, that women weren't tough enough for a new "macho" political climate and of course not tough enough to be chief executives.

Whitman provided the best response by winning and becoming the first woman governor of New Jersey. Terry lost. It wasn't just the suggested lack of toughness; after all, she had been state attorney general. There were repeated attacks on her for being single with no children.[17] A San Diego-based community organizer described to one of our convention workshops a campaign flyer in that area that said a woman candidate was "trying to pretend she's not a bitter man-hating bitch."

A number of the Democratic freshmen women realized they would need to be proactive to survive the election. They needed to describe the difference they had made in their own terms. In the past, each woman would have gone it alone, but these women represented something new. As bright young professionals with a lot of confidence and savvy, who had taken risks to run against the odds, they saw the wisdom in helping one another. They produced a video, telling the story of the freshman women in Congress, recounting their history and accomplishments, and recapturing much of the spirit of 1992. Then they took time from their own races to campaign for one another.[18] I attended some of those fund-raisers; it was very moving to watch the video, knowing how courageously many had acted in a difficult Congress, how few of the voters would ever see the video, and how endangered they now were.

There also were some very difficult races for governor that year, prompting campaign trips to Kansas for Joan Wagon, to Rhode Island for Myrth York, to Iowa for Bonnie Campbell, to Michigan for Debbie Stabenow, and to Illinois for Dawn Clark Netsch. This was another group of women who had proved themselves in legislatures and statewide office. Could they overcome the "toughness" stereotype that had been used in 1993 against women seeking to become chief executive, as well as the money advantages of their opponents?

An odd incident occurred while we were attending a press conference in Maine to announce support for Congresswoman Olympia Snowe who was running for U.S. Senate. The local NOW chapter picketed the press conference because they preferred the more liberal male Democratic opponent. We saw the world differently; Snowe was the co-chair of the Congressional Women's Caucus. She provided a moderate viewpoint among the

Republicans, and her support on issues like reproductive rights, family leave, and women's health and economic equity was extremely important. Gender was too important in this case to be put in second place.

In the long run, if women were ever going to be the majority in public office, they wouldn't all be women we agreed with 100 percent. *Washington Post* columnist David Broder called me a pragmatist in an organization whose activist base is full of uncompromising liberals. I was still the liberal who had lost a U.S. Senate race standing on principle, but now I had an additional responsibility of trying to get women fully represented in public office. One of the lessons we were learning from the 103rd Congress was that we needed everyone, Republicans and Democrats alike. Even a "year of the woman" had given us far too few supportive women of both parties.

We needed more candidates, ones we could endorse and ones we could persuade to our viewpoint. We needed to be broadening and inclusive. Women who sometimes wavered on issues we cared about might change when women were in large enough numbers to give them security. We didn't have to endorse them; but we didn't need to publicly denounce them either.

Numbers make a difference. We lost reform because there were too few of us. We needed more women to run for office. That fall, the Caucus released a study comparing the success of men and women candidates. It stirred up some controversy. It compared 50,563 male and female candidates for state and federal office between 1972 and 1993 and found that the success rates were virtually identical at every level of office.[19] It suggested that the main reason for the common perception that women have a tougher time winning elections than men is that women more often have run as challengers when men have been incumbents. When male and female incumbents were separately compared, or male and female challengers, or male and female open-seat candidates, women won as high a percentage of their races in each category as men did.

That doesn't mean that sex isn't a factor. Voters may view women's strengths and weaknesses differently; women candidates may face different obstacles and require different strategies, or they may need to turn to different people and resources. The bottom line, however, is that women can win as often as men. Women are winners. That's an important message to end an expectation of failure that discourages many women from running.

So we had two messages about difference. Women make a positive difference once they are elected to office, but we need to get rid of a negative difference caused by having too few women candidates. We needed to inspire more women to run. Just before the election, there was a brief reprise of the Hill–Thomas controversy prompted by a new book whose authors suggested that Clarence Thomas lied under oath. I hoped it might help, and I found myself and program co-host Pat Buchanan in a typical shouting match on CNN's *Crossfire*—me deploring that Thomas lied his way onto the Court and Buchanan claiming it was all hearsay. Unfortunately, there was little public response; there wouldn't be another hot-button issue in 1994.

The year 1992 had been great for progressive Democratic women. When the results came in, it was clear that 1994 was a great year for very conservative Republicans, including a few women. The women's joint press conference after the election was difficult. Ellen Malcolm, whose EMILY's List supports only pro-choice Democrats, was furious because we included a spokesperson from the WISH List, the pro-choice Republican fund, but there was no way to hide the truth of the Republican sweep, including the fact that none of the Democratic women candidates for governor had won. The only good news was that Congresswoman Snowe had won her race for the Senate and that there were five new pro-choice members in the House, one Republican and four Democrats.

Inside, I was grieving. A half dozen of our freshman reformers, the ones with marginal districts, had been swept away, including most of the stars of their own campaign video: Shepherd, English, Cantwell, Schenk, as well as Margolies-Mezvinsky. Shepherd and English had led efforts on campaign finance reform and congressional reorganization; Margolies-Mezvinsky cast the deciding vote that carried the Clinton budget package, knowing the tax increase might spell her doom. That budget package was credited later with helping launch the nation's long economic boom. By that time, these women were gone. Sometimes making a difference has a stiff price.

The actual number of women in Congress remained the same, but six of the new women were fervent ideologues in pursuit of a hostile agenda. Among them were Helen Chenoweth of Idaho, aggressively pro-life and a supporter of an antigay rights initiative; Barbara Cubin of Wyoming, who had led a pro-life initiative; Sue Myrick of North Carolina, who described herself as a "champion of religious values"; and Enid Greene Waldholtz, another ultraconservative who would, however, soon run into legal problems. They would be trying to make a difference in a different direction.

The results in state legislatures were very similar. Women would continue to comprise roughly 21 percent of legislators (1,533 women), with an increase in very conservative Republicans. The best I could say to the press was that we had held our own in numbers from 1992 and that women had won a record eighty-six statewide constitutional offices, including nineteen lieutenant governor positions.

When Congress convened, new Speaker Gingrich stripped support and recognition from all special Caucuses, including the Congressional Caucus for Women's Issues, leaving the women without staff to put together a common agenda on economic and health issues as they had in the past. On the other hand, he did bend seniority to help some women into leadership positions. He said he had learned from the women in his family "that nondiscrimination is not the same as a level playing field. Nondiscrimination fairly well guarantees that white males will win, just because of the whole balance of the system."[20]

The balance certainly wouldn't be helped by the fact that fewer women had run for state legislative seats in 1994 than in the previous cycle, for the first time in more than ten years. Was this an aberration—or an ominous turning point in women's participation in politics? We had hoped to be building on the strong record of the women of the 103rd. Instead, it appeared that something had happened to the momentum that had brought women so much progress during the past two decades.

It wasn't a failure of the women who had run; it was a failure of women who did not try.

15

Great Expectations

I had quit college after two years,
but I went back and graduated with
honors. This was done in the evenings,
and I worked in the day. . . . I am now a
professional. I am finally truly appreciated! But
more importantly, I am doing what I really want to do.

—Anonymous contributor to women's Web site, 1998

It was frustrating that the number of women running for office was so small when women's economic expectations seemed to be so great. As we reached the mid-1990s, evidence of women's progress was astounding. Women's earnings were now 72 percent of what men earned, and heading up. The old 59¢ button that we sported as late as 1981 was forgotten. We no longer attended rallies complaining about all the injustices against women. There were great expectations.

Young women were no longer looking for a job to supplement marriage, as we had done in the 1950s and 1960s; they were looking for lifetime occupations with prospects for high income and status. Since the mid-1980s, women had been awarded more bachelor of arts degrees than men, and now they were earning 55 percent of master's degrees as well. They also were earning 39 percent of doctorates, 39 percent of the MD's, and 43 percent of the law degrees. That compared to 14, 8, and 5 percent, respectively, twenty years before.[1]

Yet thoughtful surveys also revealed frustration and distress. In 1994, the Women's Bureau of the Department of Labor developed a report called *Working Women Count* that combined the results of a scientific survey with those of a widely distributed questionnaire that was completed by a quarter of a million women. In responding to the survey, fully 79 percent said they either "love" or "like" their jobs overall. There was also a strong consensus among respondents that there is something wrong that needs to be fixed in the way women are treated in the workplace and in the existing support for balancing work and family obligations, particularly in the area of high-quality child care.[2]

The report reflected the complications in women's lives. As the number of working women doubled to 60 million from the 30 million it had been in 1970, nearly 60 percent of women over age sixteen were in the labor force, including three times as many wives as in the past. One consequence was that a sizeable 58.7 percent of women in the labor force had children under age three in 1995, compared to 34.1 percent in 1975.[3] There were 10.3 million children under five whose mothers were employed, and it appeared that the numbers and percentages would continue to increase through the end of the century.

These women made it very clear to every interviewer that they were in the workplace to stay: Two-thirds were working full-time, contributing a significant 40 percent to family income. Most said they wanted to work but they found it very difficult to balance their multiple roles; at the least, they felt they deserved respect and fair treatment. A thirty-four-year-old manager from Georgia wrote the Women's Bureau: "Being a working woman is like having two full-time jobs. We're expected to be perfect in both career and taking care of the home, but without adequate compensation for either." And a forty-two-year-old mother of three from Pennsylvania said: "It's a never-ending workload. Most women have 'jobs' not careers, because of family needs. More flex-time and job sharing is needed."[4]

Women had changed their status and broadened their responsibilities, but society had not changed to accommodate their needs. Headlines told the story: "For Child Care, Mom Is Home Alone," "Family Day Care Barely Adequate," "Child Care Crunch Puts Parents Between the Kids and the Boss," "Should Corporate America Be in the Baby-sitting Business?"[5] "Child care is a disgrace in this country," wrote an Oregon mother. "On the one hand, it's too expensive for many women considering their salaries; on the other hand, it does not provide the child care provider a decent wage. Locating good child care is a nightmare."[6]

Neither their employers nor public policy adequately recognized or supported these family responsibilities. Only a few companies seemed to understand that providing family-related benefits, or more flexible hours, or home-work options would pay off in a more stable, productive workforce; many male legislators seemed stuck in the 1950s, believing that women don't have to work, and if they choose to do so, they should bear the consequences. A thirty-one-year-old sales worker, married with one child, told the Women's Bureau this: "You have to be better than any males in your job. You have to juggle family and work and still do better just to prove you are a career person and a mother. It puts a lot of stress in your life."[7]

There is also the issue of the kinds of jobs women hold. The fact that nearly 30 percent of women in the mid-1990s were in management positions was definite progress, but the vast majority, 59 percent, remained in traditionally female jobs: clerical, sales, and service positions that paid relatively little. As for benefits, 43 percent of women who worked part-time and 34 percent of those over fifty-five lacked health insurance. The percentage for the general population in 1994 was 18 percent. That is a shocking discrepancy.

The basic perception of women's status in society was at issue. A biomedical technician told the Women's Bureau that she worked as many hours with just as much dedication as male peers, yet she often felt "overlooked for advancement, travel, etc., because I am perceived by management *first* as a 'mom' who shouldn't leave her family." In other words, why offer opportunities to someone whose primary identification is related to child care? One feminist theorist has noted that the term *working mother* is used to lock women into a social structure where they always are perceived first as a mother rather than as a worker.[8] Men rarely are described as "working fathers."

All these concerns mean that women's progress carries a conspicuous asterisk: You'd better be middle class and educated to do well financially, and even then, you may have to choose between job and family. When a British au pair was convicted in the death of an infant in Massachusetts, the mother was criticized for not being at home caring for her child even though she worked only part-time as a doctor and came home at lunchtime. *Family* was being redefined in the 1990s, including how child care would be divided between two-income couples.

This isn't just a woman's problem. Men also are looking for ways to balance the pressures of work and family. Couples report meeting in parking lots to hand off children between job shifts. Men understand that they also suffer when their wives experience discrimination on the job or are denied flexibility to take care of sick children. Although many fathers are willing to play a bigger role, society still places primary responsibility on mom, and mothers anguish over the difficult choices in their personal lives.

The survey showed that some working women adjusted their expectations and have begun to stay home. "We are rejecting the male sixty-hour workweek to start our own businesses at home, work part-time, or put careers on hold while our kids are young," commented Caroline Sorensen Dixon, founder of Lawyers at Home. Two other new groups supporting the same decision were called Mothers at Home and Mothers' Home Business Network.[9] They were praised by organizations pushing family values that blamed most of society's ills on the increasing number of working women whom they accused of caring more for their careers than their children. In reality, most women were exploring how they could care for both simultaneously, or at sequenced intervals.

Working mothers surveyed in a Gallup poll sponsored by *Working Mother* magazine didn't agree that they were neglecting family. Eight out of ten said they were satisfied with how well they were doing as mothers and with how well their children were doing.[10] "The stimulation of getting out of the house, the sense of accomplishment . . . is giving women a better sense of themselves," said Eileen Shiff, head of *USA Today*'s Parenting Panel. She warned, however, that many child care situations were substandard, a particular problem to the 37 million women working for lower wages as clerks, nurses' aides, secretaries, and maids. Their wages were essential for family survival, which meant that they couldn't quit, but the options for child care at their income level often were poor.

The concerns of working families add up to a political agenda and underscores the urgency of helping women make a connection between their vital concerns and who makes public policy decisions. Outnumbered women politicians have been trying to address the issues for years with limited success. Child care long had been a priority of women in state legislatures, and the Congressional Caucus for Women's Issues has been pushing since its founding to increase availability of high-quality child care, family and medical leave, and improved health care and pensions for women. There was a burst of activity in the 103rd Congress, but progress since had slowed. So had election of women advocates to public office. That is a dangerous combination.

In 1994, for the first time since statistics were recorded in the 1970s, the percentage of women in state legislatures didn't increase with the election. That was a special challenge for us in the NWPC because we had made recruiting, training, and supporting women for office our priority mission, particularly at the state and local levels. We didn't retain staff to lobby Congress or research policy issues; we believed our assignment was to impact public decisions by getting more qualified women to run, and win. And a primary source for candidates at the federal and state levels was women in the legislature.

The question for us at the end of 1994 was this: What can we do to restart the flow into the political pipeline and find candidates who can help us achieve our expectations?

We decided to launch a special president's recruitment drive that would reach down into local communities all over the country: twenty-four cities in eighteen states in less than six months. Beginning in February 1995, the drive would carry me from New York and New Jersey to Florida and Georgia, from Minnesota and Kansas to California and Arizona, from Washington State with the highest percentage of women in its legislature at nearly 40 percent, to Alabama, with the lowest at less than 4 percent. There were speeches, media interviews, local Caucus meetings, and candidate counseling. The message was simple: "Women need a wake-up call!" It was energizing, exhausting, and very educational—for me.

It also was just like the old Senate campaign days; I hammered a single theme over and over. Progress isn't inevitable. "If you want to have power over your life, then you must make sure that more women have power to make public policy." And then looking each one in the eye: "You too can be a candidate. . . . Have great expectations."

June 13 was a typical day. There were six television interviews in Huntsville and Birmingham, Alabama, five radio interviews, three in-depth newspaper interviews that also produced photo spreads, two speeches at well-attended public meetings, and several one-on-one discussions with potential candidates. The twelve-hour day ended with my nodding over a dinner for local political women.

In every state I pointed out the similarities between the percentage of women who run for office and the number who eventually are elected. In Alabama, women were 7 percent of general election nominees in the state from 1986 to 1994 and were also 7 percent of those elected over that same period. In the state of Washington, women were 30.8 percent of the general election candidates in those years and 31 percent of the legislators elected over that time period. You can't win if you don't run.

Of course women in Alabama reminded me that there was much less support for women in a state with southern traditions and tightly held political machinery than there was in the open, pioneer climate of a western state like Washington. That certainly was true: Every state has its special challenges, but the statistical evidence remained. On average, there was an amazing match between the numbers who run and those holding office. Women were 20-plus percent of all legislative general election candidates in the country and about 21 percent of those holding office.

When women run, women win. You can't get to 50 percent with only 8, or 14, or 20 percent of the candidates. In no state were enough women running.

As a followup to our "women are winners" survey the year before, the NWPC commissioned a national study on attitudes toward public office. It showed that women were only half as likely as men to even consider running for office. Only 8 percent of women said they wanted to run—compared to 18 percent of men. The reasons for the limited interest were familiar: Both men and women expressed concerns about raising money, taking time from personal life, and the negative tone of campaigning. However, women more than men also said they wanted training and mentoring.[11] Once again, there was evidence that women felt less confident about challenging the system. Too many were accepting the kind of gender perception reported by working women in the Women's Bureau study, a perception that women had less capacity.

Our survey told us something else—that 70 percent of the voters still thought that it's tougher for a woman to get elected and, astonishingly, that the percentage believing this is higher among women.[12] Clearly women were beginning with a handicap if they felt their chances were less before they even started. They could hardly help meet the expectations of others when they had lesser expectations for themselves. We had shown in our earlier, exhaustive study that women's success rates actually equaled men's; but false belief can obscure facts, and perception can become reality.

I knew very well that not all women were in a position to run for office because of time availability, finances, qualifications, or the conditions in their life. After all, many had to focus on survival first. On the other hand, it was important not to create a stereotype of the ideal women candidate. Fannie Lou Hamer was a black Mississippi sharecropper with minimum education who gained confidence to speak for her people and had the courage to run for high public office. There are single welfare mothers with limited education who rise out of hopelessness to sit on community boards to make decisions for their neighborhoods. They stop being passive clients and begin using their own resources to help others.

We have no idea who might be ready to move up the political pipeline. Too many Americans, including far too many women, have simply become passive clients of a professional political system instead of empowering themselves to run democracy themselves. Women told the Women's Bureau they needed different policies in the workplace and more support for their double roles in life, including affordable, high-quality child care. That's a worthwhile agenda. If enough women run, and win, they're more likely to achieve it.

Traveling the country to encourage participation, moving once again among women who were focused on local problems, was energizing after spending so much time in Washington. It made me want to get back to grassroots and work on some local campaigns. Nearly four years in the nation's capital had confirmed for me that the dominating obsessions there were access and status. Who talks to whom? Whose title is the most important? It was a company town, filled with lobbyists and advocacy groups whose job it was to influence the main players and get their message out through media that itself had become part of the story. The primary business in the company town is government, but the primary concern is money—who has it, who can get it.

I liked being at the center of events, but there was a danger of confusing one's own importance with the power of the capitol itself. We had come to D.C. with a mission: to rebuild the NWPC in order to help women into positions of power; and that's how we should be judged. The recruitment drive was the final piece in a rebuilding effort that had begun four years earlier when Jody and I walked into the national office for the first time. Our great expectations might have seemed unrealistic, but just as in election campaigns, if you have a strategy and work hard, you may also get lucky. We certainly were.

Active membership had nearly doubled to 40,000; fund-raising was up 50 percent; staff had increased from eight to fifteen. We had trained 1,200 women in 1993 and increased that to 2,500 in 1994, plus we had provided special training for young women to be campaign workers. Now we set an ambitious goal of forty regional training workshops for 1995. As for candidate support, in the 1993–1994 election cycle, we provided 147 endorsed candidates with half a million dollars in PAC money we had raised through direct-mail solicitation and special events.

It would have been more satisfying if we also had succeeded in getting the Caucus reorganized for better functioning. Unfortunately, the existing leadership resisted reform. A few even seemed to resent the NWPC's success, perhaps because it made them feel less necessary. Administrative committee meetings often were unpleasant, with needless wrangling over things like the proper wording of a statement, or proposals to spend extra money while declining to help raise it. Thankfully, meetings were only four times a year.

In between, it had been a joy coming to the office every day. Jody had assembled a wonderful staff of young women who made up with enthusiasm for what they originally lacked in specific skills, and they gradually became highly effective professionals. I also had grown to know and respect women in D.C. whose lives centered on day-by-day advocacy for women. These had been good years to be in Washington. Despite political ups and downs, the Clinton White House was supportive of women, and we had been able to work together on a worthwhile agenda. There were opportunities to attend special receptions and meetings with celebrities, and the Caucus had given me a national platform to speak out for political women. I was very grateful.

But I was ready to go home. Four years of commuting was a lot, and two terms at anything was enough, on the city council, in the state senate, and now, at the NWPC. The maxim was: Don't hang on to power too long; make room for fresh ideas. The Caucus was in excellent shape to be turned over to new leadership, with several hundred thousand dollars in unexpended cash available after the NWPC convention in August to give the next Caucus president a good start. There was a caveat, however. The cash cushion would disappear in a hurry without aggressive fund-raising and good management.

Maintaining an activist women's organization wasn't easy as we neared the end of the century. Other women's groups shared the problem of building a financial base; grassroots members want strong national organizations, but they want to keep dues too low to pay for them. We filled the gap with special fund-raising events each year, a "Good Guys" dinner honoring men who support women and an EMMA's event (Exceptional Media Merit Awards) to recognize outstanding media coverage of women, but like other organizations, we found ourselves increasingly financed from donations, grants, and large gifts from unions and corporations.

Corporations were the big financial winners from the government policies of the 1980s and 1990s. They had the money. Corporate names were showing up everywhere in America where something cost big bucks: sports stadiums, university buildings, cultural institutions, parks. They all were becoming commercial billboards for sponsors, but what were the alternatives? There was little interest in the 1990s in a thoughtful review of public priorities.

It seemed foolish not to get our share. A sampling of corporate sponsors for our 1993 convention included Ortho Pharmaceutical, American Express, Avon Products, Honda North America, Inc., Anheuser-Busch, McDonnell Douglas Corporation, Sara Lee, Philip Morris Companies, and Wyeth-Ayerst Laboratories. Their executives liked us, but their motive had to be bolstering the company image and gaining access to powerful women as customers and allies. We were basically selling access.

This was not what our founders had envisioned, but it ensured that our mission continued. The challenge was finding a win-win approach that satisfied the sponsor while not compromising our programs. For example, a pharmaceutical company selling hormone products might want to sponsor a panel on health issues affecting older women. That was an important topic for our members, as long as we controlled the speakers.

It was a different world than our founders had faced, one that none of the current candidates for NWPC president seemed to understand. Our success had created complacency. As I feared when the new officers were elected at the convention, the organization lost direction and strong management. Without a disciplined plan to raise funds and maintain programs; the reserves were gone within a year, and so was almost everything we had built.

Even guessing what might happen, I knew in 1995 that it was time to leave. My sixty-eighth birthday was observed shortly before the NWPC convention. Despite the high numbers, there still was a younger woman inside who was looking for new challenges. Perhaps I would have stayed in Washington if there had been a top administration position waiting, but despite all the involvement in presidential appointments, that never had been a goal. I had never asked nor been asked, and I was very aware that the competition for major positions required a serious campaign.

Instead, I was pleased to be named by the president to something I did seek, something that would allow me to keep a presence in the center of power while not actually remaining in Washington: It was a presidential appointment to the board of directors of Freddie Mac, a private, stockholder-owned corporation that has provided funding for one in six homes in America. Like Fannie Mae, Freddie Mac originally was chartered by Congress to create a continuous flow of mortgage funds, thus encouraging more home ownership. It was a prized appointment because it gave entrée to a private corporation, but I wanted it because of a long-standing interest in affordable housing. The close working relationship on appointments with the White

House Office of Personnel certainly helped. This time, the "qualified woman" who got an appointment was me.

As I prepared to leave town, the 1996 election still was a year away. I had no idea what to expect from the intensive candidate recruitment effort of the past few months. The answer would have to wait until after November 1996. At that point, postelection analysis showed that a record number of women had run for the U.S. House, with a net increase of three new members. There also were sixty more women in state legislatures around the country, for a tiny boost, and nearly a 2 percent jump in the number of women mayors of large cities. I hoped we had helped.

As for Alabama, it still ranked last among state legislatures in percentage of women, but at least there were now six women in the legislature, instead of five.

The final days in office at the NWPC were all about expectations, great and small. It occurred to me that this would be the first time in twenty years that I wouldn't have a business office outside the home or a staff to keep my schedule and files straight. Would Jim expect me to be a happy cook preparing dinner every night? I wanted more time for family, tennis, and music—but what else? Teaching a class at the university was worth exploring, an opportunity to pass something on to another generation of men and women and to learn from them in return. There also was a possible radio show, and time for writing and giving speeches. It was energizing just thinking about all the options.

The announcement of my "retirement" was followed with the usual laudatory editorial remarks, despite the number of previous farewells the writers had offered as I left previous public positions. "Mrs. Woods' political biography is almost a textbook of the victories and defeats that women in politics have faced," *The St. Louis Post-Dispatch* editorialized. "Women can take a lesson. . . . Losing an election doesn't defeat a strong woman." *The Kansas City Star* added: "She may have contributed more to changing the political contour of the country than many of the noisy bomb-throwers who now stalk the halls of Congress. . . . Woods has discovered, encouraged, coaxed—maybe even browbeaten at times, given her take-no-prisoners personality—women candidates, helping contribute to the record number of women in office."

Those comments could be taken with a grain of salt, but I really wanted to believe *The Chicago Tribune*: "It is ironic that, as

NWPC president, she probably has made far more of a difference than she would have as a senator."

I didn't want to look backward with regrets, even if my greatest expectations had to be for others.

I was saying my farewells at our 1995 convention in Nashville when a familiar figure came walking down the ballroom aisle. It was Lela, then nine years old, and the oldest of my three granddaughters. Her father Andy had driven her several hundred miles from St. Louis to surprise me. She took the stage with perfect poise. I thought my reward was a hug. There was more. Here is an excerpt from what Lela said:

> My grandmother is a great role model for my sister and me. She
> has shown me that I can achieve anything if I put my mind to
> it. And what I want to become is very special. I want to become
> the first woman president of the United States of America. . . .

There's no way to predict the endurance of youthful dreams, but I remembered the story about Vice President Gore, President Clinton, and the inspiration of President John Kennedy. I remembered that my only role models had been Eleanor Roosevelt and my mother. Now I was Lela's.

Two year's later, Lela was elected president of the Student Council of Flynn Park Elementary School in University City, Missouri.

I was there when she was honored.

16

The Way We Were

Life is either a daring adventure or nothing.

—**Helen Keller**

Why are some women risk takers? Why do some become leaders while others are content to play more supportive roles? Those are fascinating questions as we approach a new century when there will be extraordinary political opportunities—for those who take advantage of them.

An official census of the American population is taken every ten years. That will happen in the year 2000, and based on the results, political bodies all over the country will redraw boundaries for election districts, from the local to the congressional level. In some cases, whole districts will be wiped out and new ones created. In the same time frame, barring court intervention, term limits will go into effect in many states, forcing incumbents to retire or seek new positions. The combined impact should create more seats that are wide open, or so altered as to give newcomers better odds of winning; and as we know from history, candidates have a far better chance of victory where there is no incumbent.

We also know that busy women who are turned off by negative political behavior have been less inclined to get involved in politics, especially when they don't believe they have the knowledge to succeed in an unfamiliar world. Women want to feel confident that they know what they're doing before making a commitment. And many women still tend to defer when men preempt a position in a traditionally male field. Yet a quarter century ago many of us stepped up to power in far more hostile circumstances, with less support and information. What was the difference?

When I was the age of my younger grandchildren, our family lived in a modest two-story frame home in Cleveland Heights, Ohio, on a street with similar houses, with similar middle-class families that were similarly making do during the Depression years. There was a swing on the front porch and another in a screened sleeping area in the back where I would doze off in the summer to the sound of the chains creaking against the hooks in the ceiling. The backyard was just large enough for a very small vegetable garden, a cherry tree that I loved to climb, and a lavender lilac bush whose fragrance would fill the living room as I lay on the sofa by the open window listening to my sister practice the piano.

It was a very peaceful existence that might have led to a very conventional life as a young middle-class woman: socialization, education, brief employment, marriage, children. No one could have anticipated the immense upheaval of World War II and all the subsequent social changes that would draw some of us into public life. There was no way to prepare for what was to happen, just as there is no way to look ahead now into the twenty-first century to say with certainty what awaits our children and grandchildren, and to anticipate how they will respond to whatever challenges occur. There are so many factors that influence what we are and what we do with our lives: parents, education, work, friends, public events.

There is one absolute essential for the risk taker, and that is the confidence that comes from a feeling of self-worth. Shortly after returning to St. Louis, I had a flashback to the past while listening to my six-year-old granddaughter Reina scraping her bow on the strings of a quarter-size violin. I remembered at the age of six, standing in the early morning next to the laundry chute that adjoined our kitchen, practicing on a tiny violin. The laundry chute door was open so that the sound could carry upstairs to the bathroom where my father was shaving. Every few minutes, his voice boomed down the chute: "Oh that's a wonderful E string. Beautiful!"

Listening to Reina's painfully wavering notes, I realized what my father really had heard those mornings, even though he never let me know. His praise made me believe in myself, as my parents did in so many other ways. I wanted so much to please them. To those outside our family, my parents may have seemed quite ordinary, but they were heroic to me: Dad was a model of passionate commitment, and mom, the spirit of adventure.

My father came to this country at the age of eight from Hungary, part of an immigrant family that arrived one by one by one, each working until there was enough money to send back for the next. His job was selling newspapers. He was proud as a young boy to carry home pocketsful of nickels to his mother, although once in a while, he'd hide a nickel in his cheek so he could buy candy. He loved to tell us the story of the day he was shouting his "read all about it" pitch outside a church in Cleveland when a well-dressed gentleman approached and asked him please to be a little quieter. It was millionaire John D. Rockefeller, and he gave dad a dime.

He avidly pursued the American dream, attending high school at night so he could help support the family, and paying for his college education by tutoring students in English, teaching civics to factory workers, selling men's clothing, and operating a multigraph machine. There was an old-fashioned Shopping Arcade in Ann Arbor, Michigan, with a long tile floor that he had scrubbed to earn money. I thought about him every time I walked there years later as a college student whose tuition he had fully paid.

By that time, he had become a very successful advertising salesman and a wonderful public speaker who gave a special talk to civic groups called "My America." It expressed his fervent admiration for the land of opportunity that had given him so much; it always brought audiences to their feet. When I ran for U.S. Senate in 1982, his story became the heart of my stump speech. He had given me vision, a sense of purpose beyond the purely personal.

My mother was quite a different personality, very controlled emotionally but a great risk taker. She was a natural athlete who had risen to be ranked among the top women tennis players in the country at a time when women still wore black bloomers and midi-blouses at athletic events. When she married, she gave up any thought of a sports career, but beginning when my sister Elaine and I were quite young, she escaped the tedium of the household by driving us around the country on spring and summer vacations while dad stayed home at work.

It was pretty venturesome for a woman to travel alone with young children in pre-World War II days, when there weren't any fancy motels and auto tires often went flat. Mom wanted to explore everything: We experienced the exhausting burro ride down the Grand Canyon, floated in the Great Salt Lake, stood in respect at Concord Bridge, admired Mount Rushmore—which still lacked Teddy Roosevelt's jaunty features—went up the Rockies, across the deserts, and down Mammoth Cave. She shared with us her ability to deal with the unexpected, and she left us as young adults with a self-confidence that comes from coping in strange places.

Other women leaders have their own inspirational stories. Vicki Miles-LaGrange was raised in Oklahoma City by two schoolteacher parents, who always gave her hope for the future and confidence to face any "isms." When she was sixteen, she was elected to represent her mostly white school at the 1970 Oklahoma Girls State, sponsored by the American Legion, and she was thrilled when her name was announced as winner of the governorship for the whole state. Then she was told she could not represent Oklahoma because she was a "Negro." She packed to leave, but her parents reminded her that her peers had elected her, and they insisted she attend the closing ceremony, including congratulating the new victor. They helped her turn rage into understanding of prejudice and to be inspired to bring about change.[1] Years later, she became the first African-American woman in the Oklahoma state senate, the first woman U.S. attorney in Oklahoma, and a U.S. district judge, the first African-American federal judge in the six states that make up the Tenth Circuit.

I wanted to communicate to new audiences what earlier leaders had learned, what my parents had communicated to me about courage and caring, the elements of risk taking, and what I had learned in thirty years of political give and take.

An idea for reaching younger women emerged in November 1995 at a forum for women state legislators held by the Center for the American Woman and Politics (CAWP). It was the fourth such conference that had been held over the years with good attendance. They seemed to provide just the right environment for political women to exchange ideas, partly because of the sponsorship but also because of the setting, a historic old resort, the Hotel Del Coronado near San Diego, with its Victorian architecture, flowering gardens, and seductive sandy beaches. After the years heading the NWPC, I looked forward to going there again that fall as a kind of reunion.

Women elected officials had sought one another out from earliest days to boost their expertise and their morale. No matter what the law said about equality, we knew that we were isolated inside those male institutions and needed all the help we could get. However, except for Caucuses inside larger organizations, there really wasn't a major gathering of women elected officials until 1983 when the CAWP held its first national meeting at the Coronado, drawing 350 women legislators from forty-six states, the largest number of elected women ever assembled in one place.

The forum was a great success, with good speakers and workshops and lots of sharing among the participants. The CAWP announced it would hold another conference in 1987, eventually scheduling them every four years. In 1983, I had attended as a state senator, in 1987, as lieutenant governor, in 1991, as president of the NWPC, and now in 1995, as a retired woman leader in search of a mission. It would be a wonderful opportunity to review how far women politicians had come.

Looking back, the first conference in 1983 had set a standard, perhaps because it was the first but also because of a particularly satisfying bipartisan atmosphere. All of us had to deal with so much political gamesmanship back in our home legislatures; at the Coronado we were able to talk together across party lines on all sorts of topics, from the feminization of poverty to pay equity for women state employees. We assumed that those who came to the conference were advocates for women. They were attracted by respect for the CAWP, which had been founded at Rutgers in 1971, and for its director, Ruth Mandel, who had pioneered serious academic study of elected women.

There was a spirit of camaraderie even when there were differences on specific policies. Democrats were in the majority, reflecting their greater numbers in legislatures across the nation, and the Republicans who attended were moderates, so we may have been fooling ourselves into believing there was more agreement than existed. But I remember the encouragement from Republicans as well as Democrats in 1983 for my upcoming race for lieutenant governor, just as I encouraged others to try for higher office in their states. We supported one another because we knew there still weren't very many of us.

On the final day of the conference, we put partisan differences behind us, in the words of one reporter,[2] and challenged ourselves to double the number of women in every legislature by 1987. Surely it was realistic, I said, to boost the current 15 percent of women in legislatures to at least 25 percent in four years![3]

The focus in the second conference in 1987 shifted from getting elected to achieving leadership positions. There were forty-five women holding statewide constitutional offices that year, 13.9 percent of the total, and about the same percentage serving as chairs of legislative committees. Former Congresswoman Shirley Chisholm was the featured speaker, and she told participants that moving up would take political pragmatism as well as ambition. Women were left out when they didn't learn the way things *really* worked. It was clear that political pragmatism meant partisanship, but we were confident that we could advance on separate party paths and still work together as women.

By 1991, the theme was women reshaping the public agenda; women now were more than 19 percent of state legislators and were approaching critical mass in a few states. There were major sessions at this third conference on health, violence, and sexual harassment. This was the conference where Anita Hill's appearance sparked an emotional outburst that pulled us all together and sent participants home in an upbeat mood. Even Ruth Mandel, who was notorious for her careful comments, seemed excited, and of course 1992 would turn out to be the "year of the woman," with record numbers of women elected to legislatures.

The feeling was quite different when I traveled out to San Diego in 1995. Present and past legislators were glad to see one another, but instead of enthusiasm, there was a kind of malaise. Fewer Republicans were there, partly because many moderates who normally came had been replaced with social ideologues who rejected the idea of dialogue, and partly because party leaders were discouraging women from working together across party lines. The 1994 elections had punctured bipartisanship in state legislatures as well as Congress. Fundamentalism was on the rise. The women's agenda was under attack.

Forum workshops at the Coronado had titles like "Fighting for Our Lives—Responding to AntiWoman Policy Initiatives" and "Getting Beyond the Negative" on countering negative campaign attacks. For the women who had been coming to these conferences for a dozen years, the current climate was discouraging. The CAWP based its program on the assumption that there always would be more binding us together than keeping us apart, but the increasingly nasty tone that everyone reported from all across the country was pushing in the opposite direction. After all these years of putting together the votes on issues like child care, pay equity, reproductive health services, and mental health, it didn't seem right to have our efforts drowned in bitter partisanship.

There was one very hopeful note, however, in the participation of a large number of college interns, part of a CAWP initiative to interest young women in public service. It was exactly the kind of effort I'd been looking for, and before we left San Diego, there was a discussion with the CAWP about helping us set up a similar program in the Midwest.

As it happened, Missouri women attending the conference were holding their own grievance sessions. They were furious because Sheila Lumpe, a state representative who had risen to head the Budget Committee in the Missouri House because of her ability and even-handed leadership had just been defeated in a race for Speaker by a single vote in the Democratic Caucus. Male legislators who should have supported her, including the urban and labor votes, weren't willing to give the Speaker's power to a woman. It was clear they thought she might not play their games. For Democratic women who had been loyally supporting male leaders, it was the final straw.

Listening, I wondered how many times I had sat in rooms like this over the years as women bemoaned their powerlessness. How many times had we talked about promises broken? How many times had women failed to get a commitment for their own agenda before obligingly delivering votes to others? It was time for another wake-up call. Women should stop complaining and take some action. "We're attending a conference celebrating women's political muscle—we need to start using it."

Back in Missouri, political women met to devise a strategy to negotiate from strength. Women and the pro-choice community had played a pivotal role in electing the current Democratic governor, Mel Carnahan. He was proving very popular, but the women in the room felt communication had been disappointing and appointments of women had lagged. The governor was up for reelection the next November, in 1996. We sat down with him for a frank and friendly discussion, outlining specific concerns about participation by women in his administration. We also did something else. For the first time as a group of women, we raised a record amount of money in large donations for his campaign. If you can't change the system, then learn to work it.

After the election, the Institute for Women in Public Life was established at the University of Missouri–St. Louis with combined pledges from the university, state government, and private funds. Its first major initiative was a one-week residential program for midwestern college women cosponsored by the CAWP. This later was built into the annual Leadership Academy for Missouri college women. These young women were the right audience; they declared themselves inspired as they learned everything from how to shake hands effectively to debating the pros and cons of an Equal Rights Amendment most of them had never heard of before. By the end of a week, their interest in public service needed only the right spark to turn into action.

Other institute projects would include Pipeline to Politics training workshops to prepare candidates and campaign workers for local and state races and an ongoing appointments project to help move qualified women into public positions, particularly state boards and commissions. The institute worked closely with the governor's office; the governor was a speaker in November 1998 when the institute was named in honor of the late Sue Shear, the Caucus's first election victor in 1972.

In the fall of 1996, I took a second step, starting a class at the University of Missouri–St. Louis called "Risk Takers Who Changed History—The Modern Women's Movement." The brochure blurbed that it would "develop broad social and political themes by telling the stories of women who took leaps that moved events," but it really was designed to communicate to women outside the political arena the themes of empowerment that had been so important in my political life.

There was marvelous diversity in the class, from teenage freshmen to civic leaders in their fifties, from businesswomen to homemakers. Enrollment deliberately was limited in number, and all but one of the twenty-five students were women; they were married, divorced, single, single mothers, and single mothers-to-be. Most were nervous about the word "feminist," and most were looking for some wisdom to apply to their own lives. Everyone was balancing multiple roles. I was impressed by their courage.

I told them the story of Helen Keller, who as a deaf and blind child, with the aid of a determined teacher, broke through the boundaries others tried to set for her and unleashed her own tremendous human potential. She not only learned to speak and write, but she became an inspirational leader, far exceeding anyone's expectations. Too many women still allow themselves to be limited by others' perceptions of them instead of having confidence in their own abilities.

I also told them my story, and they reminded me that not every woman had the advantage of parents who encouraged her risk taking or the advantage of wide travel and a comfortable middle-class life. How could they become risk takers?

My previous four years had been spent motivating women to run for office; now I needed to inspire women whose daily decisions were equally important even if not in the public sector: a teacher struggling with aggressive teenagers; a divorcee rebuilding her life after being abandoned in middle age; a nurse specializing in the care of AIDS patients; a Catholic sister doing social work with the indigent; young liberal arts students searching for a goal; and a whole range of others: businesswomen; computer, real estate and marketing specialists; and a religious leader in the abortion rights movement.

Risk taking is based on self-confidence and commitment to a goal. The daredevil stunt driver first establishes the ability to drive the car. Perhaps it was becoming editor of the college paper, of perhaps becoming expert on property tax relief for the elderly that gave me confidence to compete in the political system. The stunt driver wants to stretch the limits for jumping over cars. I wanted to achieve a more just and open society. You need both the vision and the belief in yourself to reach beyond normal boundaries of comfort and safety. But then it's the adventurers who venture forth to explore the unknown who move us forward, not those who stay crouched in the cave.

The "Risk Taker" class at UM–St. Louis was selected by students interested in the topic—or else hoping that it would be a snap course. Whatever the reason for being there, the learning process we went through gave me a lot of hope. We sat facing one another in a U shape that encouraged discussion; we looked at the grievances of the past but didn't linger there. We examined how media shapes women's perceptions of themselves; the myths surrounding women's voting patterns; the role of women's organizations in nurturing leadership; the emerging voices of women around the world; and the realities of our own lives.

After tracing women's progress from the 1950s, a single mother observed: "It is important to have women in positions of power, whether in public office or in the private economy. . . . As long as women 'push the envelope,' we can only continue to be amazed to see how much we as humans can attain—as scientists, as politicians, as humanists, and more!"

One young woman described how her mother had been forced to leave a job when she became pregnant; now a sister who was a middle manager in the same company had been granted pregnancy leave and went right back to work. "You can be whatever you want to be." A teenager was almost defiant in announcing that she was pregnant and planning to have her baby alone. "I am not sure I want to get married so young" when there are other things to do in life.

But another student said: "I don't think that women are going to have a level playing field until equal sharing of family responsibilities becomes a cultural norm for men and women." There was a lot of head nodding: "Time and energy can easily be exhausted meeting the needs of work and family. Many women simply cannot afford to be in public office."

They had strong feelings pro and con about women giving up work to stay home with children during early years, but their basic assumptions were worlds away from the framing of this debate in the 1950s and 1960s. This was an urban university, not Smith or Wellesley. The majority here were working mothers who also were going to school. That's a lot to manage. They had made tough decisions to put education first in order to increase their value as human beings, separate from any role as wife and mother. When they said they wanted to make something of their lives, they understood the cost.

It was the older women in the class who felt the most victimized by the past and most liberated now that they were building new lives. There were a number of reentry students in their thirties and forties who were coming back to school to finish education that had been cut off because it hadn't been a priority or affordable in earlier years. Wonderful now to be getting a college education, they said, to prepare for a meaningful future, to take control of one's own life. They joined militant younger voices in insisting that women need laws to protect them from harassment, from unfair working conditions, and from exploitation in marriage and divorce, and to assure access to family planning and abortion services.

I was deeply moved by their final papers. One wrote: "A lesson that the Risktakers class taught from the first day that the other classes I have taken failed to teach was to take responsibility for our own life and the society we live in." Another: "Our history shows what women can be and do. . . . I have learned that as a strong-willed woman, I am definitely not alone, and that is a wonderful feeling."

"If we don't take control of our own lives, somebody else will," another commented. "It is not up to men to break the glass ceiling. To pretend that all we are is victims is to perpetuate the myth that women can't fend for themselves; that we need somebody to figure for us, which is exactly the right that women have been asking for all along." "We've had to work much harder than men to prove we are capable of performing the task . . . whatever it may be. We are strong, compassionate, bright, innovative, and much more open-minded than men. Our analytical powers are superb, and diplomatically, I think we surpass men. It is an exciting time to be a woman. We all need role models; we all need words of encouragement, a sense of empowerment."

And finally: "When I ask my six-year-old sister what she will be when she grows up, I will be sure to let her know that she can do it. When I decide I want to do something, I will do it. . . . I will not settle. I will not quit. I will live as an example for others."

The women who shaped the contemporary women's movement in America were products of the New Deal and the optimistic president who believed that any problem could be solved
by government and ordinary people working together. In his
fourth inaugural speech, on January 11, 1944, not long before
his death, Franklin Delano Roosevelt spelled out an economic bill
of rights for every American, including a decent home, a good
education, adequate medical care, and the right to earn enough
to support a family. We believed it could happen, just as we
believed that we could win a war fought simultaneously on two
sides of the globe. Even though our generation had no role models for women leaders, we were sure that we could make the system work for us, or change it. We had inherited an optimistic
faith in progress.

Even many of the most militant civil rights and antiwar
activists of the 1960s and 1970s gradually shifted to public service
as a way of reaching their goals, recognizing the value of holding
power within the system as decision makers—leaders like
Congresswomen Patsy Mink of Hawaii and Maxine Waters of
California, Congressmen John Lewis of Georgia and William
(Bill) Clay of Missouri, District of Columbia Delegate Eleanor
Holmes Norton, and countless men and women at the state and
local levels. The kinds of obstacles they faced were more overwhelming, and their support systems often were different from
those of white, middle-class women from the Midwest, but the
determination to effect change was the same.

Does any of this passionate pragmatism exist among young
men and women today? The answer after a year of listening far
away from Washington was a cautious yes. There are many different "ways we were," just as there are different personalities
and different causes. Potential leaders could be anywhere, in an
inner-city ghetto, in a struggling rural community, in a working-
class suburb.

The challenge is how to nurture a willingness to lead in a
world mired in cynicism, racism, sexual myopia, apathy, bitterness, and complacency.

17

The Truth About Women and Power

It is time to unleash the full
capacity . . . of the women of the world.

—**U.S. Ambassador to the United Nations
Madeleine K. Albright, at Beijing, China, September 6, 1995**

For as long as any of us can remember—certainly back to the days when women began to vote—the big question has been whether there ever will be a woman president. In 1966, when Indira Ghandi became prime minister of India, writer Betty Friedan noted with frustration that the thought of a woman president in the United States was still so inconceivable that it seemed like a joke. Today we're in a new era. We've had a woman secretary of state and a woman attorney general. The question no longer is whether there will be a woman president but who she will be, and the precise date of her inauguration.

The problem is that it's the wrong question to be asking. In 1992, a national magazine asked Gloria Steinem to write an article to be called "Why I'm Not Running for President." In declining, she explained that she thought the presidency was chiefly a bully pulpit and that change had to come from below.[1] The focus on the exceptional heroine allows the majority of women to be bystanders; they can avoid personal responsibility for improving society while being groupies for someone at the top. Our history demonstrates that this approach won't work; leadership must start at the grassroots. Speculation on a woman president is good meat for media, but the most significant measure of women's progress isn't a woman president; it's further down the political food chain.

Unfortunately, few Americans pay attention to how many women are in local government or to what percentage of the state legislature is composed of women. But if we don't reach critical mass in state legislatures, it won't happen in Congress, and that means there will be very slim pickings to find a woman president. The prime candidates for president are governors and senators, and they tend to compete after experience in previous office. Five out of six of the new women elected to Congress in 1998 had previously served in state legislatures. As things are, a 1998 project promoting a woman in the White House had a tough time finding even one credible candidate who might have a realistic chance running for president in the year 2000; there should be dozens, as there are among men.

It's true that a woman president, no matter who she is, will be an important signal that women have achieved equal status, and it will encourage more discussion about women politicians, but as women learned in Great Britain, having Margaret Thatcher as prime minister did virtually nothing to remove barriers impeding other women's political and social progress. It took a Labor Party sweep in 1997 when Labor deliberately flooded local tickets with women candidates, to reverse years of exclusion. The number of Labor women in the House of Commons jumped from 63 to 101, pushing the overall percentage of women to 18.2 percent of total members. Stunned Tory members responded "like schoolboys," cupping their hands in front of their chests during a woman member's speech as if "they were weighing melons."[2] Margaret Thatcher never had threatened them so much.

It's popular to note that at least 20 other nations have had women prime ministers or presidents, but most were selected through the parliamentary system, and some of the most celebrated inherited power through family dynasties, such as Indira Ghandi, Benazir Bhutto, and Khaleda Zia, from India, Pakistan, and Bangladesh, respectively. Our system demands a different process of credentialing. We will have a woman president when a savvy politician with fire in her belly, and the ability to raise lots of money, has the stamina to undertake the exhausting national marathon we require to win party nomination and election.

In the meantime, as we approach the new millennium, the hard truth is that there are nowhere near enough women competing for public office. Some 75 percent of incumbents are men, and incumbents are hard to evict. Even with the possibilities of term limits and redistricting, women continue to run uphill because those in power are in a better position to manipulate events to block newcomers. There were 100 fewer women running for legislative seats in 1998 than the 2,279 who ran in 1992. What if there had been double the number of well-qualified women candidates?

What will the numbers be in the years 2002 and 2004? As few as 4,000 or 5,000 serious women candidates in winnable legislative races across the country could wake up the whole political system—especially if they have behind them tens of thousands of well-informed women who understand the power they have and how to use it, and who are committed to being part of the political process. As we have seen, the prospect of a gender gap initially terrified national leaders in the 1980s; just think of the impact of well-informed, determined women running for winnable seats in every local constituency.

Change occurs when a broad segment of society insists that it happen. That is a power question. Who has it, who uses it, for what purposes? And these are questions with which women continue to have difficulty. Just as men want to be the strong leader who is respected and obeyed, women still want to be the "good girl" who makes no one angry. We continue to view one another through gender lenses, and then respond in our behavior in a way that reinforces those signals. That means that despite new opportunities, women still face old expectations. Army generals are supposed to be manly, even when they're female; nurses are supposed to be motherly, even when they're male. Those expectations can turn into barriers.

The truth about women and power is that our status has changed but not the institutions and policymaking structures that make up our world. We should have noticed when we leveled the playing field that it still belonged to somebody else. That isn't because of some male plot; rather, the difficulty is that our institutions continue to reflect past gender stereotypes. They fail to respond to the rapid changes in our culture, and that means much of government and the corporate world seems unattractive and incompatible with our values. We don't want to get involved in government if it seems like mud wrestling, or stay in the corporate rat race at the cost of family life. We are asked to change ourselves when what should be changing are the institutions and social practices.

It is ironic. We fought so long for equal opportunity, and now that doors are open, we find new challenges behind them. There is a niggling ambivalence about men and women's roles that continues to frustrate all of us and inhibits efforts at reform. We must convince men to join us in changing structures they thought worked for them but really no longer work well for anyone. In the political world, prospective candidates tell us they want no part of a system that's drowning in money, torn asunder by ideology and bitter partisanship, and that is entered by running an obstacle course while ducking rotten eggs. In the private sector, women and men increasingly are disillusioned by a corporate philosophy that eats up personal lives. We need not accept this world when we have the power to change it.

During a business breakfast not long ago, a woman who holds an executive position in the finance field mentioned that she really enjoys her status, but she said, of course, she wasn't talking about exerting "power." She didn't like the word; it suggested bullying. Her remarks took me back twenty years to a time when a speech to women using the word "power" caused a furor. There is a major problem here. If those who control the institutions in our society feel comfortable talking about power, with whatever meaning they give the word, and women don't, because of whatever meaning they give to it, then there is a serious disconnect.

I suggested to my breakfast companion that she might be overreacting to a false idea of power; the term just means an ability to get things done, to influence others to act in a way we want, a measurement of effective energy. It doesn't automatically involve force, confrontation, or any other negative quality. Indeed, many men and women provide a different power model that is more strategic, persuasive, and collaborative and that should be valued as much or more. She listened politely, clearly still disinclined to take any risks with her reputation.

"Women see [power] as a means to an end and men see it as an end,"[3] commented former Congresswoman Leslie Byrne of

Virginia. She thought it might have something to do with the mothering role that requires women to put another life ahead of their own. Hillary Rodham Clinton told Congresswoman Margolies-Mezvinksy for her book that it might have something to do with boys' experience in sports and the early goal of playing to win. Generalizations are dangerous, but it would seem that many girls have learned to prefer winning because they are liked rather than because they beat someone else out. Gold medal women's soccer and hockey teams may provide a different model. They beat someone else out *and* they are liked.

"We willingly submit to this societal brainwashing [about power] until we realize [it] is directly in conflict with our own good,"[4] Congresswoman Margolies-Mezvinsky observed about women. To be liked isn't the same as being given power, former Governor Madeleine Kunin remarked. Women too often are appeased by compliments. She recalled a news commentator telling her that he was with her in his heart. "It wasn't his heart I wanted. It was his vote."[5]

Like my businesswoman friend, many women in the 103rd Congress were conscious of being viewed differently because of gender, but unlike her, they understood that women's attitudes in the power debate had very real consequences. "We have to be aggressive without looking aggressive," Karen Shepherd said. "We have to be fierce without looking bitchy."[6] Some didn't want to discuss power, but Congresswoman Carrie Meek of Florida had no problem in talking about it: "I think as [women] begin to push to get more power—and that's what we're doing . . . because power isn't anything that people want to give to you all the time—sometimes you have to take it."[7]

Here is the heart of our dilemma. If women are going to have a bigger voice in decisionmaking, confrontation is inevitable, but women's comfort level makes confrontation unacceptable. They believe that mixing it up in the political arena, whether as candidate or identified supporter, or facing someone down in the executive suite will exact a price they don't want to pay: the loss of peer approval. These women rarely allow themselves to acknowledge the satisfaction that comes from exercising power. They use power every day at home and at work, but they call it something else, so they can say no when asked to use their influence in more controversial arenas.

It is infuriating when one woman after another declines to lend her name to candidates or causes, let alone write a check, while men respond with alacrity in order to further their interests and their power relationships. The "good girl" complex leaves women vulnerable to manipulation by those who understand power very, very well and have reason not to want to share it. These people delight in labeling activist women with such unattractive adjectives as pushy, bitchy, and femi-nazi, to make others hesitate to emulate them or even to be involved in their causes. They've worked to make "feminist" a worrisome word. Even when women know these labels are distorted and agree with the goals of the women being attacked, they may join in the chorus blaming the women for being too conspicuously aggressive. Good girls don't stir up trouble.

What I failed to communicate to my breakfast companion is that power, like public service, can be tremendously satisfying. It can produce feelings that are downright euphoric. I can remember the first time it happened to me, during the solo flight as a student pilot. I was just seventeen and a few months earlier had discovered a small airfield on the outskirts of Chicago with a makeshift hangar, a few worn single-engine planes and—it was still wartime—a couple of instructors who looked like Air Force washouts. There was money in my pocket from a job in a record store, and I figured that learning to fly couldn't be much more difficult than learning to drive. After all, there were women aviators in the military ferrying airplanes across the country; it seemed like an adventure.

My parents were taken aback at first, but I always could count on mom. She agreed to take a test flight before saying an absolute no; the flight school used its best plane, the one least likely to leak gasoline on a passenger's feet, and the ride was a persuasive success. It wasn't long before my first solo flight. Going up was easy, but looking down at the plane's small shadow moving over the ground evoked a fresh realization of the fragility of the plane, and of life itself. Everything depended on bringing this machine safely down, and that depended on me. I had never felt such power, and such responsibility.

But it was power that served a very narrow purpose. A few years later, there was a different power experience as managing editor of *The Michigan Daily,* a daily campus newspaper in Ann

Arbor. *Look* magazine ran a feature on college life in 1949 that included a telling photograph of me sitting on the copy desk, puffing a cigarette and looking tough. I thought that was the appropriate look for a woman boss. Clearly there still was some learning to do. What was important about this powerful position wasn't intimidating everyone as Big Woman on Campus; it was the ability to shape information for thousands of readers. That could change events.

The final lesson came years later on the day the traffic stopped speeding through our residential street. The door-to-door petition drive had been successful in pressuring authorities to act where an individual complaint had not. There was power in empowering others. The women who changed America in the 1960s and 1970s understood this very well. It would be a mistake to read our history as a chronicle of famous personalities; these women had power because they inspired others to take action, communicating ideas, convening meetings, confronting authority, and educating women to take leadership. The world changed because those taking the lead spoke to greater dreams than any one individual's personal advancement.

It is unclear whether a younger generation understands that kind of power, which is born of a passion to end injustice. The more fortunate of today's women believe they already have the power to control their lives and need nothing more. They believe all barriers are down and there is no reason why they shouldn't reach any goal: Should I design buildings, be a judge, sell insurance, become a minister, a surgeon, master teacher, professional basketball player, or program a computer? Do I start a family now, or later? Or never? Go back to school, work at home, start a business?

The most fortunate women are not just holding jobs; they're doing interesting things in business, the professions, and community organizations. Most expect to work at least part-time during their lifetime, and that gives them a different view of their own value. They can't believe women ever put up with blatant gender discrimination. Patriarchy? What's that?

We rejoice for them, but it's unclear if they really understand their power, or what they can do with it. Will they use their muscle solely for personal goals, or are they also conscious of a responsibility for those less able to act on their own behalf? How much of their political capital are they willing to risk to improve the world around them? Do they understand that they can change conditions that limit them, instead of adapting to them? Former Texas Governor Ann Richards has commented, "You have got to be willing to step up and use the power—not just acquire it."[8]

Conservative groups argue that women are doing wonderfully and need no further interventions. They scold that women should stop acting like victims when they're not. They accuse feminism of creating present work-family tensions by pushing women into careers that require twelve-hour-day schedules with no time to bear or care for children. The conservatives don't propose changing the working conditions; they blame the women and advise them to stop trying to balance job and family, something that is economically impossible for the majority, who depend upon their work income.

We all should celebrate women's progress. The statistics are impressive; it's been only a generation since women couldn't get credit cards in their own name, didn't have coaches and uniforms for team sports, could be battered by husbands without legal recourse, and were often fired for getting pregnant. We can be proud of what we have accomplished. We've proved we aren't passive victims. It hasn't just been religious fundamentalists who have tried to block us or only the hard line conservatives who now praise our progress in order to stop it. Labor unions once opposed the Equal Rights Amendment as a danger to protective provisions in labor contacts. People have been trying to manipulate or control women's choices throughout history, always claiming to be helping us when the real agenda was something else.

Now we're told that gender problems ended with the passage of antidiscrimination laws. There's a great story demonstrating why that's a myth. It spread like wildfire on the Internet in 1999.[9] It seems that three tenured women professors in the School of Science at the Massachusetts Institute of Technology compared notes in 1995 and decided that they were being treated differently from male colleagues, in a way that discouraged their professional advancement. Indeed, their lives were being made miserable; they received less space, salary, awards, resources, and committee assignments than the men did. No one had spoken out because each woman feared being labeled a radical troublemaker in an institution that valued good behavior. Besides, discrimination was illegal, so how could it exist?

They conducted a survey in which other senior women faculty members confirmed their findings, although junior, untenured faculty women with less seniority did not, saying they sensed no discrimination and felt supported on the job. The junior faculty's big worry was the long-term impact on their careers of trying to combine family and work. The feelings of marginalization apparently began as women moved up, assuming tenured positions that placed them in competition for resources.

The surveyors were fortunate to have a sympathetic dean of science who set up a committee to formally pursue the inquiry. The committee's report not only confirmed that inequities existed for tenured women but it found also that the percentage of women faculty (8 percent) had not changed for at least ten years, despite rapidly increasing numbers of women science students. "The pipeline leaks at every stage of careers."

Throughout the inquiry, despite their discontent, the women encouraged a collaborative process that "could serve as a model for increasing the participation of women and also of underrepresented minorities." Their approach led to a reasonably hopeful ending, when the dean took specific actions to improve the status of senior women as well as to address the family–tenure concerns of the junior women, and to also establish a long-range process to increase the number of women on faculty.

"I was unhappy at MIT for more than a decade," a senior woman said. "I thought it was the price you paid if you wanted to be a scientist at an elite academic institution. After the committee formed and the dean responded, my life began to change. My research blossomed, my funding tripled. Now I love every aspect of my job. It is hard to understand how I survived all those years—or why!"

The MIT story struck a chord with women all over the country who knew something was not working in their corporate or professional settings but hesitated to complain. The MIT women were "gifted scientists [who had] themselves convinced that gender had nothing to do with their careers," but ran into a new discrimination that is "subtle but pervasive, and stems from unconscious ways of thinking that have been socialized into us, men and women alike."[10] We want to believe competence will be rewarded, but for that to be true, women must be prepared to expose and remedy the less obvious discrimination that results when we are measured "through the eyes of prejudice," with expectations based on unconscious stereotypes.

An important finding of the study was that different perceptions of gender bias by junior and senior women repeat themselves over generations. Current senior faculty said they too had begun by believing gender discrimination no longer existed. "Gradually, however, their eyes were opened to the realization that the playing field is not level after all, and that they had paid a high price both personally and professionally as a result."[11] Apparently the greater their stature, the greater the threat and the greater the inequities.

What finally propelled this small group of women to action was "the feeling of an injustice, the anger that accumulates from this recognition, and the strong desire to change things for themselves and for future generations of women."[12] They were able to feel that they were using their power not just for personal advancement, but for everyone.

When critics deride continued concern about discrimination, they miss the impact of conscious and unconscious gender judgments that can produce quite different experiences for men and women. We don't want to admit that we may still have different expectations of one another as men and women and that we can and must deal with this. There's a big difference between telling women that they have an equal chance to win in comparable circumstances to men, as we did in the National Women's Political Caucus, and telling them that comparable circumstances always exist, which is nonsense. There's also a big difference between viewing oneself as a passive victim and as someone with the responsibility to confront inequities and bring about change.

Women in America, just like men, are tremendously diverse in their political and social views, but it is astonishing what women can achieve when we do find common cause. For example, millions of women have joined together to fight breast cancer, rallying across political and ideological lines to raise money, insist on better research and care, and to lobby elected officials. True, it is a socially acceptable cause; no one had to explain the life-and-death urgency or manufacture emotion when word spread that congressmen wouldn't even listen to women's concerns. Indignant women didn't worry that they would be labeled "pushy" for their efforts.

A different example of women's collective strength occurred in Missouri in 1998 when an overwhelming turnout of women defeated a ballot measure to expand the legal right to carry concealed weapons. Women's resolve was remarkable given the adverse factors: Television was swamped with commercials favoring the proposal; it was presumed that the National Rifle Association would triumph in a conservative state. Pollsters reported that men were saying yes, and then noticing that their wives were saying no. Still, analysts were amazed when the measure was defeated, and they attributed the loss to a massive turnout of urban and suburban women voters who believed the proposal would mean more guns and simply didn't want any more. They could have stayed home, accepting "the inevitable," but they didn't. They used their political muscle.

What if we applied that muscle to assuring quality child care, universal health care, family planning funds, flexible working conditions, and wiser military policies? In the workplace, the home, the ballot box, and civic causes, women have power to make a difference. This is more than a matter of numbers in polling places. Women today have technical skills, financial resources, and key positions in the private and public sector where they can be persuasive opinion-makers—if they are willing. Women are making the workplace a more humane environment, and they are providing models for collaboration in legislative negotiation. They are building effective partnerships across all kinds of old barriers. That is power. Why are we so reluctant to give success that name?

My sons are kind and caring human beings; I'm confident that my grandsons will be the same. Younger women can join with a new generation of men who share their concerns about family, workplace, and world, who welcome a society where duties and responsibilities are shared, and who are free of gender bias. Men need reassurance that change won't cost them their opportunities, and that we appreciate their contributions in all appropriate roles. They need, in turn, to appreciate our leadership. Together, we must reach out more aggressively across traditional barriers of party, race, class, culture, and nationality. Too many remain within arbitrary social boundaries, limiting their effectiveness. The struggle to transform society must benefit everyone, or it won't produce permanent benefits for anyone.

Women are rising up all over the world, particularly in third-world nations, where for so long they have been denied equality and dignity. Hillary Clinton's stirring charge in a speech at the Beijing UN conference that women's rights are human rights has brought new attention to issues such as rape as a tool of war, genital mutilation, sexual slavery, economic inequity, murder of girls in the name of family honor, and other forms of intimidation and violence. There are societies in which girls are denied education and women still are denied the vote. We cannot be complacent; fundamentalism is a danger everywhere, including in this country, where a veil of religion is used to give standing to proposals that would return women to second-class status.

Women throughout Africa, India, and Latin America are taking very real risks to speak up; they are surprising everyone by becoming candidates for major office, challenging deeply ingrained cultural patterns. Women are providing differing styles of leadership in a shattered world. In Ireland, in the former Yugoslavia, and in Somalia, women have organized themselves to overcome ethnic and religious hatreds and create dialogue, while traditional male-led groups continue to kill one another. Here at home, we have set our own examples: Women give direction and energy to crisis centers, to overburdened child care centers and clinics, to struggling public schools, and to training programs that teach alternatives to violence as a way of resolving disputes. There is plenty for us to do in the new century.

For American women, there's been a millennium issue for years. Think of the slogans "50–50 by 2000." "A woman president by 2010." Or just the perennial "Wait 'til Next year!" For the past fifty years, women have concentrated on changing an unsatisfactory present into a more perfect tomorrow. We've had to be futurists. Now we're told that the future is here. There's not much point talking about what we want the future to look like if we aren't ready to talk about using the power we have to achieve it. For those who want to have an impact, here are some ideas on how to start, reflecting the lessons of one lifetime's political voyages:

1. Make the connection between your life and the political process. What vital interests of yours need attention? Legislatures write divorce and child-support laws, tax codes, environmental laws, health and mental health regulations, standards for public schools, regulations for small business, and penalties for crime.

2. Make the connection between your own life and the lives of other women. All issues are women's issues, but common sense tells us that women have different life experiences that they share. Get involved in the campaign of a woman candidate whose views are like your own.

3. Have a long-range plan. There's no magic formula for attaining and using power, but those most likely to succeed have thought about where they want to go and who can help them get there. You also should think how you can use your resources and influence in connection with points 1 and 2.

4. Understand that money is power. Until we find a way to curtail the dominance of money in politics, women must learn to use it to get their voices heard. It's a matter of leveraging resources strategically. Governor Richards used to tell women at fund-raisers to donate the value of the clothes they currently were wearing.

5. Be inclusive. Progress isn't about challenging men; it's about empowering ourselves to achieve more together.

The late Barbara Jordan, congresswoman from Texas, wrote: "Things are changing and they are changing fast. Get active in politics wherever you are at whatever level you choose. Get out there and do what you are able to put more of us where we need to be. We will not rest until more women speak for the needs, worries and interests of women. It's about time."[13]

For those who are moved by Barbara Jordan and want to try public service, here is some additional advice culled from the wisdom of women who have reached public office:

1. Begin with a commitment to something you really care about. If you don't believe in what you are doing, neither will anyone else.

2.   Start with something you know about. It doesn't matter
     whether it's school tax campaigns, trash disposal, or man-
     aging money—knowledge is a rallying point for leadership.
3.   Start where you are. Even if you really want to be gover-
     nor, begin in your own neighborhood or your own work-
     place. There's a lot to learn, and it's better to make
     mistakes in friendly territory.
4.   Do your homework. It is amazing how many people
     expect to be leaders without knowing much about the
     people or area they want to represent. Listen a lot before
     you start talking.
5.   Reach out beyond your present social circle. Broaden
     acquaintances to other religious, social, and civic groups;
     spend time with have-nots as well as haves. If you want
     to be a party's nominee, make the effort to become active.
6.   Be strategic. Several years ago in California, women
     activists adopted an acronym, DIRE, for Death,
     Indictment, Retirement, Expectation, to evaluate incum-
     bents likely to create openings for future seats. Do the
     research to build a base where you have the best chance
     of winning.
7.   Be a risk taker. Opportunities arise; the question is who
     has the courage to use them. Don't jump off cliffs, but
     saying no is less risky only if you want to stand still.
8.   Maintain a sense of humor. It will make others more
     comfortable and save your sanity. Women politicians have
     a reputation for being humorless. The answer isn't telling
     jokes; it is taking criticism less seriously.

I truly believe that women can make a difference by providing principled leadership with a mission: achieving a more
humane and equitable society. We'll feel more comfortable about
power when we can see it through our own gender lens and
understand that the reason for insisting on change is not just personal. We are at our best when we feel we're helping others.
American women fought to end sex discrimination thirty years
ago because we understood that if a hostile system was going to
change, we would have to change it. Today, too many women
expect unresponsive institutions to change without their commitment. It isn't going to happen.

The reason we recall the past is not to dwell in it but to inspire women to take what is useful in order to move forward. Personal success has given younger women much more power than they seem to realize that they have. We want them to use it. Some time in the next millennium, women finally will reach a critical mass of leadership in public and private sectors, in corporations and legislatures. It would be a tragedy if this younger generation of women should sleepwalk through its good fortune.

We have been largely absent from history; government, money, and politics were considered men's business, so women could deny responsibility for failures. That is no longer true. Women are the majority of the voters. Women are major fundraisers for both parties. Women are holding together neighborhoods. Women are making critical decisions on war and peace and at every level of law and business. It is true that we still are far from fully represented in decisionmaking bodies and that politics remains a male game; but that's no excuse for failing to use the power we have to make this a more livable world.

We will prevail. "Enter any community in any country, and you will find women insisting—often at great risk—on their right to an equal voice and equal access to the levers of power." Those were the words of Madeleine Albright in Beijing at the UN Conference for Women, a gathering that did much to inspire women elsewhere to believe in their own human rights and to encourage them to put their own strengths to work. Here in this country, we have had a head start; society has been transformed over the past thirty years, and that means opportunity is everywhere.

Somewhere, at this very moment, in some neighborhood in America, a woman very like my younger self is confronting a problem that affects her life and family. Perhaps it's the need for a playground for her children; maybe it's a threat to clean water from rural animal waste. She has spoken up, but no one is willing to take action. She's never been a public person, and famous women senators seem a world away. Still, she cares deeply about finding a solution. After agonizing thought, she makes a crucial decision.

She will step up to power, and another woman leader will be born.

Appendix

PERCENTAGES OF WOMEN IN ELECTIVE OFFICES

	1977	1979	1981	1983	1985	1987
Congress	4%	3%	4%	4%	5%	5%
Statewide	10%	11%	11%	11%	14%	14%
Legislatures	9%	10%	12%	13%	15%	16%

	1989	1991	1993	1995	1997	1999
Statewide	5%	6%	10%	10%	11%	12%
Legislatures	14%	18%	22%	26%	26%	28%
Congress	17%	18%	21%	21%	22%	22%

SOURCE: Center for the American Woman and Politics.

Notes

Chapter 1

1. The White House Office for Women's Initiatives and Outreach, *Female Presidential Appointments*, January 1996.
2. Donnie Radcliffe, "The Women's Hour," *The Washington Post*, February 9, 1994.
3. Ibid.
4. Ibid.
5. Amelia Earhart, letter to husband, George Putnam, 1937. Quoted in Susan Ware, *Still Missing* (New York: Norton, 1993), p. 232.
6. *A Century of American Women*, edited by Alan Covey (Atlanta: TBS Books, 1994), p. 51.
7. Janet Reno, speech to the National Women's Political Caucus Convention, Los Angeles, July 10, 1995.
8. Eleanor Clift, "Shards of the Glass Ceiling," *Newsweek*, February 22, 1993.
9. Sheila Tobias, *Faces of Feminism* (Boulder: Westview Press, 1997).

Chapter 2

1. Brett Harvey, *The Fifties—A Woman's Oral History* (New York: Harper Collins, 1993).
2. Betty Friedan, *It Changed My Life; Writings on the Women's Movement* (New York: Random House, 1976).
3. "If Women Ran America," *Life*, June 1992, p. 40.
4. Margaret Mead, *Male and Female, A Study of the Sexes in a Changing World* (New York: William Morrow & Company, 1949), p. 335.
5. Friedan, *It Changed My Life*, p. 16.
6. "How To Be a Woman," *Seventeen*, quoted in Harvey, *The Fifties*, p. 73.
7. Mead, *Male and Female*, p. 333.
8. Louis Menard, *The New Yorker*, October 26, 1998.
9. Gloria Steinem, *Outrageous Acts and Everyday Rebellions* (New York: Signet, 1986).

Chapter 3

1. Michael Harrington, *The Other America* (New York: MacMillan, 1962). Harrington said between 20 and 25 percent of the American people were poor, with inadequate housing, medicine, food, and opportunity, p. 182. An earlier

influential book underscoring the contrasts of wealth in America was John Kenneth Galbraith's *The Affluent Society* (New York: Houghton Mifflin, 1958).

2. David Farber, *The Age of Great Dreams* (New York: Hill and Wang, a division of Farrar, Straus and Giroux, 1994), p. 57.

3. Ibid., p. 111.

4. David Burner, *Making Peace with the 60s* (Princeton, New Jersey: Princeton University Press, 1996), p. 207.

5. Farber, *The Age of Great Dreams,* p. 67.

6. Ibid., p. 63.

7. Kay Mills, *This Little Light of Mine, The Life of Fannie Lou Hamer* (New York: Dutton, 1993), p. 121.

8. Ibid., p. 45.

9. Susan Tolchin and Martin Tolchin, *Clout—Womanpower and Politics* (New York: Coward, McCann & Geoghegan, 1973), p. 74.

10. Farber, *The Age of Great Dreams,* p. 246.

11. *A Century of American Women*, edited by Alan Covey (Atlanta: TBS Books), 1994, p. 52.

12. *Urban Decay in St. Louis,* a report by six authors and analysts in the *Washington University Magazine,* summer 1972.

13. Ibid., p. 16.

14. Ibid., p. 16.

15. Ibid., p. 16.

16. The Feminist Majority Foundation, *Feminist Chronicles,* 1998.

Chapter 4

1. Susan Ware, *Still Missing* (New York: Norton, 1993), p. 80.

2. Clarissa Start, "The Four Careers of Harriett Woods," *The St. Louis Post-Dispatch,* May 2, 1967.

3. Madeleine Kunin, *Living a Political Life* (New York: Alfred A. Knopf, 1994), p. 103.

4. Ibid., p. 223.

5. Center for the American Woman and Politics, "The Impact of Women in Public Life," Eagleta Institute of Politics, Rutgers, New Brunswick, New Jersey, 1991.

6. In 1973, there were just 12 women mayors out of 752 positions in cities with populations over 30,000. *Factsheet on Women's Political Progress,* National Women's Political Caucus, 1993.

7. Thomas Amberg, "Highway Department Is Unaccountable, Secret, Imperious," *The St. Louis Globe–Democrat,* June 11, 1978.

8. Pat Schroeder, *24 Years of House Work and the Place Is Still a Mess* (Kansas City: Andrews McNeel, 1998), p. 46.

9. U.S. Department of Education, National Center for Education Statistics, "Degrees and Other Formal Awards Conferred," surveys and Integrated Postsecondary Education Data System (IPEDS), "Completions" surveys. 1996.

Chapter 5

1. The National Women's History Project, "The Path of the Women's Rights Movement, Detailed Timeline," Windsor, California.
2. Ibid.
3. Susan Tolchin and Martin Tolchin, *Clout—Womanpower and Politics* (New York: Coward, McCann & Geoghegan, 1973), p. 173.
4. Columnist Peter Hamill.
5. Tolchin and Tolchin, *Clout,* p. 174.
6. Bella Abzug, *Gender Gap* (Boston: Houghton Mifflin, 1984), p. 158.
7. Liz Carpenter, *Getting Better All the Time* (College Station: Texas A&M University Press, 1993), p. 130.
8. Abzug, *Gender Gap,* p. 21.
9. Irene Cortinovis, interview with Harriett Woods, Oral History Program, University of Missouri–St. Louis, July 20, 1977, p. 11.

Chapter 6

1. Jane Mansbridge, *Why We Lost the ERA* (Chicago and London: University of Chicago Press, 1986).
2. Fred W. Lindecke, "Panel Expected to Favor ERA," *The St. Louis Post-Dispatch,* February 3, 1977, p. 16A.
3. Deborah Smith, "Women Legislators," *St. Louis Globe–Democrat,* March 8, 1978.
4. Center for the American Woman and Politics, *Reshaping the Agenda: Women in State Legislatures,* Eagleton Institute of Politics, Rutgers, New Brunswick, New Jersey 1991.
5. Randy McConnell, "Power Is No Prerequisite for Capital Media Stardom," *The Missouri Times,* May 10, 1981.
6. Richard A. Seltzer, Jody Newman, and Melissa Voorhees Leighton, *Sex As a Political Variable* (Boulder/London: Lynne Rienner Publishers, 1997), p. 31.
7. Mary Kimbrough, *St. Louis Globe–Democrat Magazine,* May 23–24, 1981, p. 5.

Chapter 7

1. Jack Flach, *The St. Louis Globe–Democrat,* March 8, 1982.
2. Tim O'Neill, *The St. Louis Globe–Democrat,* March 7, 1982.
3. *The Kansas City Times,* Editorial, March 10, 1982.
4. Judy Mann, column, "Strength," *The Washington Post,* August 13, 1982.
5. Elizabeth Bumiller, "Senate Showdown in the Show-Me State," *The Washington Post,* October 15, 1982.
6. Jim Willis, Associated Press, September 30, 1982.
7. *The St. Louis Post-Dispatch,* October 1, 1982.
8. Mann, "Strength."
9. *The St. Louis Post-Dispatch,* November 3, 1982.

Chapter 8

1. Associated Press, Washington, D.C., November 4, 1982. Reprinted in Lafayette, Indiana, *Journal and Courier*.

2. Center for the American Woman and Politics (CAWP), *Sex Differences in Voter Turnout*, Fact Sheet, July 1995.

3. CAWP Fact Sheet, derived from U.S. Bureau of the Census Current Population Surveys.

4. American National Election Studies (NES).

5. Rosalie Whelan, Executive Director of the National Women's Education Fund, *Women's Political Times*, December 1982.

6. Margaret W. Freivogel, "Women Make the Difference—in Some Races," *St. Louis Post-Dispatch*, November 14, 1982.

7. *Newsweek*, November 1, 1982.

8. Peggy Simpson, "Helping Women Win in '84," *Working Woman*, November 1983, p. 60.

9. Thomas W. Ottenad, "Women Leaders Warn Democratic Hopefuls," *St. Louis Post-Dispatch*, April 20, 1983.

10. Jacquelyn Mithcard, "Democratic Candidates Pay Homage to Women Voters' Clout," *The Capital Times*, July 11, 1983.

11. Howell Raines, "Democrats Line Up on Feminist Issues," *The New York Times*, July 11, 1983.

12. Georgia Duerst-Lahti and Rita Mae Kelly, *Gender Power, Leadership and Governance* (Ann Arbor: University of Michigan Press, 1995), pp. 68–69, 85.

13. Fred W. Lindecke, "Mrs.Woods Plans to Run for Lieutenant Governor," *St. Louis Post-Dispatch*, March 2, 1983.

14. Linda Witt, Karen M. Paget, and Glenna Mathews, *Running As a Woman—Gender and Power in American Politics* (New York: The Free Press, a Division of MacMillan, 1994), p. 162. They named the initial "A Team" as Ranny Cooper, Nanette Falkenberg, Eleanor Lewis, Millie Jeffrey, and Joanne Howes. Joan McLean also was a key player.

15. See the chapter "The Gender Gap" in Richard A. Seltzer, Jody Newman, and Melissa Voorhees Leighton, *Sex as a Political Variable* (Boulder/London: Lynne Rienner Publishers, 1997).

16. Witt, Paget, and Matthews, *Running As a Woman*, p. 167.

17. Patricia Rice, "Women Are Cool to No. 2 'Flirtations,'" *St. Louis Post-Dispatch*, December 11, 1983.

18. Witt, Paget, and Matthews, *Running As a Woman*, p. 162.

19. Geraldine Ferraro with Linda Franke, *My Story* (New York: Bantam Books, 1985), p. 102.

20. Ibid., p. 109.

21. Ibid., p. 79.

22. Kathy Wilson, *Women's Political Times*, vol. 9, no. 7, November/December 1984.

23. Voting numbers and turnout rates are from CAWP, *Sex Differences in Voter Turnout*.

24. CAWP, *The Gender Gap* Fact Sheet, using data from *The New York Times*.

25. Subtracting Reagan's women's vote of 54 percent from the men's vote of 62 percent gives an 8-point gap. Some analysts use a different method, subtracting the spread in the women's vote, 10 points, from the spread in the men's vote, 25, which would give a 15-point gap. What is important is using the same method from one election cycle to another.

26. Wilson, *Women's Political Times.*

27. Ferraro, *My Story,* p. 295.

28. Duerst-Lahti and Kelly, *Gender Power,* p. 31.

Chapter 9

1. Maureen Dowd, *The New York Times Magazine,* December 30, 1984.

2. Julie Johnson, *The Baltimore Sun,* October 17, 1986.

3. Marilyn Adams, *USA Today,* December 31, 1984.

4. Margaret W. Freivogel, "Woods Cheered at Convention," *The St. Louis Post-Dispatch,* June 30, 1985.

Chapter 10

1. For example, it was a fledgling Center for Women's Policy Studies that conducted the original research for the Equal Credit Opportunity Act of 1973, which made it illegal to deny credit on the basis of sex. It was research by women economists like Barbara R. Bergmann and Heidi Hartmann, who founded the Institute for Women's Policy Research in 1987, which provided support for the economic equity package of the Congressional Caucus for Women's Issues. There also was the Women's Research and Education Institute (WREI), led by Betty Parsons Dooley. Legal centers included the NOW Legal Defense and Education Fund, the Women's Legal Defense Fund led by Judith Lichtman, and the National Women's Law Center, led by Marcia Greenberg.

2. U.S. Department of State, *U.S. Report to the UN on the Status of Women 1985–1994,* p. 1.

3. Secretary of Labor Robert B. Reich, *Good for Business: Making Full Use of the Nation's Human Capital.* A fact-finding report of the Federal Glass Ceiling Commission. Washington, D.C., March 1995.

4. U.S. Department of State, *U.S. Report to the UN,* p. 16.

5. Ibid., p. 17.

6. Ibid., p. 34.

7. Office of the Lieutenant Governor, Jefferson City, Missouri, *Homelessness in Missouri,* June 1987.

8. U.S. Department of State, *U.S. Report to the UN,* p. 15.

9. Examples are the National Association of Women Business Owners and the National Association of Female Executives.

10. U.S. Interagency Committee on Women's Business Enterprise, in cooperation with the National Women's Business Council, Expanding Business Opportunities for Women, Washington, D.C., January 1996, pp. 2–4.

11. Mary Feingold, "Walking the Walk," *Madison* Magazine, August 1999, p. 31.
12. Expanding Business Opportunities for Women, p. 4.
13. U.S. Department of State, *U.S. Report to the UN*, p. 20.
14. Pat Schroeder, *24 Years of House Work . . . and the Place Is Still a Mess,* (Kansas City: Andrews McNeel Publishing), p. 185.

Chapter 11

1. Anne N. Costain, *Inviting Women's Rebellion, A Political Process Interpretation of the Women's Movement* (Baltimore: Johns Hopkins University Press, 1992), p. 96.
2. Ibid., p. 97.
3. Susan Levine, *Degrees of Equality—The American Association of University Women and the Challenge of Feminism in the Twentieth Century* (Philadelphia: Temple University Press, 1995), p. 144.
4. Ibid., p. 144.
5. Ibid., p. 144.
6. Bella Abzug, *Congressional Record-House*, July 13, 1971, p. H 6699.
7. Ibid.
8. Rona F. Feit, "Organizing for Political Power; the National Women's Political Caucus," *Women Organizing* (Metuchen, New Jersey and London: Scarecrow Press, 1979), p. 187.
9. Levine, *Degrees of Equality,* pp. 162–163.
10. Susan Tolchin and Martin Tolchin, *Clout—Womanpower and Politics* (New York: Coward, McCann & Geoghegan, 1973), pp. 29–30.
11. Tim O'Brien, "Women Organize for More Power," *The Washington Post,* July 10, 1971. *Congressional Record,* p. H 6701.
12. *Congressional Record,* p. H 6701. The steering committee: Betty Friedan; Bella Abzug; Congresswoman Shirley Chisholm; Gloria Steinem; plus Mary Clarke, California Women's Strike for Peace; Shana Alexander, then editor-in-chief of *McCall's* magazine; Nikki Beare, Dade County, Florida, Women's Commission; Liz Carpenter, former press secretary to Mrs. Lyndon B. Johnson; Virginia Allan, former chair of President Nixon's Task Force on Women's Rights and Responsibilities; LaDonna Harris, Native American rights leader; Joan Cashin, National Democratic Party of Alabama; Elinor Guggenheimer, New York Child Development advocate; Myrlie Evers, California civil rights leader; Dorothy Height, president of the National Council of Negro Women; Fannie Lou Hamer, Mississippi civil rights leader; Olga Madar, vice president of the United Automobile Workers; Beulah Sanders, vice president of the National Welfare Rights Organization; Wilma Scott Heide, president of the National Organization for Women; Midge Miller, Wisconsin state representative; Elly Petersen, former vice chair of the Republican National Committee; and Jill Ruckelshaus, White House aide to President Nixon. There were an additional two dozen women, from even more diverse backgrounds who made up the complete National Policy Council when it began to meet.

13. *Congressional Record,* p. H 6700.
14. Feit, "Organizing for Political Power," p. 189.
15. Tolchin and Tolchin, *Clout,* p. 47.
16. Ibid., p. 49.
17. Theodore H. White, *The Making of the President 1972* (New York: Atheneum, 1972), p. 168.
18. Bella Abzug, *Gender Gap, Bella Abzug's Guide to Political Power for Women* (Boston: Houghton Mifflin, 1984), p. 49.
19. Feit, "Organizing for Power," p. 202.
20. *Winning with Women,* a 1991 survey commissioned by three women's organizations.

Chapter 12

1. Judith Resnik, "From the Senate Judiciary Committee to the Country Courthouse: The Relevance of Gender, Race and Ethnicity to Adjudication." In *Race, Gender and Power in America: The Legacy of the Hill–Thomas Hearings,* Anita Faye Hill and Emma Coleman Jordan, editors (New York: Oxford University Press, 1995), pp. 178–179.
2. Ibid., p. 189.
3. Ibid., p. 190.
4. Ibid., p. 190.
5. Timothy M. Phelps and Helen Winternitz, *Capitol Games, Clarence Thomas, Anita Hill, and the Story of a Supreme Court Nomination* (New York: Heparin, 1992), pp. 179–180.
6. Resnik, "From the Senate Judiciary Committee," p. 185.
7. Jane Mayer and Jill Abramson, *Strange Justice, The Selling of Clarence Thomas* (Boston/New York: Houghton Mifflin, 1994), p. 209.
8. Ibid., pp. 219–221.
9. Ibid., p. 234.
10. Ibid., p. 222.
11. Ibid., p. 198–199.
12. Senator Paul Simon, *Advice & Consent: Clarence Thomas, Robert Bork and the Intriguing History of the Supreme Court's Nomination Battles* (Washington, D.C.: National Press Books, 1992), p. 121.
13. Phelps and Winternitz, *Capitol Games,* pp. 266–267.
14. Barbara Boxer, California, Nita M. Lowey, New York, Patsy Mink, Hawaii, Eleanor Holmes Norton, Washington, D.C., Patricia Schroeder, Colorado, Louise Slaughter, New York, Jolene Unsoeld, Washington.
15. Mayer and Abramson, *Strange Justice,* p. 270.
16. Ibid., p. 270.
17. Ibid., p. 271.
18. John C. Danforth, *Resurrection, The Confirmation of Clarence Thomas* (New York: Viking, 1994), p. 159.
19. Anita Hill, *Speaking Truth to Power* (New York: Doubleday, 1997), p. 139.
20. Ibid., p. 202.

21. Mayer and Abramson, *Strange Justice,* pp. 302–303.

22. Simon, *Advice & Consent,* p. 112.

23. Mayer and Abramson, *Strange Justice,* p. 304.

24. Simon, *Advice & Consent,* p. 117.

25. Hill, *Speaking Truth to Power,* p. 141.

26. Resnik, "From the Senate Judiciary Committee," p. 200.

27. Hill, *Speaking Truth to Power,* p. 124.

28. Danforth, *Resurrection,* p. 161.

29. Simon, *Advice & Consent,* p. 113.

Chapter 13

1. Toby Eckert, "Moseley-Braun: Political Survivor or Accidental Senator?" Copley News Service, October 14, 1998.

2. *Time,* May 4, 1992, pp. 35–36.

3. Judi Hasson, "Women: Watch out, Washington," *USA Today,* June 3, 1992.

4. Paul Houston and Marlene Cimons, "To Women, '92 Could Be *the* Year," *Los Angeles Times,* April 30, 1992.

5. *Time,* May 4, 1992, p. 36.

6. Steve Daley, "Wallets Open for 'Year of Women,'" *The Chicago Tribune,* October 25, 1992.

7. Houston and Cimons, "To Women, '92 Could be *the* Year."

8. Center for the American Woman and Politics, "Women Candidates for Congress Fact Sheet," Eagleton Institute, Rutgers University, New Brunswick, New Jersey.

9. Charles Trueheart, "Politics' New Wave of Women," *The Washington Post,* April 7, 1992.

10. Harriett Woods, letter to Patricia Ireland, December 11, 1991, National Women's Political Caucus files.

11. *Los Angeles Times,* January 19, 1992.

12. Debbie Howlett, "Women Launch an Assault on 'Old Men's Club'," *USA Today,* March 26, 1992.

13. Houston and Cimons, "To Women, '92 Could Be *the* Year."

14. Ibid.

15. Tanya Mellich, *The Republican War Against Women* (New York: Bantam Books, 1995).

16. Ibid., p. 261.

17. Ibid., p. 272.

Chapter 14

1. Kristin Huckshorn, "Playing by the Rules," *San Jose Mercury News,* October 31, 1993.

2. Maureen Dowd, "Growing Sorority in Congress Edges into the Ol' Boys' Club," *The New York Times,* March 5, 1993.

3. Rachel Leahey, "47 Women in Congress, 170 To Go," *Equal Times*, August/September 1994.

4. Ibid.

5. Ibid.

6. Debra L. Dodson, Susan J. Caroll, and Ruth B. Mandel, *Voices, Views, and Votes: The Impact of Women in the 103rd Congress*, Center for the American Woman and Politics (CAWP), Eagleton Institute of Politics, Rutgers, p. 4.

7. Ibid.

8. Huckshorn, "Playing by the Rules."

9. Andrea Stone and Dee Ann Glamser, "Lawmakers and Laws Change— As Women Gain Power, Bills Reflect Their Influence," *USA Today*, February 12, 1993.

10. Rachel Leahey, "47 Women in Congress, 170 To Go," *Equal Times*, August/September 1994.

11. Ibid.

12. Dodson, Carroll, and Mandel, *Voices, and Views, Votes*, p. 24.

13. Ibid., p. 14.

14. Ibid., p. 15.

15. Voter News Service (VNS) survey, November 8, 1994: Men disapproved of Congress 84 to 13; women, 74 to 19.

16. VNS survey: Men disapproved of Clinton in percentages, 57 to 40; women approved Clinton, 48 to 46.

17. "What Role Did Gender Play in the '93 Races for Governor?" *Women's Political Times*, winter 1993–1994.

18. Congresswoman Maria Cantwell of Washington initiated the video. The others were Lynn Woolsey and Lynn Schenk of California, Karen Shepherd of Utah, Elizabeth Furse of Oregon, and Eva Clayton of North Carolina.

19. National Women's Political Caucus, *Perception and Reality: A Study Comparing the Success of Men & Women Candidates*, September 1994.

20. Elinor Burkett, *The Right Women* (New York: A Lisa Drew Book/Scribner, 1998), p. 190.

Chapter 15

1. Census Bureau Facts for Features, February 23, 1999.

2. Women's Bureau, U.S. Department of Labor, *Working Women Count, A Report to the Nation*, 1994.

3. *The New York Times*, August 23, 1998. From Bureau of Labor Statistics.

4. Women's Bureau, *Working Women Count*, p. 28.

5. *USA Today*, January 17, 1995; *The Washington Post*, April 8, 1994; *The Wall Street Journal*, October 12, 1994; *Working Woman*, February 1995.

6. Women's Bureau, *Working Women Count*, p. 31.

7. Ibid., p. 29.

8. Zillah R. Eisenstein, *The Radical Future of Liberal Feminism* (New York & London: Longman, 1981), p. 207.

9. Karen S. Peterson, "In Balancing Act, Scale Tips toward Family," *USA Today,* January 25, 1995.

10. Karen S. Peterson, "Working Moms Are Upbeat," *USA Today,* January 14, 1994.

11. Mellman-Lazarus-Lake, Inc., December 7, 1994, survey for the NWPC.

12. Ibid.

Chapter 16

1. Nancy M. Neuman, editor, *True to Ourselves,* a publication of the League of Women Voters (San Francisco: Jossey-Bass Publishers, 1998), pp. 222–223.

2. Broder.

3. The figure was still 22 percent in the year 1999. CAWP Fact Sheet.

Chapter 17

1. Carolyn G. Heilbrun, *Education of a Woman* (New York: Dial Press, 1995).

2. Sarah Lyall, "Parliament Defines Itself in Gestures of Chivalry," *The New York Times,* December 22, 1997.

3. Marjorie Margolies-Mezvinsky, with Barbara Feinman, *A Woman's Place* (New York: Crown Publishers, 1994), p. 75.

4. Ibid., p. 78.

5. Madeleine Kunin, *Living a Political Life,* (New York: Knopf, 1993), p. 280.

6. Margolies-Mezvinksy, *A Woman's Place,* p. 82.

7. Ibid., p. 80.

8. Mark Clayton, "When the Good Ole Boy is a Girl," *The Christian Science Monitor,* February 10, 1998.

9. *A Study on the Status of Women Faculty in Science at MIT,* 1999.

10. Lotte Bailyn, MIT faculty chair, Comments on the Study, March 1999.

11. Ibid.

12. Ibid.

13. Margolies-Mezvinsky, *A Woman's Place,* p. ii.

Bibliography

Abzug, Bella. *Bella! Ms. Abzug Goes to Washington*. New York: Saturday Review Press, 1972.

Abzug, Bella, and Mim Kelber. *Gender Gap*. New York: Houghton Mifflin Company, 1984.

Burkett, Elinor. *The Right Woman: A Journey through the Heart of Conservative America*. New York: Scribner, 1998.

Burner, David. *Making Peace with the 60s*. Princeton, New Jersey: Princeton University Press, 1996.

Cantor, Dorothy and Toni Bernay, with Jean Stoess. *Women in Power: The Secrets of Leadership*. New York: Houghton Mifflin Company, 1992.

Carpenter, Liz. *Getting Better All the Time*. College Station: Texas A&M University Press, 1987.

Cassidy, Robert. *Margaret Mead: A Voice for the Century*. New York: Universe Books, 1982.

Clark, Judith Freeman. *Almanac of American Women in the 20th Century*. New York: Prentice-Hall Press, 1987.

Costain, Ann. *Inviting Women's Rebellion: A Political Interpretation of the Women's Movement*. Baltimore and London: The Johns Hopkins University Press, 1992.

Covey, Alan. *A Century of American Women*. Atlanta: TBS Books, 1994.

Danforth, John C. *Resurrection: The Confirmation of Clarence Thomas*. New York: Viking, 1994.

Dodson, Debra L., Susan J. Carroll, and Ruth B. Mandel. *Voices, Views, Votes: The Impact of Women in the 103rd Congress*. New Brunswick, New Jersey: Center for the American Woman and Politics, 1995.

Duerst-Lahti, Georgia and Rita Mae Kelly, editors. *Gender Power, Leadership and Governance*. Ann Arbor: The University of Michigan Press, 1995.

Eisenstein, Zillah R. *The Radical Future of Liberal Feminism*. New York and London: Longman, 1981.

Farber, David. *The Age of Great Dreams*. New York: Hill and Wang, 1994.

Ferraro, Geraldine, with Linda Bird Francke. *Ferraro, My Story*. New York: Bantam Books, 1985.

Ferree, Myra Marx and Beth B. Hess. *Controversy & Coalition: The New Feminist Movement Across Three Decades of Change*. New York: Twayne Publishers, 1994.

Friedan, Betty. *The Feminine Mystique*. New York: W.W. Norton, 1963.

——— *It Changed My Life: Writings on the Women's Movement*. New York: Random House, 1976.

Galbraith, John Kenneth. *The Affluent Society*. New York: Houghton Mifflin, 1958.

Harrington, Michael. *The Other America*. New York: MacMillan, 1962.

Harvey, Brett. *The Fifties—A Woman's Oral History.* New York: Harper Collins, 1993.

Hill, Anita. *Speaking Truth to Power.* New York: Doubleday, 1997.

Hill, Anita Faye, and Emma Coleman Jordan, editors. *Race, Gender and Power in America: The Legacy of the Hill–Thomas Hearings.* New York: Oxford University Press, 1995.

Howard, Jane. *Margaret Mead. A Life.* New York: Simon & Schuster, 1984.

Klatch, Rebecca E. *Women of the New Right.* Philadelphia: Temple University Press, 1987.

Kunin, Madeleine. *Living a Political Life.* New York: Alfred A. Knopf, 1993.

Lamson, Peggy. *In the Vanguard, Six American Women in Public Life.* New York: Houghton Mifflin Company, 1979.

Levine, Susan. *Degrees of Equality.* Philadelphia: Temple University Press, 1995.

Mandel, Ruth. *In the Running. The New Woman Candidate.* New Haven and New York: Tickron & Fields, 1981.

Mayer, Jane and Jill Abramson. *Strange Justice, The Selling of Clarence Thomas.* Boston and New York: Houghton Mifflin Company, 1994.

Mead, Margaret. *Male and Female.* New York: William Morrow and Company, 1949.

Mellich, Tanya. *The Republican War Against Women.* New York: Bantam Books, 1995.

Mills, Kay, *A Place in the News: From the Women's Pages to the Front Page.* New York: Dodd, Mead and Company, 1988.

Mills, Kay. *From Pocahantas To Power Suits.* New York: A Plume Book, 1995.

Mills, Kay. *This Little Light of Mine. The Life of Fannie Lou Hamer.* New York: A Dutton Book, 1993.

Morris, Celia. *Storming the Statehouse. Running for Governor with Ann Richards and Dianne Feinstein.* New York: Charles Scribner's Sons, 1992.

Neuman, Nancy M. *True to Ourselves.* A Publication of the League of Women Voters. San Francisco: Jossey-Bass Publishers, 1998.

Newman, Jody, Richard Seltzer, and Leighton Voorhees. *Sex as a Political Variable.* Boulder and London: Lynne Rienner Publishers, 1997.

Patt-Corner. *Risks and Rewards.* AAUW Outlook, Spring, 1997.

Phelps, Timothy M. and Helen Winternitz. *Capitol Games.* New York: Heparin, 1992.

Reich, Robert B. *Good for Business: Making Full Use of the Nation's Human Capital.* Washington, D.C. Federal Glass Ceiling Commission, U.S. Department of Labor, 1995.

Robertson, Nan. *The Girls in the Balcony: Women, Men, and The New York Times.* New York: Random House, 1992.

Schroeder, Patricia, with Andrea Camp and Robyn Lipner. *Champion of the Great American Family.* New York: Random House, 1989.

Schroeder, Patricia. *24 Years of House Work and the Place is Still a Mess.* Kansas City: Andrews McNeel Publishers, 1998.

Simon, Paul Senator. *Advice & Consent.* Washington, D.C.: National Press Books, 1992.

Steinem, Gloria. *Outrageous Acts and Everyday Rebellions.* New York: Signet, 1986.
Tobias, Sheila. *Faces of Feminism.* Boulder, Colorado: Westview, 1997.
Tolchin, Susan and Martin Tolchin. *Clout.* New York: Coward, McCann and Geoghehan, 1973.
Ware, Susan. *Still Missing.* New York: WW Norton & Company, 1993.
White, Theodore H. *The Making of the President.* New York: Atheneum, 1972.
Witt, Linda, Karen M. Paget, and Glenna Mathews. *Running as a Woman, Gender and Power in American Politics.* New York: The Free Press, a Division of MacMillan, Inc. 1994.

Index